A Pilgrimage Beyond Belief

Spiritual Journeys through Christian and Buddhist Monasteries of the American West

DENNIS PATRICK SLATTERY

A Pilgrimage
Beyond Belief

*Spiritual Journeys through
Christian & Buddhist Monasteries
of the American West*

Preface by
Peter C. Phan

Foreword by
Thomas Moore

 Angelico Press

Revised and expanded edition of the work
originally published in 2004 by Jossey-Bass as
Grace in the Desert: Awakening to the Gifts of Monastic Life
© Angelico Press 2017

For information, address:
Angelico Press
4709 Briar Knoll Dr.
Kettering, OH 45429
angelicopress.com
info@angelicopress.com

ISBN 978 1 62138 300 0 pb
ISBN 978 1 62138 301 7 cloth
ISBN 978 1 62138 302 4 ebook

Cover design: Michael Schrauzer

INCIPIT

The way of writing is straight and crooked.
Heraclitus, *Fragments*

CONTENTS

DEDICATION

To my parents, Roger and Mary, to my sister Mary Beth and brothers Marty, Bob, Bill. To our sons, Matthew and Stephen, and to Francesca, our daughter-in-law; to our granddaughters, McKenzie-Jean and Eleanor Ann.

Most especially, however, I dedicate this book to my wife, Sandy, who has given me a life of freedom to pursue what I felt called to and who has been my ever-faithful companion and strength. She is the reason I come home.

ACKNOWLEDGMENTS

Parts of the published writings listed below appear in modified form in various sections of this memoir:

"No Sense of Peace." *Sacred Journey: The Journey of Fellowship in Prayer.* Vol. 52, No. 4. August 2001. 39–44.

"From Silence to Sound: Poetry and Prayer as Portals to the Eternal." *The New Zion's Herald: Opinion, News and Reflections for 21st-Century Christians.* July/August 2001. 19–20.

"Poetry, Prayer and Meditation." *Journal of Poetry Therapy.* Vol. 13, No. 1, 1999. 39–45.

"The Soul's Soundings: Joys of the Aural Life." *The Salt Journal.* Vol. 2, No. 3. January/February 2000.

Casting the Shadows: Selected Poems. Kearney, Nebraska: Morris Publishing Co., 2001.

"Poetry as Portals to the Sacred." Conference on Portals to the Sacred. Santa Barbara, California. 31 May–3 June 2001.

"A Retreat? From What?" *The Roll. Magazine-Newsletter of the Schola Contemplationis.* Vol. 13, No. 4 (50) December, 1996. 139–141.

"Monastic Retreat Gives Life Clearer Order." Viewpoint. *The Texas Catholic.* September 27, 1985. 41–B.

Grace in the Desert: Awakening to the Gifts of Monastic Life. San Francisco: Jossey-Bass, 2004.

Preface

D EVOTIONAL LITERATURE often describes life as a pilgrimage through a vale of tears to the eternal home, a "journey of the soul," a growth from spiritual infancy to saintly maturity. As part of this interior pilgrimage, some devotees journey to the holy places of their religion: Hindus to Ban'ras, Buddhists to S'n'rth, Jews and Christians to Jerusalem, Muslims to Mecca, just to mention some of the holiest cities. For those not able to travel to these distant places, a trek to a local sanctuary is a pilgrimage in miniature where they hope to experience the same transforming power of the transcendent or the divine.

Because Dennis is a dedicated pilgrim as well as a compulsive writer, he made not only a "pilgrimage" but also a "pengrimage." So, you are now holding in your hands one of the most deeply reflective, richly poetic, and yes, spiritually uplifting "journals of the soul" I have been privileged to read. I trust you will find out for yourself what a spiritual treasure this book is by perusing it from cover to cover. Here I will only briefly describe the many pilgrimages that are narrated in these pages.

There is of course a physical pilgrimage to various centers of prayer and spirituality. Some of these are well known, others less so; some prospering, others on the way to extinction. An experienced traveler, Dennis is a perceptive tour guide to these places and the people who run them. Some of these centers offer only the bare minimum of creaturely comforts, sometimes with a friendly mouse as a daily visitor; others offer the conveniences of a modern motel. Some look out over breathtaking scenery, with deer grazing nearby; others a drab parking lot, with "retreatants" partying with pizza and beer. At some places, food is Spartan; at others, the nuns try to fatten you up with special meals marked "For the Hermit"! In many pilgrimages the devotees "circumambulate" upon arriving at and leaving the holy site to absorb, as it were, its sacred atmosphere.

Dennis, a modern pilgrim, rode in his truck up and down the west coast and the Midwest, but he never missed the chance to walk in the woods surrounding the monasteries in solitude and find his God there (and once, attacking dogs!). For readers who desire to visit these places they would do well to take note of Dennis's unique information on them in addition to the usual guides sold on the market.

There is next an ecumenical and interreligious pilgrimage. One of the monasteries Dennis visited is Holy Transfiguration Orthodox Monastery, also known as The Monastery of Mount Tabor; another is Sonoma Mountain Zen Center outside Santa Rosa. At one place, the once-altar boy, raised in Catholic schools, was introduced to the strange world of icons and Byzantine Divine Liturgy. At the other, he was initiated into Zen meditation through a series of minute rituals and the practice of mindfulness by raking the gravel and dirt ("I rake; therefore, I am"), practices that his church looked upon with suspicion not so long ago. In this way the Catholic pilgrim's eyes were opened to the wealth of spiritual riches of other religious traditions.

There is thirdly a pilgrimage in the company of saints and scholars of the past. Though solitude was the most pervasive feature of Dennis's pilgrimage, he was never alone. Spiritual masters such as Pseudo-Dionysus, Benedict, Meister Eckhart, John of the Cross, Teresa of Avila, Julian of Norwich, Hildegard of Bingen, and contemporary writers such as Thomas Merton, Thich Nhat Hanh, David Steindl-Rast, William McNamara, Anthony De Mello, and Thomas Berry kept him constant company. Through Dennis's meditations, we are introduced to these spiritual teachers whose wisdom continues to nurture humans in their journeys to God.

There is a fourth pilgrimage, and a most pleasant one. It is the journey with novelists and poets and psychologists, from the venerable Dante, whose *Divine Comedy* is a spiritual pilgrimage itself, to Dostoevsky, whose insights into the evil of the human heart continue to haunt us, to C.G. Jung, whose reflections on dreams illumine the secrets of the human soul. But these are not the only creative writers present in the book. Dennis himself is an accomplished poet, and so here and there he regales us with his own poems, when mere prose is unequal to the deep emotions stirring deep within his heart.

Finally, there is a fifth pilgrimage, and a most painful and difficult one. It is Dennis's journey back into his own past, between memory and imagination, a past traumatized by his father's alcoholism and rage, and by his own demons of anger and self-doubt. It is an unflinching and searching gaze of his memory into the depths of his soul, but a memory washed over by the unabashed tears of joy and gratitude in the quiet of the early morning in the chapel and in the silent vigil before the Blessed Sacrament. Joy and gratitude, because now the memory is redeemed by the imagination of the possibilities of God's transforming forgiveness and love. Only a person who has experienced God's gratuitous love can write the following words: "Grace, I suddenly understood, is a gift of freedom, of a full liberation from one's self. It does not ask that anyone or I deny ourselves; in fact, grace becomes a way of moving closer to who one is, but by a route that does not depend on one's will but on the will of God. And it visits one in love. Love liberates in its gentle but powerful force."

Belden Lane's *The Solace of Fierce Landscapes*, which Dennis cites, refers to the desert, the mountain, and the cloud as the geographical symbols of the three stages of the spiritual life, namely, purgation, illumination, and union. May we who read Dennis's book also move through the desert of the dark night of the soul, to the mountain of the light of divine knowledge, to the cloud of unknowing which wraps us in the radiant darkness of divine love.

PETER C. PHAN,
Ellacuria Chair of Catholic Social Thought,
Georgetown University

Foreword

HUMAN CREATIVITY is vast and diverse. Artists make and shape all kinds of material, from paint on a canvas to the body in motion. In the area of spirituality and religion, this creativity gives rise to modes of living, themselves art forms of a sort in search of meaning and purpose. That is how I see monastic life, as an art form of the spirit. Generally, its aim is to shape a life—it's sometimes called the "regular" life because it is based on a rule and is highly regulated—so that eternal and timeless matters come to the foreground. The monk's day is set according to precise times, allowing for periods of meditation, study, work, prayer, and silence.

In a certain sense it is an easy life: someone does the financial books, makes the money, cleans the buildings, and cares for the gardens and lawns. Usually it is the monks who do these chores, but they are spread around, so that usually no monk is responsible for the whole, except for the abbot or prior. There is also instant community, plenty of people in a monk's life to share problems and be available for entertainment and friendship. Silence can be a blessing, and even freedom from marriage and family has its rewards.

I speak as someone who lived the life for thirteen years in my youth. I was not in a strictly monastic order, but one that was half monastic and half active in teaching and pastoral work. In a sense, I had the best of both worlds: the cloister and life in society. My memory of that life is mixed, as is every human endeavor. I enjoyed community life, liturgy, silence, and the solitude. I didn't care much for my vow of obedience, having to do whatever some wacky superior thought was good for me. On a few rare occasions I longed for a sexual partner, and I wanted more freedom to think and to travel.

I can understand how ordinary people long to have a taste of that life, to go on retreat or to live near a monastery and share some of its benefits. I try to make my own home as monastic as possible, as much as you can with demanding work and children. Tasting the monastic life can be a spiritual practice. It keeps alive in you the value of community, solitude, and a focus on spiritual issues. Such a practice is especially meaningful in today's world, so materialistic in its thought and so frenzied and loud in its style. Silence and solitude are major items that recommend the life.

I think of silence not as the absence of sound but as a lack of chatter and noise that allow you to hear things you otherwise never hear. A monastery is like that. It's a place intentionally set apart from worldly life so that you can discover the world. Monks sometimes take a vow of poverty, and yet their life is rich and complete. They may take a vow of celibacy, and yet they know a level of love and joy in being together that any couple might envy. A monastery seems to be a walled cloister, and yet it turns out to be an extraordinary window on nature and human living.

A monastery is not just a building or a tract of land. It's a community of people, a tradition, a philosophy of life, a kind of love. When you enter a monastery, you know you are now in a special place. The very atmosphere is different. It is alive in ways you would never expect. It is full, precisely because it is empty. You can appreciate quickly how such an atmosphere would have a strong impact on people living there.

I enjoyed reading Dennis Slattery's account of his many visits to a variety of monasteries. I appreciated his simple openness to his experiences. He would go through the door of a monastery, not knowing what to expect, and make himself at home there. In every place he became attached, a sign that he entered these communities with an open heart, without guile and without much emotional distance. What we don't find in Dennis's experience, and you wouldn't expect it of a visitor, is any sign of the struggles monks go through. The truth is, it is not always an easy life.

But Dennis does tell a remarkable story within the story of his visits. As he emptied himself in one place after another, his recently deceased father became present to him, and he was able to work through mostly disturbing memories and reflect on his own role as a father. This ghostly relationship is the soul of the book. We don't really need a travelogue of monasteries. Well, maybe we do, but we also need a deeper experience of their mystery.

Foreword

I also appreciated Dennis's attention to animals and to nature. He understood that a monastery is not really an isolated place. Its typical remoteness—felt somewhere even in city settings—is really a doorway onto nature. Nature offers the real silence, the real mystery, and the real community. Myself, I doubt that I would travel far from a monastery I was visiting, but he knew better. He went out of his way to see the natural beauty associated with the monastery, even if it required a car to get there.

Today people tend to separate religion from spirituality and prefer spirituality. To me, spirituality is the experience and religion the method and style. By religion, I don't mean church or organization, but a concrete means for entering the world of spirit. I hope that Dennis's fine, honest, beautiful book inspires readers to imitate him in their own way, to discover how deeply satisfying a life in the spirit can be, how it doesn't have to exclude ordinary, normal, and pleasurable life, but can actually intensify it.

We live in a world where spirituality is often misread as ideology. Belief is overdone at the expense of experience. In a monastery, you learn your theology by rising early, chanting, sitting calmly, reading often, and keeping quiet. It is by no means anti-intellectual, but in intelligence there is a full body-soul-mind-spirit-emotion experience. It's inspiring to see monks from different religious traditions meet and discover they have so much in common as monks, if not as believers.

The variety of spiritual styles Dennis met on his tour might teach you that spirituality is better understood as spiritualities. There are many ways to the spirit, and to be spiritually alive it helps to be open to the diversity of religious styles. I suggest setting aside your worries about the niceties of belief for a few years and discover in your body and in your heart how spirit can bring you to life. I'd recommend a trip similar to Dennis's, and be sure to take home a good measure of the values and forms you learn on your journey. More than anything, the world today needs this education in spirit, a softening of the heart to make it open to every creature, which, you discover in your monastic passage is your neighbor, your family, and your very body.

THOMAS MOORE, August 2003
Author of *Care of the Soul*, *The Soul's Religion*, and others

Introduction I

THIS BOOK is a revised and expanded version of *Grace in the Desert: Awakening to the Gifts of Monastic Life* published by Jossey-Bass in 2004. The book has enjoyed some popularity and been well received. But to pass into publication, the manuscript had to be trimmed by some 50,000 words. While I was delighted to see a modified version of the book find the light of day, I carried a yearning and a grieving for those stories that had to be jettisoned to satisfy the parameters set by the publishers. I thought one day that I might publish a full version of my monastic journey.

Now, some eleven years after the original, the volume you hold is as close to the original as I could wish for. I have changed a good deal of the original and replaced some changes made by the editors of the original volume. I have also expanded the "References" and "Further Readings" sections. I believe now that it tells a fuller story of my double pilgrimage: into the interior geography of my life and out to some fourteen monasteries, each of which carried, like a unique container, its special blend and brew of the monastic imagination. I hope you, the reader, gains something of your own spiritual life through these stories and prayers.

Introduction II
To the Reader

You should carry the monastery in yourself. The desert is within you. The desert calls you and draws you back. . . . Truly, I prepare you for solitude.
— C. G. Jung, *The Red Book*

WRITING IS A FORM of pilgrimage. Let me fess up. I came to this idea *before* I read it recently, so I am going to claim it as my own. But Patricia Hampl deserves acknowledgment here when she ends the best chapter in her book, *I Could Tell You Stories*, entitled "Memory and Imagination." The memoirist is an "older sort of traveler, the pilgrim, seeking, wondering" (37). Amen. We entered the same imaginal space in recognizing that not only writing, but reading as well are pilgrimages so long as one is not bent on murdering to dissect. I love neologisms so here is mine: "pengrimage." From pilgrimage to pengrimage. A weak attempt to capture something of the hermitage quality, even the hermetic quality, of writing from memory. To pengrinate is to move across the page, often helter-skelter and let the writing, the motion, have its way with memory so that the sorting of what is relevant and clamors to be included is allowed to have sway as much through the body as through remembrance. Yes, there exists in each of us a story to be told, but before that, perhaps there is a story to be toured. This book will be a tour and a telling of what became a pivotal journey in my spiritual evolution.

The tour begins when the self-shelved is dusted off and remade, re-visioned, and given a voice. Memoir writing unshelves the self. Memoir writing is a kind of tour through the drawers of the memory: open this one, then that, some contents leap forward, dying to be discovered, uncovered, and recovered; others lie dormant, uninterested, refusing to be nudged into narrative. Let that plot rest in peace.

As I age, memory ripens. I love the title of Vladimir Nabokov's autobiography: *Speak, Memory!* In the memory the meaning lurks, like a cat behind the couch, crouching. Or a coyote sheltered behind a scrub bush. Memoir writing pokes a stick at history, like thrusting a big pen around and then observing closely and with fascination at what scurries forth. In parts of my story, shame steps aside, demurs to desire. My desire to tell is stronger than my shame to deny. My fingers work the keys, like running in place on the treadmill at the health club, while inside the journey is fluid, sometimes linear, more often spiralic, but always surprising. Writing what lies ahead mingled within me a curious blend of recollection and desire— something erotic stirred to arousal in the telling.

I love those film advertisings that try to entice us to see a new release by proclaiming: BASED ON A TRUE STORY! What lunacy. All stories are true, whether based on facts or the fabrication of imagination or an amalgam of both and more. The following words, recollections of meanderings, peregrinations, procrastinations, and more than one perturbation are true; all have emerged from out of the chaos of a true story. The Greek word, "paroikia" means, "to sojourn in a foreign land" (Aivazian, 336). I cannot know what the terrain is filled with, familiar things or foreign elements, until I write them out. These chapters are my own journey into what I thought was going to be familiar terrain; writing brought out instead the most unfamiliar faces and some very maiming memories.

I greet and salute a handful of people who helped me to shape this story into some coherent form while avoiding formula: I thank Christine Downing and Maureen Murdock, both memoir specialists, for reading the manuscript and making innumerable suggestions for improvements; gratitude I extend to Peter C. Phan, Allen Tate Wood, Larry Allums, and Evans Lansing-Smith, for reading and commenting on the overall design of the work. I also thank Mark Kelly, Reference Librarian and computer guru at Pacifica Graduate Institute for assisting me in locating website listings of monastery information.

I also thank Pacifica Graduate Institute for granting me my first sabbatical after teaching there for three years, so that I might go on the road and into the spirit of pilgrimage. Finally, I wish to thank all my teachers, including my parents, who from the time I was old enough to crawl and speak, have guided me toward who I am today. I include among these teachers all the voices of the past that found their words to me in books, tapes, and conversations. This pilgrimage is theirs as well as mine. And to my father, who after he died, decided to accompany me, most unexpectedly, on the pilgrimage; he added a deeply satisfying dimension to my sojourn.

1

When the World
is Too Much With Us:
A Monastic Pilgrimage

Idleness is the enemy of the soul. Therefore, the brothers should have specified periods for manual labor as well as for prayerful reading. —*The Rule of St. Benedict*

I HAVE BEEN THINKING of this story of monastic living for some time now. But not until I was washing the floor in the kitchen a few days ago, and feeling that being down on all fours was a good position from which to ask for a sign from God if I should begin this process of recollection, did I accept that I would lift the story from my hands and give the decision over to Him. I use the pronoun "Him" even though I do not believe God is gendered. "It" does not seem to work and "He/She" is the worst form of doggerel imaginable. I am a traditional Catholic and was raised to accept God the Father as the image of God. So *Him* it shall be. When I learn differently, I will be the first one to tweak the gender and align myself with the new revelation.

Having asked for a sign, I let it go and made sure that I scrubbed each corner of the kitchen floor, especially places where the dirt seemed to congregate most aggressively. Then, a day later, I visited my place of work, Pacifica Graduate Institute in Carpinteria, California, to fetch my mail. There, in a puffy yellow envelope, was a packet from The Fellowship of Prayer Organization housed in Princeton, New Jersey. I opened it, not knowing what to expect, and sure enough, wrapped in their August, 2001 issue, was an article of mine entitled "No Sense of Peace," under the heading, "Pilgrimage." It was a five-page essay I had written after I returned from a pilgrimage of a little over three months' duration which allowed me to visit, meditate, and read in eleven monasteries and one Zen Buddhist Center, a desire I had nurtured for years before actually finding the time and the courage to step off the porch and begin it. The theme of the essay was "solitude" and its definitive loss in many communities of prayer, to say nothing of the secular world.

The strange part of finding this essay in the journal, along with a photo of me in the front of the article, is that I had completely forgotten sending it to them for consideration. But there it was, out of the blue. I remembered almost immediately being down on my knees scrubbing the kitchen floor just hours before, and asking from this lowly posture for a sign on whether to go ahead with this recollection, now two years old, or move on to another project. So, the sign has signaled, the floor is as clean as I can make it, and I have launched this chronicle of my experiences.

I do my most creative work, including writing, early in the morning, between four and eight. I like to be up and in my chair or at my desk when it is still dark and the world is full of the silence that shapes it for the new day. With a coffee cup in hand, and having lit a candle to the goddess Hestia, patron saint of focusing, hospitality, and illumination, I read or write with only a small lamp on so that the darkness is right there in quiet pulsation as it brushes against the light and spars gently with it. Any sacred presence is most intensely in the room then, helping me to see something necessary or inviting. If the rooster from across the creek by the lemon and orange tree groves begins his squawking and high-pitched call to the sun, that only deepens the silence that surrounds his determined cries. I feel called in these dark hours; the sacred exists most intensely in the serene silence, in silent darkness and this time, where the boundary between dream time and waking life is as thin as a communion wafer and about as fragile. I am most susceptible at these times to what wants to be heard and recorded. So I write beneath the little light of my lamp, toward the darkness and away from the quotidian. It is my daily ritual of approaching the mystery in the commonplace.

When the World is Too Much With Us

For this book, I imagine the monks up at their early hour, chanting, praying, or shuffling in single file in their robes, all looking about the same; my morning reading and writing participate in their prayer life, separated from them by distance but not by time. For me it comprises the most sacred part of the day. Colleagues laugh when I mention to them that for me all the serious work of the day is generally over by ten a.m. and I then turn to the work of a more practical nature. The one exception to this rule is teaching, which may stretch to nine p.m. on certain days. But the imaginal work, the work that beckons to sacred presences, is finished by now; when the pickup truck drives by the house with radio blaring and newspapers thunking onto asphalt driveways on both sides of us, I know that my time alone and in silence, perhaps in front of the glowing white light of the computer screen, is dimming, so I best keep moving as time's subtle but relentless flow begins to cross the inky cloak covering my study window.

Memory for me works best in the darkness of the morning hours, when I cannot see the outside world and the neighborhood has not yet stirred with neighbors preparing to leave for the day, driving up out of our canyon just a quarter of a mile from the Pacifica ocean to earn their keep before returning some nine hours later. This is my time, a kind of monastic hiatus or spirit hours preserved for the real work of learning, be it through writing, meditating, or reading. It is the time of meditation, not analysis, of contemplation and journal writing, not grading papers or preparing lessons for class. It is the most fruitful time of my life and I do not take any morning for granted, for this is the time when the secrets that lie dormant in the rest of my life have a chance to emerge slowly, like a rainbow trout rising vertically toward the surface of a lake. Once it is past for the day, it cannot be retrieved, and so I engage it seven days a week because each slot holds a promise of something precious potentially offered. None should be lost or sacrificed to any other activities or engagements. Not showing up is a cardinal offense, a transgression worse than writing a bad sentence.

In like manner, a carefully-chosen monastery or retreat center becomes a wonderful and still mysterious place of refuge from a world that continues to accelerate in its distractions and demands on me and others to do more and to reflect less. *More* can be a monstrous assault on simply Being. William Wordsworth, a magnificent nature poet, wrote in 1807 the sonnet that follows; it expresses my state of mind that sent me pilgrimaging. I want to share the entire poem with you here because it expresses some of the feelings that pushed me out the door and onto the road.

The World is Too Much With Us

The world is too much with us; late and soon,
Getting and spending, we lay waste our powers;
Little we see in nature that is ours;
We have given our hearts away, a sordid boon!
This Sea that bares her bosom to the moon,
The winds that will be howling at all hours,
And are up-gathered now like sleeping flowers,
For this, for everything, we are out of tune;
It moves us not.—Great God! I'd rather be
A Pagan suckled in a creed outworn;
So might I, standing on this pleasant lea,
Have glimpses that would make me less forlorn;
Have sight of Proteus rising from the sea;
Or hear old Triton blow his wreathed horn.
(*The Norton Anthology of Poetry*, 559)

His poem retrieves something essential for human survival that has been lost in the modern world; it also offers some reasons for its rejection. The poem reclaims a mythic and imaginal ability, a gift we all possess but perhaps do not often deploy. The ensuing pilgrimage is motivated as much by a desire to recollect this mythic sensibility, so tied as it is to the life of the spirit, as it is to move closer to God as a fully human and transcendent presence.

Making a journey is one of the oldest activities of human beings. From first bumping up against the idea to planning it, to organizing all of its parts as much as one can anticipate the unknown, to carrying it out, all excited my blood, something I wanted to feel palpably—the heated blood flowing in the veins, some excitement that would stir me out of the ordinary and invite the unfamiliar into my life. A deadening lethargy and inertia was the price tag for a security that was numbing me.

When the World is Too Much With Us

Once, when I was contemplating a new teaching position that would pull me from a secure tenured position as a full professor in one state where we lived with our sons, and moving almost 1800 miles away to a new institution that promised very little security, I at first shrunk from making the move permanent. One of the folks working there, a gracious woman, Susan Santini, in whom I confided my concerns about leaving a secure teaching position, answered without blinking an eye: "If security is what you are seeking, then you are already partly dead." Ouch. She was right. The need for security was so strong in me that the thought of relinquishing or jeopardizing it did more to keep me from pursuing what deeply burned in me. We made the move and were never even tempted to look back.

Embarking on a journey so insistently challenged my need for security to such an extent that some new sense of freedom was kindled in simply planning it. Going it alone added to the hollow feeling of insecurity. Making the act of the will to do it was already, before even packing or making the initial arrangement, to cross a major threshold. The imagination, now free from its normal restraints, began to envision possibilities not hinted at before. I recalled the German poet and botanist Goethe's wonderful admonition to the faint of heart:

> Until one is committed, there is hesitancy, the chance to draw back, always ineffectiveness.... [But] the moment one definitely commits oneself, then Providence moves too. All sorts of things occur to help one that would never otherwise have occurred. A whole stream of events issues from the decision....
> Whatever you can do,
> Or dream you can, begin it.
> Boldness has genius,
> Power and magic in it.
> (qtd. in *Rag and Bone Shop*, 235)

Making the decision to engage the journey stirs Providence to cooperate in its implementation. Of course it is a matter of faith that the monastic journey will expose possibilities and pain—of loneliness, of solitude, of vulnerability, of being wounded, of past afflictions—all those elements that seem to be necessary for a deeper understanding of who one is. The deepest suffering grows from sacrifice, from giving up, from letting go of what offers comfort; from there the deepest growth may emerge. I now believe that suffering into who and what one is, is also to witness the working of God in one's life.

Despite a friendly and humorous outgoing presence in the world, I have always loved solitude. As a young child I would find ways to fool my mother into thinking I was ill so I could avoid school for a day or two because I knew that she, an avid reader herself, would drive our only car, a beat-up grey '51 Chevrolet to the library and fetch me some 8–10 books, which I would then gather around me in bed, like soldiers around a fort. I had the habit of building a citadel in the bed, keeping a flashlight handy, and pulling my small wood-grained radio into the inner sanctum of a heap of covers. There, hidden in darkness except for the directed beam of my flashlight, I would read adventure stories of horses, boys growing up on a ranch, and sea narratives. Maybe Nat King Cole, Patti Page, or the McGuire sisters would be crooning on the radio. I would read these marvelous tales of places and persons that transported me, like a barefoot Hobbit, into climates far more gentle than the harsh Cleveland winters that blasted across Lake Erie from Canada, frequently beginning at Thanksgiving and lasting through April, holding us all in a deep freeze. I rode with the Hardy boys on their X-Bar-X ranch and swam with them in the cool pools of Montana. I loved the Walter Farley series of Black Beauty tales and could smell the horsy pungent odors of my own horse while I read. I loved any story where someone was on the road, for that is what I longed for.

But most of all I remembered the solitude, the aloneness of these magical days with snow covering everything outside as Lake Erie froze over once again and went serenely dormant till spring. Usually two days was the length of time I could sustain the charade; then back to school and the noise and racket of hundreds of children, Ursuline nuns in swishing black robes and veils below starched wimples, and small wax-coated cartons of chocolate milk at midday to stave off the hungers of an eleven-year-old. I missed my fort, the hollow in the blankets, and my radio playing softly while I read. I was already monastic as a youngster, my hermitage an army blanket from World War II one of my uncles had come home with, and a cotton spread as thin as crepe. But I was abbot and humble monk and given *carte blanche* in solitude. I founded the celibate Order of Radio-Reading-and Listening. Total number of monks blanketed in solitary cells: one.

2

Origins of the Monastic Call

Origins of the Monastic Call
O Lord, turn your ear to my cry.
Do not be deaf to my tears.
In your house I am a passing guest,
a pilgrim like all my fathers.
Look away that I may breathe again
Before I depart to be no more.
—*Psalm* 38

WHEN I WAS SIXTEEN I lived in a home that was quiet all week, with little conversation between family members; but all went consistently berserk on the weekends with the manic gyrations of a raging alcoholic father who terrorized us all. His reticent but friendly self would begin to crumble sometime between nine and ten p.m. on Friday night. He would begin drinking in earnest and with keen purpose around six p.m. Our mother and my brothers and sister could all feel the impending blast that gathered steam at the beginning of the weekend. Saturday mornings he was up early to clean the house. By Saturday night he would be in a rage and carefully intent on dismantling all that he had carefully straightened and cleaned in the sober part of the day. We would all fly out of the house to the homes of friends or relatives, or to a movie theater—anywhere to escape the wrath of a man deeply in pain and suffering his own infernal shame until Sunday, when he would try to sober up enough to make it to Monday morning Mass and then to work downtown by eight a.m. This pattern had remarkable stamina; it remained charged, at rough calculation, for decades. It was the life we all learned to resent and to fear, a sustained repetition of ferocious discontent.

So when a wild-eyed friend of mine, Rick, asked me one July day when I was not yet seventeen, if I wanted to ride on the back of his BSA motorcycle from Cleveland to Long Island, New York, my bag was half-packed before I answered "let's go." We left his house on two wheels, in white t-shirts, no jackets, no rain gear, and no helmets for the hot northern Ohio summer ride. Early in the evening we threaded our way south to the Ohio Turnpike and pointed the handlebars east. With every mile distancing me from another underworld weekend, I grew calmer, feeling the freedom from the domestic friction that haunted me all week. We rode all night. I spent many hours looking mostly at Rick's black hair and funny long neck with three brown moles on its right side as we cruised hour after hour at sixty-five mph. The throttling groan of the dual exhausts pulled me into alternate periods of dozing and then suddenly jerking awake for fear of falling on to the cement pavement skidding underneath us at a dizzy rate.

Somewhere around three a.m. we paused at a Truck Stop cut into the mountains of Clarion, Pennsylvania for an early breakfast at just about the time a ferocious thunderstorm that had been pursuing us east for hours caught up to us and crashed on our exposed heads, delaying our trip and adding more danger in the form of slippery cement. After breakfast, and impetuous by nature, we waited just long enough for the storm to abate, then continued our journey on the now empty and quiet turnpike at four-thirty a.m.

The rain stung our faces and hair and the air turned cold so that within minutes we were soaked and shivering. No helmet, no windshield, and no riding goggles; nonetheless, Rick forged ahead, with me a close second, hugging him now to try to keep us both warm. After a few hours, I fell asleep; I woke with a start just soon enough to prevent my toppling sideways onto the slippery concrete road and perhaps pulling Rick with me. We made it into the dawn and sunshine, dry now from the morning air that tumbled us through the spin cycle and let us forget about a shower, at least for that night.

We drove into New York City, along 5th Ave. in Manhattan, past the Empire State Building and many curious New Yorkers busy with getting to work but pausing a moment to gaze at our raggedy appearance. We had hung some of our wet clothing on the handle-bars and mirrors to dry and so looked the part of vagabonds blown in from the sea. We then headed toward Long Island. Only then did I ask Rick what the point of the trip was because up to now I had not cared why we were making the journey, only that we were. I knew what it was for me: to escape for a blessed week my home-grown violence punctuated by a dull routine. He told me he wanted to revisit the house where he had grown up and to see who lived there. He told me he missed his house, his bedroom, the neighbor-hood and some good friends; perhaps all of these things were still there. Now, in retrospect, I realize that I had entered most fully, impetuously and mostly ill prepared, my first pilgrimage. We had returned to a sacred place for Rick; he spoke with great reverence tinged with nostalgia of the streets on which he used to play. His current home life was something like mine, but his alcoholic-in-res-idence was not just his father but both parents. We had exchanged moments of domestic terror while riding the New Jersey Turnpike so that when we arrived on Long Island I felt like I knew him much more intimately. Telling traumas in travel, now there is a form of therapy that one could take on the road. We were both regularly traumatized by one or both parents. This journey of six hundred miles on the back of a motorcycle, I discovered so many years later, was a modern motorized version of an ancient practice and one that would set a pattern in my life from then to now, over fifty-five years later. My second pilgrimage was destined to be much shorter and closer to home.

Attending an all-male Catholic High School, St. Joseph's in Cleve-land, we seniors were required to make a weekend retreat in the spring of our senior year. No real sign of blessedness; rather, no choice. All of us signed up to participate from Friday afternoon through Sunday lunch. The Marianist brothers and priests who comprised most of the faculty in the early sixties smuggled in their own grand design: they strategically placed us in various rooms close to them and invited a few of us into their rooms for conversa-tions. At the time I did not realize that recruiting for the order was afoot as well. It was, in fact, a recruitment weekend and some of the promising civilians like myself were being encouraged to consider joining the Marianist order after high school. If nothing else, we were at least influenced to consider The University of Dayton, a Marianist-operated school, in hopes that we might change our minds.

Next to the high school on Lake Shore Boulevard along the shore of Lake Erie was the diocesan retreat house; attending the weekend retreat was almost like heading to school for classes. We checked in at the front desk of the old, dark, brick building and were in some cases assigned roommates. I was given a room to myself between two of my teachers, both Marianist priests—while my classmates were delighted to be sharing rooms with friends. I really had no sense of who or what I was at that time in my eighteen years, so I was unconscious of the fact that I was being singled out; my thought was that I got the luck of the draw and thought no more about it.

We settled in, explored our surroundings, were given a schedule of the weekend events and told quite clearly that we were expected to participate at each of the services during the day. Our freedom was limited and securely monitored, but I found that I did not mind this at all; in fact, as I settled into my spare room with faded green and grey linoleum on the floor, a small bed, a desk with a reading lamp on it, and a modest wooden upright chair, along with a stuffed and pathetic-looking lounge chair to sit and read in, I did not mind. In fact, I felt a delight, even a growing feeling of joy emerge in me that this room, my own for two days, was a treasured lair. Growing up in a small house with many brothers and a sister, I never really had my own space; this room, by contrast, was paradise, though I don't want to overwork that word. I felt the same rush of ecstasy when I was able to stay home from school and build my fort/reading warren in my bed; my retreat room had the same feeling of safety, privacy, and solitude, like a blessing bestowed gratuitously. I suddenly realized I liked the fact that I had no roommate, except for the silent and companionable one from early childhood: solitude.

During those glorious three days from Friday evening to Sunday afternoon I was invited, actually summoned, into one or another of the priests' or brothers' rooms for consultation. At first, guilty by nature and ashamed by training, I assumed I was being called to visit them because of something I had done wrong at school but had overlooked until now. This retreat was really a time of reckoning, of balancing the ledgers. But once the conversation began, I realized that the priest was interested in what I was planning to do after graduation. Then began the subtle but insistent pitch for the priesthood or brotherhood in the order. It was gentle, soft, and had not the grit of a used car salesman's clamoring; but it was clear what outcome was desired.

I took in their words and for a time contemplated becoming a brother; I had witnessed so many good men in the classes at the high school, fine first-rate and dedicated teachers, so joining the order and perhaps teaching others had a certain appeal. The weekend concluded without any clear decision on my part, but I kept close to me for many years the satisfying feeling of having the solitude of my own room for three days and the generous concern of several teachers. Perhaps my monastic journey began there, as an eighteen year old, in Cleveland, inhabiting a room between two Marianist brothers. They were far more successful than they realized in planting a desire in me, one which was to recreate a space for silence and solitude. In these two atmospheres lay the ground of a mystery whose insistent presence I could only sense.

Gethsemani Monastery: Initiation

Years passed. I married my wife Sandy, now of forty-seven years, finished an undergraduate degree in literature and psychology at Kent State University, and then began a Master's degree in Comparative Literature while beginning a teaching position at an elementary school in Ravenna, Ohio, some twenty miles east of Kent. I taught Special Education students for two years as I completed the graduate degree. Then a long-time high school friend recommended me for a high school teaching position at Lorain Catholic High School. I drove up from Kent for the interview and was hired to begin teaching in the fall of 1970. My wife, Sandy, was also offered a position teaching at St. Peter's elementary school. After almost eight years of thinking not one thought about monasteries or the life of solitude, I began assisting Father Bill Snyder, the school chaplain, at Mass in the morning.

One day, while Father Bill was hanging up his vestments after Mass, I asked him, with no forethought, if there was any place in the area where one could make a retreat. He did not hesitate: "Gethsemani Monastery, south of here in Kentucky," he responded. "You would enjoy the drive down there and the countryside that surrounds the Trappist retreat." It was early May and the school year would soon be over, so I called for a mid-June reservation. Classes completed, I drove my recently-purchased BMW motorcycle down to Trappist, Kentucky, twelve miles south of Bardstown, a road trip that was to put me on a monastic path that has lasted for forty-five years.

From this journey, retreating to monasteries more often on two wheels rather than four, began in earnest. Anyone who has seen or stayed in this magnificently inviting place will never forget coming on its fortress-like structure sitting just off of Farm Road 31 E. Whitewashed Gothic architecture with its sharp pointed spires, it looks like a transplant from France or Germany. My mood changed when I drove up the driveway to the Guest House entrance—not my mood, really, but the atmosphere, the aroma of the air, the feel of the geography shifted. Tucked into the farm country of Kentucky, with its large stone statue of Christ at the top of a small hill greeting every car that passed and anyone who drove through the cloistered gate, with the blue grass mountains in the background, the oppressive summer heat with no breeze that made one wish immediately for a thunderstorm to loom up and clear the air—all these sensations rushed over me as I parked my BMW and took my bags to the entrance, rang the bell and was greeted by the monk who was Guestmaster for this season.

He was a Benedictine brother, I learned, who had been making retreats here for years, but after his wife died and with his children grown, he had come to make a one-week retreat and had stayed. He was in his sixteenth year at Gethsemani; I was entering the gate for the first time. When he learned that I had studied literature, his hands immediately disappeared into the top desk drawer where he was sitting. With a smile on his face, he pulled out a volume by the poet Rabindrinath Tagore and began reading a poem to me. How he loved this poet and wanted me to experience that same love! I stood amid my backpack and duffel bag and listened to him, saw the shine come across his face and knew that I would be right at home in these surroundings: a Trappist monk greeting me at the threshold with a poem. Such was my introduction to the monastery, through the portals of a poet's words. I suddenly felt embraced by the place and realized that this was a part of my life I had missed intensely even though I did not know it.

I also learned from him that the works of the Swiss psychologist, C.G. Jung (1875–1961), were also an integral part of their monastic instruction. They loved the mystical Jung, the Jung of archetypes and of the four functions, the Jung of *Mysterium Coniunctionis* and writer on Christianity, the symbolism of the Mass, the image of Christ as symbol of the Self, the writer who mused about death and immortality, not the analytical Jung of personality types and word association tests. They found in his mysticism a companion soul to their own spiritual work, a process led over the years in large measure by a man whose name fills my bookshelves today and remains the best-known monk of this monastery or any order: Thomas Merton.

The Guestmaster instructed me to grab my bags and follow him to my room on the second floor of the guesthouse, a plain and harmless looking structure just behind and to the right of the guest office. I loved this well-worn old place so much more than its upgraded version, which I experienced years later. My tiny room was so narrow that if I stretched my arms out my fingers would touch each wall. This for me became the physical measure of intimate monastic space. In it was a small bed, short so my feet stuck straight out over the end; a small reading table, with a tiny lamp on it that cast a very sickly yellow glow at night or early in the morning hours; and a stiff wooden chair in front of it. On the wall was a clean sink with a towel on the rack and a light overhead with a metal string dangling from it. When I pulled it the first time, I felt the oily residue from a hundred other occupants who had performed the same act over many years. There was a small recessed cavity next to the bed with a few hangers on which to drape clothes and tuck a suitcase or two into. Bathrooms and showers were down the hall, lit only periodically by small bulbs so that the hallway day or night seemed to maintain a quiet dark atmosphere, which suited the intentions of the place.

One set of stairs led down and out to ground level, while another headed through a labyrinth of stairs and short hallways, to the balcony section of the chapel. Down below were the main floor of cement, altar, and a large banner of Christ in iconic style, with a splashing gold background against which was a slender figure in white who looked to be dancing an Irish jig. To each side were the stalls for the monks to enter, where they would sit or stand to pray and chant the psalms several times a day or worship during the Mass. The walls—high, somber and stuccoed—were whitewashed so that a clean austerity pervaded the entire grand space of the chapel. If anyone coughed or sneezed, the sound would reverberate for a short time, breaking the deep silence that pervaded its sacred space.

However, it was to the silence, so deep and unfamiliar, that I was most drawn. It had such weightiness that I felt my ears could hear a deep hum, the hum of solitude. Silence, deep and dark became over many years one of the elements or qualities that drew me to many different monasteries during the next several decades. Silence with great subtlety opened on to a different dimension of existence, at once friendly and formidable, like the existence of a force that one lived amidst but never grasped or possessed. I felt the silence like a nugget of gold at the center of a huge ball of yarn, some essential feeling at the heart of a spiritual life. I could already feel its hardness when I squeezed the ball of yarn; I just could not see its blazoned glimmer, nor did I need to.

After settling into my room, I wandered into the library, a dimly-lit and musty place that invited me to bring a book and find one of the overstuffed chairs in between the stacks to sit and read under a lamp with a light bulb that was inadequate for reading; it required of me to concentrate intensely on the words of each page. In the center of the room was a glass case extending some ten feet and about four feet high. In it were letters to one Thomas Merton, a new name to me at the time. Letters displayed were signed by the southern fiction writer, Flannery O'Connor; the philosopher and theologian, Jacques Maritain; the writer Howard Griffith; President John F. Kennedy; the Dalai Lama; and by other leaders around the globe.

At just this moment one of the monks came into the library and found me with my face practically pressed against the glass, as if I were in a plush jewelry store looking to buy some precious gems. He introduced himself as Brother Patrick Hart, Merton's personal secretary and assistant for decades. He asked if I wanted to see Merton's grave, so we walked out to the grassy plot of ground that ran along the outer wall of the chapel. I had missed Merton's presence by only two years—he died in 1968. Here in the early summer of 1970 was his grave, marked simply "Father Louis" to the left of the chapel and in with the other Trappist monks buried close to him. His grave, with its flat and wide white metal cross, was not distinguished from all the others.

Brother Patrick generously suggested a few of Merton's books for the beginner; two shelves in the library were lined with multiple copies of his work as well as several volumes of his poetry. I began then with *Conjectures of a Guilty Bystander* and have continued to read his numerous books for the past fifty years.

Amidst all this discovery, after a few days a question demanded to be heard: "What was I doing here?" I was not really seeking God. God would find me whenever He chose; I did not need to go after Him. Some deep draw from within was the magnet that attracted me to Gethsemani. I asked myself what I enjoyed about being here and found the following circumstances that came immediately to mind: the ascetic beauty of the life here. By that I mean the simple austerity of each day, beginning with the monks singing the psalter together in Gregorian chant at Lauds, followed by Mass in the early morning hours, when the windows lining the great high walls were filled with the darkness of a new day not yet fully birthed. I also loved the simple meals in the dining hall where we helped ourselves to the food, then walked to one of a series of long tables to enjoy our meal in silence. We pulled out from under the table a small wooden stool with a rectangular hole in the center for our hand to grip it and set it upright. We all faced the large floor-to-ceiling windows in front of us and, side by silent side, enjoyed the nourishment. At cer-

tain meals the monks would play a tape of either Merton instruct-
ing the novices or another speaker's words on contemplation,
silence, a life of prayer, or the monastic life. All of them invited a
deep meditation within me, which I settled into as I ate the nour-
ishing, simple vegetarian food. I felt for the first time how body and
soul both relish being fed regularly and moderately, that a certain
unique quiet joy ensued if one nurtured both at the same time: food
garnished with faith.

During these early days of monastic living, I especially remember
Merton's voice and manner of teaching. His speaking was much
higher in pitch than his thick body and strong, kind face would
indicate. He also grew animated easily and quickly when he spoke.
He was passionate about what he was saying; his delivery quickened
when he tripped over an insight that accelerated it. Completely
engaged, I would listen and eat and later wonder where the food had
gone, so preoccupied was I in following the lines of his thought and
the quick wit and spontaneous laughter he displayed freely and
often. He loved to laugh. In part, I suspected, because he found
learning an act of joy. Secretly, when I came to the next meal, I
hoped that the monks would again play a tape of him teaching or
preaching, for I seemed to learn quickly and easily in this medium,
as I knew others did also.

I also loved the walks in the woods surrounding the monastery. In
the hot summer months the humidity was high, the air heavy and
sultry, and the sun through the haze that typifies Ohio and Kentucky summers scalded the forehead. Mosquitoes were everywhere.
I was grateful for remembering to bring a can of repellant with me.
During the day the air always contained a low buzz from all the airborne insects that accompanied me wherever I wandered. At night,
the air would cool enough for a deep and restful sleep. No air conditioning at that time permitted the tiny cells to heat up during the
day, but at night the cool white-washed walls and the screened window inviting in the night air allowed me to sleep soundly, until of
course we would all wake with a start when the sound of the bells
punctuated my and other retreatants' slumbers. All of us were called
to the chapel by the bells but only a few were self-chosen and hearty
enough to shake off the miasma of sleep to join the monks. The lit-

tle, white, plastic alarm clock with its green glow hands and numbers seemed to wake me each morning before the alarm went off. As I rose I heard the wake-up buzzes of several other clocks down the hall.

From the beginning I liked being up well before dawn; I discovered that being awake in the early hours was as pleasant as it was rare for me in my life. These new hours of conscious waking comprised virgin territory, a timely terrain that radiated a strong peace and tranquility in the silence. Disheveled, unshowered, and wearing the rumpled clothes of a vagabond, I negotiated the labyrinth with the help of low-wattage lighting and shuffled to the balcony of the chapel, there to settle into a trance-like worship somewhere between dream and devotion. The monks moved silently, appearing in the dimness like apparitions in their white robes and cowls. Their heads were bowed, their feet sandaled and their posture reverent and perhaps a little fatigued as well. They shifted around, avoiding bumping into one another as they negotiated their circular path from their stalls to the main altar and back again, always in silence. Even from as far away as the balcony where we retreatants participated, I could hear the subtle swoosh of their cotton robes brushing against them and the floor. I counted in these mornings thirty-two monks in all.

I also enjoyed later in the morning crossing the highway and walking to the high cornfields of summer with their wispy tops, fine filamented hair swaying slowly in the summer breeze. I would enter these rows and walk through them, the stalks higher than my head; here I felt very protected and cocooned between the stiff rows softly hissing to one another. I loved the smell of this place, hidden and secure between sentinels of corn. I loved equally visiting the dairy where the herds were milked early in the morning in clean, sterile, bright rooms with concrete floors and a bank of skylights. The monks did not mind my being there as long as I stood back from the machines. In their blue Farmer-John overalls and high, black rubber boots, they would simply motion to the cows, who—in a silence not unlike the monks at service—obediently moved into a single stall. There, the electric milkers were then attached to their udders and the milk would miraculously begin squirting in thick jets through the glass or clear plastic pipes into large spun-aluminum holding tanks to begin the pasteurizing process. Monastic moos from the now depleted and contented cows would punctuate the silence and the low drones of the machines.

The stream of cows all lowing impatiently seeped out of the building and along its sides; the cows moved in morning procession, a well-rehearsed ritual to offer up their gift of milk to the machines. Later much, if not all, of this milk would go through its own transformation and become one of four or five different textures, tastes, and sharpnesses of cheeses that the monastery created and shipped all over the world. For years I bought and sent to my parents' home in Euclid, Ohio the famous and popular "Four-pack" containing a large wedge of four kinds of cheese superb in texture, taste, and price. This commodity had only one serious competitor: the famous fruitcake that the monastery had made for decades to generate income. I laughed once when I read Merton admonishing his brethren: "We are not in the cheese and fruitcake business. That is not why we exist!" St. Benedict, looking on, would of course applaud his monk's reminder. Apparently sales were becoming too good and from his vantage point, the business end of monastic living was gaining too much in popularity over the contemplative life. Leah's active life needed to once again concede to the more contemplative Rachel.

Yet, as I watched this work and spoke to the friendly monks who took such pride in their work, I noticed something: their working, their movements seemed to me a form of prayer. They worked with a quiet contentment, and as I watched their faces I could not help think they never left the contemplative life of their vocations; rather, they made their daily work with the cows find an accord with their contemplations. Something serene in their faces I found attractive and desired. I visited the dairy daily to discover their secret, their calmness, their love of God and serving the world through Him each day. Certainly the cows in their care reflected a serenity that pervaded even this busy building. Work as another form that prayer may assume slipped into my awareness.

But above all, what brought me back to this monastery and to subsequent ones stretching now over a period of fifty years was the overpowering sense of mystery and serenity that permeates most monastic settings, the more austere the better. I discovered in each visit a richness, even abundance, in austerity, in a life spare and clean and dedicated to serving others. This discovery was one of so many paradoxes that I began to understand accompanied the life of spiritual largesse.

After two years of teaching high school I was exhausted, as was my wife teaching 7th and 8th grade students at St. Peter's elementary school. My initial searching for graduate schools where I could pursue a Ph.D. and move into college teaching yielded a new program at a small Catholic liberal arts university in Irving, Texas: the University of Dallas. The school was beginning a new program of interdisciplinary thought within what was called The Institute of Philosophic Studies and offered a Ph.D. in a rare area of psychology: Phenomenology. I interviewed for a position in their graduate program, was accepted, and in July of 1972 we moved to Texas on the far side of the planet from Ohio. Just a few months before our move, my wife had been experiencing abdominal pains, which her doctor diagnosed as a stomach virus. On February 11, 1973 we named that virus Matthew Damian, a healthy nine-pounds-plus son, making us wonder once more how low a level of competence some medical staff are able to descend to and yet maintain their license. As I write this our son is forty-two with a beautiful daughter, aged fourteen.

After the first year of graduate school I again felt this call to Gethsemani. Something else needs to be added here: since my interstate ride with my friend Rick to Long Island on his motorcycle so many years ago, I harbored a dream to own one someday. Three months after Sandy and I married in 1968, I bought my first motorcycle. When I decided to end the academic year by spending one week with the monks, their cows and prayer in Kentucky in late spring of 1973, I chose to travel the 1000 miles from Dallas to Trappist, Kentucky on two wheels, taking only minimal clothing, a pup tent purchased at Kmart for $17.00, a used sleeping bag from a second hand store, a few cans of Campbell's Pork-n-Beans, some metal cooking and eating utensils, five carefully chosen books, a rain suit for the southern storms I knew I would encounter, some tools, an extra tire tube for flats, a tire pump, extra spark plugs, and a sparse stash of cash. Robert Pirsig's *Zen and the Art of Motorcycle Maintenance* had just been published and a friend told me to take it with me. I packed it in one of the Craven travel bags of a still fairly new 1971 BMW R75 and loaded the bike till I could not see the seats or the back tire. I was giddy with the prospect of a 1000-mile road in front of me.

I always enjoyed the excitement of preparing for a journey, a thick and leisurely ritual that I was beginning to understand more as a pilgrimage. Memories of my first stay at Gethsemani all began to surface as I prepared for the road trip, all with my wife's blessing and our son Matt's look of confusion, then pain. Did I feel a bit selfish? Yes, indeed, but I submerged these feelings beneath the anticipation of recapturing a sense of peace and contentment that the monastic experience coaxed from me. Hardened by a year of competition with other graduate students and far too intent on proving myself worthy, I felt unmoored. I knew that returning to the monastery would help me reclaim parts of myself that had scattered over the fields of books and lectures of this past year. Most of all, I remember the feeling of peace, serenity, and solitude that would come over me after about two days immersed in this sacred space, a temenos of sorts, that was liberating after a year chasing relentless schedules and demands of study and work. To be on the road, alone, with no helmet on my head and bare arms being burned under the Texas, June sun was a joy to contemplate.

I took two to three days to travel the distance, checking the map for back roads that more-or-less paralleled the Interstate's monotony. The journey to Gethsemani rode in tight competition with the time at the monastery and only occasionally would I ask myself what the true motives for going there were. I do not think I honestly answered that question because I simply did not know. Subsequently, with a bit of maturing, I have a better sense of my motives, which I will explore later; for now, it was enough to fire up the motorcycle and head out Interstate 30 toward Louisiana. I watched my wife Sandy and our new son Matthew grow smaller in my rear view mirrors.

I had discovered KOA campgrounds in previous camping trips; they were close to the main highways, safe, family-oriented, had hot showers, a swimming pool, a little food court, were operated by good people and welcomed motorcyclists into the camping area. Foolishly, in those days, I rode without a helmet, without suntan lotion, with rolled up sleeves, or alternately taking my shirt off and riding through the hot air at 70 mph. Years later, from such careless exposure and earlier ones, I have had two dozen procedures to remove basal cell carcinomas that would appear overnight. But heading to the monastery, I was twenty-seven years old and free as a bird living out some updated version of the film, *Easy Rider*. I also felt very virtuous because I was heading to a monastery. Now whether Gethsemani gave me a reason to travel a long distance by motorcycle or whether the motorcycle was my ticket to the monastery has never been sufficiently sorted out. I only knew I wanted to go and perhaps that was reason enough at this stage of my spiritual questing, which now takes the form of a spiral questioning as I try to turn into some meaning what was at the time an authentic but unformed experience.

Something deeper, however, drew me to the monastic life, some unspoken impulse or urge to enter the silence of spiritual living, with its simplicity, its peeling away of what faded into unimportance after a day or two in this altered condition. No, it was not just about escaping to the road. But that fantasy was the engine that I kick-started to get me going.

The days and nights camping allowed me to cook a little meal for myself after building a respectable fire at my campsite, eat, and then climb into the blue tent, which I had succeeded in anchoring in the dirt with metal stakes. Occasionally I would listen to the quieting voices of other campers, the birds rustling and settling into the trees for the night, and, if I was truly blessed, a light cool breeze that seeped through the thin canvas.

So moved was I by philosopher Robert Pirsig's *Zen* book on humanity and machinery that I read on breaks and in the evening, and so seduced by his various Chatauquas on philosophy that I had to act on it. So, the second morning of my camping out, I awoke just at sunrise, pivoted the BMW motorcycle on its center stand to the east, removed the tool kit, and unfolded the covering to reveal a surgeon's network of utensils, uncorked the valve covers on either side of the horizontally-opposed piston engine now stone-cold from sitting all night, removed the feeler gauge and requisite wrenches from the roll-up tool kit, and with great reverence in complete silence adjusted the valves as a ritual taken from the pages of his book. Pirsig would have been proud of me, I thought, as I replaced the covers and stowed the tools under the seat in the small black fiberglass cradle designed for them.

I was not conscious, exactly, of the ritual I had performed as being a ritual, nor did I find anything particularly extraordinary about what I had just done. I only knew that my morning action was a proper response to the Zen book and seemed to fit into the overall tenor of this journey, or more appropriately as I look back, this pilgrimage to Gethsemani. Ritual was gaining a toehold in my imagination as something to be acknowledged, practiced, remembered, and repeated, always in the spirit of contemplation and reverence. The idea of these motorcycle trips to the monastery began to assume a consciousness of ritual at this moment. Adjusting the valves was a small ritual inside a larger ritual journey. Pirsig's book had made me more conscious of the journey itself as a response to a need and a hunger for ritual that I believe exists in the soul of each of us. Some never acknowledge its existence or importance. I believe now that I was entering with a fuller awareness the power of ritual as a way of making sense of actions that seemed rather flat or mysterious as to their purpose. It was a defining moment for me and I made the rest of the trip to Gethsemani shifting both the gears on the motorcycle and my consciousness to engage another way of thinking about my own destiny within a fuller spiritual awareness. What I would realize later is that I had entered with some authenticity the world of myth and its presence as a conveyor of meaning and purpose for a life.

Subsequent motorcycle trips to Gethsemani over the years became increasingly fatiguing under the hot Texas sun and the monotony of Interstate travel. So beginning on the second trip and on each subsequent one I would include as part of my preparation buying inexpensive poetry anthologies at a local used bookstore. I made certain that it and a roll or two of scotch tape was packed in one of the hollow places of the fairing, which was mounted to the frame and held the windshield in place as well as offered deep hollows on either side for storage. I would tear out two pages from the volume and tape them to the gas tank, one above and one below the gas cap. When fatigue or boredom set in, I would read and memorize the poems, repeating them aloud until they had been committed to memory. At a rest stop or when pausing to fill the gas tank, I would tear those poems from the tank and replace them with two others. In this way I learned what poet's verse was most conducive to gas tank reading and most directly memorable.

I called them "Road Verse." They traveled well, but some poets travel better on a gas tank than others. W. B. Yeats fast became a favorite gas tank poet of mine and I loved to memorize his high-octane verse. Wallace Stevens was most difficult and Emily Dickinson's obsession with the dash made me dizzy, as if I were breathing gas fumes, since I was forced to look down and then back to the road to ingest her poems line by line. Her poems began to take on the shape of a hyphenated road map and I lost the thread of the journey by the time I reached the last line.

Metaphysical poets, however, were my favorite and there was no comparison to reading the poetry of Henry Vaughn or Robert Herrick to promote meditation; but John Donne's sonnets were the best to prepare one for the monastic experience. Consider, for example, part of Sonnet 14, "Batter my heart, three-personed God":

> Batter my heart, three-personed God; for You
> As yet but knock, breathe, shine, and seek to mend;
> That I may rise and stand, o'erthrow me, and bend
> Your force to break, blow, burn, and make me new.
> (*Norton Anthology of Poetry*, 222)

Donne's poetry, especially, allowed me to see how close and intimately compatible was poetry to prayer, a coupling I explored often.

Shakespeare's sonnets also traveled well because they offered such wonderful material with which to contemplate love in all of its forms. Even at high speeds, I found him eminently readable; he seemed to play best through Arkansas and Tennessee. While I wanted to, I never succeeded in composing poetry while driving but instead contented myself to reading the masters under the bright light of the southern sun.

37

Entering Sacred Space

When I arrived days later at the end of the driveway to the monastery, two Cistercian monks of the Benedictine order came out to greet me and ask what I wanted. Few if any retreatants show up here on less than four tires, they told me. I was a novelty, perhaps even a dangerous one, so they were cautious. Storm clouds were forming in the north and I was glad to have arrived just before it unpacked its contents on the parched land suffering a sustained drought. I asked one of the monks if there was any form of a shelter where I could park the motorcycle. They turned from me and took a few steps back to converse for a moment. After a minute one of the brothers told me I could take it through the enclosure gate, which he would open, so that I could park it along the inside wall of the post office. Its floor was concrete, its space massive so that it would not interfere with the general flow of daily commerce that took place there.

I was overjoyed to have my transportation out of the elements during my stay and promptly wheeled it through the gate and into the side entrance of the post office, parking it exactly where they had designated, where it would remain in silence for the duration of my stay. I cancelled all plans to tour the countryside during my days here; such a move forced me to settle in more completely into the rhythm of the place rather than using the monastery as a pit stop between touring excursions.

The monks were surprised to learn I had driven a thousand miles from Texas. I might just as well have come from Bulgaria, so incredulous were their looks. I felt good about my initial impression of them. After checking in with the guest master about my reservations, I returned to unload all of my gear. I hesitated when I entered the post office, however, for there three monks had surrounded the BMW and were pointing at one part or another and whispering quietly to one another. One even tried the throttle grip and gave it a good turn to feel its resistance. I gave them a minute and then made more noise than was necessary on entering so that they stepped back and bowed their heads and smiled as I took first the sleeping bag, then my duffel bag and books from a worn out and broken Samsonite attaché case I had bungy-corded onto the ribbed luggage rack on the back of the bike. In subsequent days I made several trips down to fetch one item or another from the bike's fiberglass saddle bags and was always amused to find a couple of monks gathered around it while one or the other pointed to something that interested him. I felt like some curious apparition that had descended into their midst and they were trying to interpret, by my means of conveyance, what I could possibly be doing here.

It was the same question I posed to myself every time I came to Gethsemani, which numbered eleven retreats in a sixteen-year span. This annual pilgrimage became a necessary part of my life. I did not always travel by motorcycle, but in the half dozen times that I did, the monks always allowed me to park in the post office. That event established my identity as we joked that I had the only reserved parking space in the monastery's history.

I never left Gethsemani or any of the monasteries transformed. I don't believe God works in us so dramatically, though He may. What I did leave feeling was rested, refreshed, more focused, more ordered, with a clearer sense of purpose in what I was doing, a much fuller gratitude for my life, which felt closer to a state of prayer that my daily life often pushed out, and more connected to an awareness of the invisible powers governing the world's motion. Daily prayer became a corridor into a sense that mystery was the dominant force governing the world's order. I might call that presence God, but I did not feel a necessity to. I was conscious, however, that my awareness of myself *and* the world as well as myself *in* the world, had increased and deepened in crucial and permanent ways.

For example, I began to sense that by stepping out of the familiar and everyday world of student, worker, husband, and father, I could enter through the doors of the monastery what was unfamiliar terrain in me. Finding the safe structure of a monastery allowed me to ask myself questions about what I was doing in the world—questions that did not have a chance to live and breathe in my daily round of schedules and obligations. The monastery's atmosphere and serene pace, its quiet and its absence of demands, allowed a field to open in me that was at once frightening and attractive, unnerving and energizing.

This monastic atmosphere began at first as simply a felt sense, which then over time became a voice, subtle and quiet, that reminded me of the presence of love in the world. How we move into that love, I began to imagine, is what grace guides us toward. These truths were gifted to me in moments of quiet meditation, so I began to look forward to periods of sustained quiet to listen to what else would be revealed. What surfaced were not ideas but images: my brothers and sister, my parents, my own family of wife and child in Texas, my pursuit of a doctoral degree. So much of what I took for granted became strange and unfamiliar, as if I were looking at someone else's life. I believe it was the beginning of what in some religious traditions is called an unattached mindfulness, a way of seeing without emotional engagement so to discern and feel more deeply. Most of all was the most precious boon of wanting or desiring nothing. Life itself as it was given contained more than ample abundance.

A little irony creeps in here, for it may be that monasteries may not even be the best places to stay at if one is engaged in a concerted and even urgent search; perhaps they are the places of rest during the search rather than the arenas for the search itself. I was content to pray, to attend the various prayer and chanting gatherings, to participate in the Mass, to take naps, to read to my heart's content, to write in my journal daily and to occasionally check in on the BMW in the post office to be sure a monk had not slipped it out the back door for a quick ride up to Bardstown with a load of monk's cheese and fruitcake to peddle.

I felt also that I had dared in these retreats to explore some of the more destructive elements in my life: my anger, my hot temper, my uncanny ability to be easily bruised or hurt by any slight done to me, intentional or unintentional, a tendency to become depressed and to stay in a blue funk for days, a general obsession with taking care of myself first, my friends next, my school work next, and my wife and son somewhere after that if enough time remained. These all surfaced of their own accord in a series of what I call "reckonings." I did not need to send out invitations for them to visit nor did I greet them with a welcoming gesture to enter and settle in for long periods. "Batter my heart, three-personed God." They knocked on the door of my heart with each day I spent at the monastery and I always felt somewhere in the process a very strong and unavoidable feeling of remorse, along with a firm purpose of amendment to do better, to be more compassionate, to practice generosity to my own family first before radiating it out to others. And to allow all these good intentions to emanate from my own ability, accompanied by grace, to be more compassionate with myself; let it begin at home, I was advised.

I do not know if this shift into a more honest introspection was God working on me, in me, or not. I do know that it happened there at the monastery and that whatever book I picked up in the library, or chose to pack and bring to read during my stay, inevitably directly addressed one or the other of these weaknesses in me, as if I were being directed by some invisible guiding hand to face and entertain these scars on my soul and to consider ceasing to reopen afflictions that needed a final and permanent cauterizing.

In the face of this anguish, I remember what one of the monks, Brother Peter, told me as we strolled one day in the thick summer heat of a June afternoon inside the stone walls of the guest house property. We passed alongside the dark waters of the pond where magnificent goldfish swam, where bullfrogs grunted the evening away, and where the Stations of the Cross carved out of cedar wood circled the inside walls along a gravel pathway. Brother Peter observed: "people make such a big mistake coming here hoping to find God or have a beatific vision, when all we ask is that people show up, take naps, eat good but simple food, hike in the woods, listen to the birds and leave replenished. Often that is what people need more than seeing God."

I liked his simple and profound observation because it helped me to lower my expectations to a human level and to give up, at least in the way I was pursuing it, the need for a transcendent experience. "That," the brother told me, "would come of its own accord if one were ready to receive it." "So what is it to pursue God, for you?" I asked him. His reply astonished me: "By doing nothing more than walking with you around the grounds and noticing the beauty in the commonplace." The simplicity of his faith was so grounded in the world that I began to lose the belief that "spiritual" meant "ethereal" or "unearthly." He was one of my strongest guides at this or any other monastic setting. Grace walks into our lives on the most unexpected feet.

I have kept his words close to me in all subsequent retreats over the years when I have walked through the entranceway of many monasteries and retreat centers since then, both in the United States and in Italy. It reminds me of Emily Dickinson's insightful observation about poetry, in which the poet must claim, "to tell all the truth, but tell it slant." Don't try to pursue certain things head-on, for it invites failure or only partial success. Let the slant of things have a chance to play, let the spiral spin itself out, not through a direct frontal assault but by means of a more subtle circling motion that paradoxically often becomes the most direct route. The sacred is life slanted, I thought. Not a slippery slope but a slanted plane of vision may be the most effective presence of the holy.

Hiking in the woods one time with my younger brother Bill, who had driven down from Cleveland to spend five days at Gethsemani with me, we found a footpath on the same side of the road as the monastery but north of it. Ambling along with no destination in mind, we came upon a clearing. There, in the center of it, backed up to the woods that loomed darkly behind it, even in the midday sun, was a cinder block building, a cabin of sorts, with a deep concrete-slabbed porch in front. We had both heard that Thomas Merton, after years of negotiating and not a little wrangling with the abbot, had finally received permission to build a structure not too far from the monastery—about a twenty-minute walk—and to live there for extended periods of time in complete solitude. Bill and I did not know if this was indeed Merton's cabin nor if it was occupied, but our curiosity proved too great, so we proceeded slowly and with respect toward the porch in case a monk would suddenly emerge from the front door. The surrounding was full of silence; one could hear grasshoppers chirping in the field in front and a thicket of birds from the woods. The setting was serene and quiet; the house seemed enveloped in a deep stillness. Excited about the prospect of having stumbled on Merton's hermitage, and not seeing or hearing anyone within, we stepped on to the porch and peered into one of the front windows.

Origins of the Monastic Call

Inside was one large room with a fireplace against the back wall, a writing desk, a few pieces of spare furniture, a cement floor with a few dimly-colored rugs lying about, a simple wooden crucifix on one wall, and a cloth-covered reading chair. The overall effect was of a simple but engaging austerity, sparse but welcoming. What I liked about its coziness was its feeling of bare essentials being just enough, actually more than adequate, for one to live there full time. Simple bare essentials characterized the insides, dark in corners but lighted by the several windows around its outside. As I peered into his room, I felt the presence of a subdued freedom, a space of liberation, where so few objects in it allowed one to move and think in an expansive liberty.

We did not try the door but turned instead to sit on the white wooden chairs arranged on the porch to face the mountain range directly before us. When we positioned ourselves and looked out, the deep green Kentucky landscape took our breath away. We knew instantly why Merton had built his simple domicile here and facing the direction he had chosen.

The porch looked out to a string of mountains overlapping one another far into the distance. It was easy to imagine him, or any monk who would use this hermitage subsequently, gazing out in the evening or the morning toward the majestic silent row of mountains stretching to eternity. This afternoon as we sat there in a hazy summer heat filled with sounds of crickets, birds, and a slight breeze in the enormous trees behind us, we saw how the mountains were covered with a gauze of haze so that their contours were delicately softened. They appeared almost like dark ghostly forms that invited the eye to meditate on them, to lose oneself in reverie there on the porch, a wonderful liminal pocket between the interior of the hermitage and the deep distance of nature, unencumbered by power lines, billboards or other buildings—nothing but a clean field newly-mowed in front of the hermitage and stretching out some one hundred feet, and then the meadow extending farther down a gentle slope into the dark woods just ahead. The smell of new-mown grass was sweet in our noses and the gentle buzz of insects filled out the solitude. How powerful was the impulse to meditate outdoors here in the natural beauty of a Kentucky hillside. How strong was nature's invitation to contemplate in easy breaths as my eyes slowly closed.

I don't know how long Bill and I sat there in silence. But I remember promising myself that if I came back to Gethsemani, and if the hermitage was unoccupied, that I would again make the pilgrimage up here to the porch, simply to sit for a part of the day and to feel the presence of Merton, the other monks who rotated staying here, and the deep warmth of the summer afternoons that gave this carved space out of nature a sacred feel and security rarely felt by me in any other locale. Later, in photo books of Merton and the monastery, I would see him dressed in blue denim work clothes, sitting right where my brother and I were now. He would be looking out, faintly smiling or standing by the side of the building or reading or writing inside, a large bulk of a man, a thick farmer whose fingernails, I imagined, always carried a bit of earthy dirt under them that may have peppered the keys of the typewriter he hovered over. Soil and soul, dirt and divinity, earth and eternity—all congealed in my imagination of Merton and place.

Being this close to him, and to the building that he constructed, emanated a feeling of consolation and made the man more incarnate. Merton once wrote of solitude:

> Why write about solitude in the first place? . . . Those who are to become solitary are, as a rule, solitary already. At most they are not yet aware of their condition. In which case, all they need is to discover it. But in reality, all men are solitary. Only most of them are so averse to being alone, or to feeling alone, that they do everything they can to forget their solitude. (qtd. in *Echoing Silence*, 25)

After a time, my brother broke the silence. "Do you want to head back to the monastery?" "No," I said, "not yet. Do you?" "No," was his immediate reply. He then said what I felt: "Sitting here so close to where Merton composed some of his best writing, I feel like I know him as a person rather than as the most popular monk writer/ poet of this century." I agreed. The memory of Merton was so strong that we were both content to sit looking at the mountains and feel his presence. We felt quite palpably the spirit of the man and his work, as well as a certain peace that overcame us both in the presence of God's creation.

Origins of the Monastic Call

A pacifist with a fierce obligation to live and speak of the life of contemplation, Merton wrote at one point about his own writing: "There is no question that the activity of writing and the thinking that goes with it all is for me healthy and productive—because, I suppose, it is my most normal activity" (*Turning Toward the World*, 31). Perhaps he wrote these words on the other side of the cinderblock walls only feet from where we were sitting. This may have been the place where he discovered the deep confusion and turmoil of his vocation, a confusion I currently feed off of because it gives me solace and hope. One hears the anguish in his voice when he writes: "Action, however, can and must be taken in my own life which has become confused, distracted, sloppy, off center" (*Turning Toward the World*, 41). No, the monastery is not the place one heads for as a spiritual equivalent of Club Med. Naïve and foolhardy it is to think, as some do, that in the cloister of monastic life all strife, confusion, and anguish dissipate. It can just as easily become the place where all forms of weakness, resentment, pettiness, and wounding escape through the fissures of silence and worship. Spirituality is not immune from the need, on occasion, for therapy.

Merton's anguish illustrates plainly that monastic living does not exonerate one from life's pollutions; in fact, in some ways it may exacerbate them. I like his words of anguish and confusion—if he is courageous enough to admit them, who am I to deny their destructive and yet guiding presence in my own life? Monastic living is like a magnifying glass of sorts: it exaggerates and makes big what the rest of us in our daily lives often try to ignore or bury or deflect by a din of distractions. In moments of quiet contemplation I often felt a pageant of inadequacies line up and march right into my attempts at prayer—all forms of remembered hurts, failures, attempts at perfection not achieved, silly fights with my wife, ferocious attempts to be right, an inability to listen to another from his/her point of view, the need for recognition and success, to name a few. Tremendous courage is needed to enter the monastery even for a few weeks, let alone a lifetime, if one is called by the voice of blind faith.

Bill and I enjoyed one another's company intensely at this moment; we grew closer not as brothers but as friends sharing these moments of silence with Merton. Later I was to read in his journals—my God, did the man do nothing but write!—dated September 4, 1960: "Perhaps what is required is blind faith that in spite of everything God works in His own time, [He will] lead me to a more fruitful place, where I really belong, where I can serve Him more truly" (*Turning Toward the World*, 41). The idea captivated me: to move in the world to the right place in order to serve Him truly. But where and what is the right place and how does one know one is moving in the right direction or is instead really being instructed to stay put? These questions cannot be answered; they require the (e)motion of blind faith. Perhaps my visits to monasteries over the years, undertaken in blind faith and in the spirit of unknowing, have been to do the right thing, to submit to place and time where certain responses will be called for.

Dissolution

A couple of other events caught my attention. The first occurred after several one-week visits to Gethsemani; it marked a shift in my attitude and reason for returning to this religious setting and subsequently to many other retreat centers. I had given up directly searching for God. "When he wants to find me, he knows where I am," I told myself as I lifted that burden off my shoulders and felt freer to settle in as best I could to the rhythms and patterns of the monastery. Perhaps God comes to us, like Truth as told in Dickinson's poetic lines earlier: Slantwise. I knew that I was working far too hard on staying busy, determined to plan each day so as not to have to meet up with the vacuum of non-doing. I pledged to slow down in order to give Life more space to unfold on its own terms and conditions.

Then, one morning, early, as I found a place by myself in one of the pews of the balcony where I could look down and witness the monks entering, I felt a faint flush of some presence moving in me. I had by now, after several visits, fallen in love with the psalms, especially when they are chanted by the monks in the Psalter, alternating responding to one another across the aisle as first one, then the other group of monks, sang part of the verses. I still have my own copy of the one used by the monks and have read it often during the ensuing years. I remember being moved by the psalm being sung that morning in the dim light before dawn. The atmosphere had something of the uncanny about it, an expectation even, as I listened closely to the chants:

> Lord, hear a cause that is just,
> Pay heed to my cry.
> Turn your ear to my prayer:
> No deceit is on my lips.
> From you may my judgment come forth.
> Your eyes discern the truth.
> You search my heart, you visit me by night.
> You test me and you find in me no wrong.
> My words are not sinful, as are men's words.
> (*The Psalms*, 36–37)

I felt suddenly as if I had pilgrimaged inside the chanting as it embraced me; at that instant, and without any warning, I began to weep. No reason surfaced, just the weeping, which part of me was embarrassed by and another part of me did not care—I needed to weep. I put my head down and those that I loved began to appear before me with the words, "These are your gifts which you must cherish." I knew on a deep level that if God was to appear in my life tangibly, that this was one of those moments, when a rush of some sweet and stinging force became suddenly so present that everything around me dimmed and disappeared. I stopped resisting my emotions and allowed them to wash over me fully, for I sensed that this was a visitation from another realm that was thoroughly in this realm of listening to the chanting of the psalms, as if the monks' singing had conjured some strange and powerful force into our midst, like a field of faith newly seeded. Such is the power of the Psalter; for the first time I recognized chanting and singing's supernatural power.

I was grateful that only a couple of other retreatants had risen early to be present for the psalms before Mass. Something broke down in me at that moment, some dissolution of hardness, some calcified part of me melted down and allowed me feelings I had not experienced for a very long time, and least of all in public. I wept for the pain I had caused others, for the harshness with which I often treated myself, and with the unforgiving quality of my thoughts and feelings toward those who had offended or wounded me in some way. My soul felt called to something at this moment, however unidentifiable it would remain. The small part of me, the part that is so sensitive and easily offended, the part that resents, grows angry, feels remorse, is extreme in seeking perfection—that part of me broke open and I felt called to a larger sense of myself and others than I had ever acknowledged.

Such an experience was to happen many times while staying at other retreat centers. A terrible feeling of isolation merged with a felt sense that I was not alone in my suffering and that joy was possible even in this anguish, which had a melancholy sweetness about it. It surfaced and lingered with me long after I had left the place. I knew something important had occurred to me but resisted the urge to analyze it—in it was a sensed presence of a reality that had no boundaries and resolved all feelings and thoughts of contradiction, all dichotomies and differences. I knew that some altered awareness of who I was had a permanence, even a necessity about it that frightened me because it arrived, like many of my aggressive and angry outbursts, completely out of the control of what I desired or anticipated. I think its power frightened me, yet I longed for it to reoccur, knowing in the moment the foolishness of pursing it.

Later, after breakfast, I sought the outdoors. I walked the woods daily and ate meals with the other retreatants with a new shifted awareness of what, I could not language. But the place was different now, more hospitable, less foreign. I felt for a moment that some layer of the monastic world had been peeled back, if even for an instant, and that I had peered into some dimension or terrain that may, I say *may*, be closer to where the monks live every day. So powerful was this experience of being flooded with so commanding an emotional rush that I wrote about it in my journal for days after and thought about it often on my drive home. How, I wondered, could reality contain such profound emotional life that felt at once sacred and numinous and frightening? I knew that instead, it had to seep in, like one of those garden hoses with a million holes in them, called a "soaker" that lets the hard ground soften over time as it absorbs tiny trickles of water. Absorption, not an excessive deluge, was the slow pace of understanding.

In those days at Gethsemani only men were allowed to stay at the monastery. One of the monks told me that they had allowed couples to make retreats at one time, but the atmosphere had quickly become too social, too much of a festive and collective gaiety, so the monastery dropped this option. If spouses came, they could stay in a room across the road on the property and meet with their husbands or partners during the day. Since that time, women are now allowed to make retreats alone at the monastery, something I found to be true in virtually every place I stayed or read about.

One of these men appeared in the library one morning just after I had settled into a chair for a long read. He was excited and wound up rather tightly for such an early hour. He told me, without hesitation, that he had just been released from state prison after having served a number of years for killing a man in self-defense while serving time. His initial charge was robbery, but killing another inmate in a knife fight had extended his stay. Now paroled, Paul had made an appointment with the abbot to request entrance into Gethsemani as a novice. From his prison days he knew in his heart that becoming a monk was his vocation and he was anxious to begin. His interview was in one hour. We talked for a while and then I wished Paul well as he returned to his room to prepare for the interview.

Later that day, after dinner, we met and walked along the roads and on to a footpath that led along a drainage ditch for a quarter mile, then headed back toward a beautiful grove where there was a statue of Jesus in a position of anguish as the artist imagined him in the garden at Gethsemani. About fifty feet away was a clustered statue of Christ's three disciples all asleep, unable to stay awake with him as he prayed for the cup of his own sacrifice to pass from him. I identified much more sympathetically with them, for my inability was closer to theirs.

Paul and I sat there in the grove as the light receded behind the thickness of maple, sycamore, and cottonwood trees. He told me the abbot was very kind but was very emphatic that it would not be a good idea for Paul, newly out of prison after many years, to begin life as a novice with the Trappists. He suggested instead that perhaps in a few years he could visit again and reapply. Paul was devastated. He had planned with absolute certainty that he would be accepted and had therefore no backup plans. His future appeared before him as a gaping vacuum. He had hitch-hiked to the monastery with only the few belongings he had brought from a Kentucky prison, so certain he was that he would be accepted.

As we looked together in silence at the anguished and suffering expression of Christ facing the cruelty of his own future, there in the woods, every day and every night, with no one watching with him except those of us who were willing to sit for a while and witness his future, I felt a deep compassion for this man. "Now," he said, "I guess I will go to my sister's in Lexington, but I am out of money and have no transportation. The few dollars the prison gave me for bus fare is gone. The abbot said I could stay for free at the monastery for a few days, but then it would be best if I left."

I told Paul that my stay was up in two days and that I was then heading to Cleveland on my BMW and could take him as far as Lexington. I thought I could make room for him if I repacked my gear to free up the passenger seat. He agreed and for the next two days Paul seemed more content. He had called his sister and she had told him to come to her home.

My stay at Gethsemani came quickly to a close. Time always accelerated during these quiet days outside of the pulsing routine of responsibilities at home. Paul and I loaded our belongings on to the BMW and headed northeast, both bare-headed, for in those days helmet laws had not gone into effect, or, unfortunately, been repealed under the pressure of motorcycle riders who claimed restrictions on their right to whack a bare noggin against a tree or street surface as one of their options. So together, and with Paul screaming into my ear most of the trip in an attempt to have a conversation amidst Peter Built semis and swarms of cars and campers whizzing past us on the interstate, we cruised toward his sister's home. I would welcome our separation and my solitary ride hundreds of miles north to Cleveland.

I left Paul at an intersection in downtown Lexington, and we promised to keep in touch after exchanging addresses. I wanted to know if he was accepted into Gethsemani on his next try. Even as we spoke and waved goodbye, I knew I would never see or hear from him again, which proved to be true. But I thought of Paul often, especially as he embodied so compactly the mysterious intimacy between violence and the sacred, between killing and a deep spiritual quest and how that coupling has been part of human history and given dramatic expression in the first murder of Abel by Cain in the Biblical tradition to the suicide bombings of the World Trade Towers in New York and the Pentagon in Washington, DC, as well as a global up swelling of violence in the name of God, religion, and salvation.

I also thought of how I was being used by God to help this pilgrim on his way, to transport him from the monastery into a new life, a new beginning, closer to where he was to be true to another calling that he did not yet sense. Perhaps Paul had to pass through Gethsemani to be guided by the abbot toward another future, another vocation, and that I had been used as a vehicle in the form of a two-wheeled motorcycle to transport him a few interstate miles closer to his destination. How can one know without a deep faith that this possibility might be the true one? And that is part of the mystery of divine action, invisible but palpably real when it is embodied in human enactment, that brought me back repeatedly, as if called by a divine voice, silent but heard, to the monastic way of life.

Helping Paul on his own journey made me feel even more deeply God's presence and design in my life. I felt a burning recognition that I was being called every day to serve others, not myself. The monastery was for me an opening, a door to walk through, so that I could perceive another ground of being, one that put others before my own desires.

3

The Extended Pilgrimage

I don't want to go on being a root in the dark, / insecure, stretched
out, shivering with sleep, / going on down, into the moist guts of
the earth, / taking in and thinking, eating every day.
                                    —Pablo Neruda, "Walking Around"

THE PRECEDING CHAPTER outlined my initial interest in and
participation in the monastic life, a beginning that is still
with me over fifty years later. In addition, it was the period
of seed planting, harvested many years later when I decided to use
a sabbatical to venture on a three-and-a-half-month pilgrimage
through five states and twelve retreat settings. What follows is the
record of those life-altering months.

In my life I have been blessed with a host of guides, mentors,
angels, and psychopomps along the road who have both pointed me
in directions I should take and repelled me from roads I should
avoid. They have appeared in many guises: as people, as animals, as
books, as ideas, and as poets.

Planning this sabbatical pilgrimage incited a great thirst in me,
with a corresponding hunger, to seek out a personal God that speaks
directly to me within a unique spiritual life that serves as mentor and
guide in this life, one which allows my footing to be a bit more secure
in a very unpredictable and slippery world. The lens of understanding began to focus just a bit more on the image of my desire.

Some ideas die with a struggle. Other ideas, desires or inclinations have a longer shelf life in the soul. After cultivating a careful
rhythm of an annual pilgrimage to Gethsemani for many years, I
stopped visiting monasteries for the next fifteen as my personal and

professional life skidded and careened with no clear anchor grounding me in one place or one secure teaching position. I alternately drifted and was guided by a sure invisible hand.

Then, after teaching at a small Catholic university in San Antonio, Texas, for several years, I was promised a sabbatical, my first in twenty-five years in the classroom. Such is the price tag attached to changing jobs and institutions: one is forced each time to reset the sabbatical clock. In a bookstore one day and not looking for anything in particular, I came to the travel section and there, glancing down, I saw, with some astonishment, a two-volume set of paperback books entitled *Sanctuaries: A Guide to Lodgings in Monasteries, Abbeys, and Retreats of the United States* by Marcia and Jack Kelly. Without even a thought, I impulsively bought both volumes and took them home. One of the two volumes was dedicated to the West Coast and Southwest, the other to the East Coast and Southeast. Each contained descriptions, addresses, directions and histories of hundreds of retreat centers in the United States. Since the publication of these volumes in 1992, the Kellys have updated both volumes in a supplemental book published in 1998, followed by a revision in 2010.

In my study I began to dream of putting together a sabbatical pilgrimage that would allow me to stay at several retreat centers in various parts of the country I had never visited. The idea both felt right and excited me, sending my imagination forward to the time when I could step out of the routines of teaching, meetings, essay grading, family responsibilities and enter once more the terrain of solitude that for many years I had bracketed in order to secure an academic career. Dormant for so long, the memory of monastic living scooted back into my memory with a force that was both exciting and demanding.

At just this time, however, I received a phone call from the Provost of Pacifica Graduate Institute to come to southern California to teach full time in their Counseling and Mythology programs. I eagerly accepted the offer and soon found myself packing the two volumes of *Sanctuaries* in boxes, along with the thousands of other books in my library, and preparing, with my family, for another journey that had not been planned or expected. I left the possibility of a sabbatical behind me and with it, the fantasy of retreats. But while the books were packed, the idea wasn't. It occupied much of my time even while my family and I made the transition from one saint's city to another: San Antonio to Santa Barbara.

What I did not count on, however, was that the time accrued teaching that led to a sabbatical at this institution was shorter than most universities; before too many years had passed, I was offered time off during the following academic year. The Kelly volumes had been placed prominently on a bookstand close to my important books; with this offer from the school, I once more pulled them from the shelves, this time to actually plan a three-and-a-half-month pilgrimage into unknown terrain.

Preparing for the trip infused me with new life and thoughts of unforeseen skirmishes with the unknown. And yet, thinking of the voyage, I was not really choosing it as much as I was being hand-picked by it. Some other presence was guiding what I tentatively called "my" decision. Nothing else presented itself as a suggestion for another kind of sabbatical project. Only this. It was less that I chose to participate in the religious life of various communities in several states on the western side of the United States as much as I was called to this participation. I decided to trust this awareness, to listen and to meditate on the pages of the volume as I slowly turned them; they described the various places in the six states listed: Arizona, California, Colorado, New Mexico, Oregon, and Washington. Since I had trusted this process of renegotiating a monastic pilgrimage, I would then make my decision on how each place felt and how it called to me and to trust that I would journey to those places that I needed to discover and to be present at just those times they slotted into my itinerary. I also knew on a more visceral level that this journey would be an interior one as well and that the terrain I traversed in my spiritual life could prove to be more hazardous a landscape than any exterior wilderness I found myself in. Was I to imitate on some critical level Dante the pilgrim's own birthing awareness when at the beginning of his 14th century poem, the *Divine Comedy*, he finds himself conscious, perhaps for the first time, but nonetheless lost in a dark wood (*la selva oscura*) midway through his life? The interior dark woods both frightened and attracted me. I felt that this trip was a necessity, not a luxury. Feeling connected to it in this way encouraged me to hasten my plans and solidify the reservations.

In February and March of 1998 I began each morning perusing the lists of retreat centers in each state as I prepped for the sabbatical, which would run from August to December of the same year. I was excited and anxious when I thought of the length of time away as well as the chagrin I might feel if I returned home early because I lacked the moral stamina or the psychological and emotional energy to sustain such a sojourn. I wasn't going skiing in the Alps or backpacking through Greece. I was going to drive my truck to the entrance of a dozen monasteries. Then what? Sit and read? Bother other retreatants because the experience of being alone proved too overwhelming? Sulk, slip, and slide into a deep depression? Smuggle some bottles of Merlot into my room and drink myself silly until vespers or matins where I could then slur the Psalter with indignation? As the time to depart grew closer, all of the above as well as other options became very real. But they rested smaller than my desire to venture forth, having heard and heeded the call.

I thought of asking my wife to give me some accelerated lessons in cross-stitching so I could make a mural of Rome, something big and, above all, time-consuming, for time is what I was giving myself and I feared not having it filled to capacity with a busy schedule for each day. So habituated was I that I could not even bear the possibility of having days unstructured, open-ended, unplanned, full of holes. I felt compelled to fill them out with activity before I even left home. If I was not going to be constructive, productive, and busy, then why go? I can see in retrospect that the motives we use to avoid experiences of God, the sacred, and numinous, are legion, infinite, and subtle. I succeeded in part in staying busy, but there were days when I allowed the deep silence and open space of what I came to call God's Dark Presence to seep into my life, unscheduled and unannounced. Love and terror at first accompanied these moments and hours. Being alone and feeling lonely soon made their own distinctive presences; I wanted the former and would be very comfortable without the latter.

The above unease at having too much unstructured time forced me to contemplate the deep fear that can generate much of my daily activity. As some historical periods have been called The Age of Reason, or The Age of Anxiety, I want to dub mine "The Age of Activity" or even "How to Avoid the Silence of the Sacred in Everyday Life." Answer: Keep Busy and hunker down just below full or partial consciousness. Such a futile response.

I also felt a certain shame growing in me, the shame of leaving the trip only partly completed. I could simply abort the pilgrimage after a week or two and drive around, intrude into the homes of relatives, to my sons' apartments in San Antonio, familiar places where friends would invite me out to dinner and ask how I am doing. At this stage I began to think of canceling the handful of reservations I had secured and to make it a 3-week instead of a 15-week journey. I could play it safe and pull out on a much shorter leash and then visit the Grand Canyon, the Grand Tetons, the Grand anything, then simply point the truck toward home and drive until I found my driveway.

But faith comes in all forms and grace intrudes in such subtle variations. I believe that it was a sense of grace that gave me the courage to persevere, to complete the reservation dates at each place and to buy what I needed in order to make the extended journey that by now had taken on a life of its own. So against this force that said "give it up, modulate your vision of things, back down on the intention to stay on the road and in the monasteries for the times planned," I pushed on and secured a solid three-month schedule, remembering to give myself some breaks of up to three days between monastic sites. I therefore chose places that seemed to invite me with a certain hospitable feeling as I read of their facilities. I allowed the journey of reading through *Sanctuaries* as its own pilgrimage to shape the contours of the road journey. Not science but a certain blind faith led me to direct my course in this way.

My intention in crafting the grid I would follow was a simple ritual. I was to remain as calm and silent as I could and to meditate for a few moments before opening the guidebook. I would then jot down the names of places that seemed to have an energy or a calling that presented themselves more than others, and then to simply trust this response. Some of those places that selected themselves, however, were not available when my schedule would allow me to be there, so after a phone call, I let them go as possible sites. I trusted that they were, for whatever reason at this stage, not places that I needed to stay in. After almost five weeks preparing the list of retreat centers, I arrived at the schedule outlined in the Table of Contents. In retrospect, the plan, with all of its blemishes, imperfections, and shortcomings, worked. I could then plot another pilgrimage using the same intuitive faith method.

But I was still trapped to a large degree in the "keep-this-trip-full-and-busy" mode of retreating, so, foolishly, I scheduled myself in such a way that I would take various breaks in the journey to fly to Vancouver, British Columbia and give a talk and a poetry workshop at their C.G. Jung Center. Then, as if that were not enough, I would fly to New Orleans weeks later to give a talk at the Parker Institute, fly back and resume my pilgrimage. I did both of these, but I felt as if I had removed a major organ like my own appendix in the process, because I did not foresee or even calculate what a powerful hold the various retreat centers would have on me individually and then in a collective accretion, or even how I would enter into the spirit of the monks' lives, into their contemplative and prayerful, meditative existence. In short, I left no room for exiting out of the contemplative life or reentering it. The abrupt transitions were therefore painful and very unsettling. This process of wrenching myself back and forth between worlds was a hard lesson to learn about the power of interactive fields. When one enters a field deeply, its energy arena must be respected; abruptly pulling out of one field into another had a shattering effect on the entire pilgrimage.

It is a subtle slippage. The contemplative life is not something one steps into, as if entering a building or a Jacuzzi: one moment you are outside, the next you are securely ensconced within. I did not even feel the slow tug of the places working on me until I found myself at the airport prepared to fly to the cities in which I was scheduled to talk. Only then did the whole cacophony of modern life slap me sober as I realized how far I had retreated from this frenzy. Advice to myself: do nothing more than settle into the places chosen so that the schedule of other events does not intrude and rupture whatever peace and discovery you have experienced. My ceaseless activity almost ruined the entire experience and under-scored how the desire or compulsion to remain busy is not a sign of progress but a symptom of a deep fear of silence, contemplation, and even one's self, wrapped, for a time, tightly in God's presence.

As I prepared for the journey that was fast approaching, I contin-ued to read in areas new to me. I read in the *Upanishads* what I should have taken to heart; instead it remained outside of me: "when the five senses of the mind are still and reason rests in silence, then begins the Path supreme; this calm steadiness of the senses is called Yoga and emerges when all the desires that cling to the heart are surrendered, when all ties that bind the heart are unloosened, then a mortal becomes immortal" (*The World's Wisdom*, 14). My ambitions were so much lower than attempting to move to immor-tality. I wanted to think about and define for myself my own mortal-ity, why I was the way I was, why I had had this desire for the sacred all my life and what it covered up or what was covering *it* up. I knew that I could not make a resolute decision to enter into the religious life with the right spiritual attitude, accompanied by a willingness to yield to its presence more fully.

I thought more honestly about human freedom and being liber-ated from destructive emotions, patterns of behavior like those fueled by resentments, envy, a need for success, anglings for popu-larity, desire for success, and recognition through teaching and publishing. I was, in short, a driven person who fed ferociously, sometimes addictively, on success and recognition. I began to fear that that was all I was and had, in the process for gain, in fact short-changed more essential, if not more satisfying, qualities: a good husband, a kind and nurturing father, a faithful friend and a good brother to my immediate family, and a son my parents could be proud of. Would I receive answers to any of these questions? It did not matter, for I was being called to pilgrimage and had to yield to this voice in order to complete something in my life. In retrospect I would call it a quest, for I was full of questions in my mid-fifties and some threshold was calling me to be crossed, to bridge parts of myself. In traveling over eight thousand miles by truck and plane, I would in some small measure make the crossing over the largest freestanding bridge of my life.

Reflecting now on my life plot, I see that its major motif as well as its central archetypal figure was that of a journeyer, a voyager. In forty-six years of marriage we have lived in seventeen different homes. Sojourning to the next life station has been palpable and frequent, so this monastic journey was another chapter in a travel plot that allowed for only short respites of dwelling in place.

The *Bhagavad-Gita* helped me immensely at this crossroads. In fact, as the patterns of a life begin to emerge to reveal their invisible powers, I notice that my guides throughout my life have been as often a book or a passage I tripped across at just the time I required to hear/read it, as if they have been persons who gave me words I needed at a strategic moment of a profound shift in direction. A few weeks before the pilgrimage, I was to meditate on the idea of non-attached action. It suggests: go ahead and act, but remain free of its consequences. The problem is not the action but the quality of mind with which one acts. To identify with one's actions in desiring certain results, one is then bound, trapped in effect, to that pattern of action. It is best, this wise text cautions, to act earnestly but without attachment to results (*World's Wisdom*, 31). The language of this wisdom helped me realize that I desired to enter into the monastic life with some unarticulated results already at hand. I needed to surrender something of my own desires to the larger reality of the pilgrimage: once I succeeded in doing so, if only partly, it would be enough to free me for the journey. From this point on I never looked back.

The entire trip was undertaken with a few insights into my own character: I consider myself a spiritual person but do not know what that means fully. I have witnessed clergy—nuns and priests—exact the cruelest behavior on others and I have witnessed kindness from those who profess no religious beliefs. I also continue to learn how to pray, but its action remains a mystery. I am easily distracted and have a hard time meditating, calming the mind, eliminating desires, dissolving destructive thoughts, curtailing anger, stifling resentments, moderating, comparing myself with others, or squelching mean or self-lacerating thoughts. Armed with such a panoply of deterrents, I made the pilgrimage anyway. I thought that if I waited to salve all the wounds and lacerations of my psychic and emotional life, I would probably decay in the very spot I wished to begin from. Go with the wounds, thought I, for your present condition may in fact be the best it is going to be for the time being.

Even with all of my blemishes showing and becoming more chronic and acute, I nonetheless felt the call to spirit, a spiritual unconscious, perhaps, that however imperfect and half-formed, was mine to work with and be worked on. Who knows what might bubble up and be revealed to me through the cracks and fissures of my own fallen and fallible nature? That was not mine to control but to be present to. Feeling deep within me a form of spiritual anorexia, I knew that there was a fuller nourishment possible; I had just not found the right table to sit at so that I could discover it on the menu. Perhaps my inner life is spiritual first, psychological and emotional second and third.

I realized too that the language of the Catholic Church in its homilies and sermons had long ago lost its connection to mystery for me. It seemed divorced from any imaginal grasp of how and what I lived; it was rational and uninspired in its descriptions, as if it had lost its source of inspiration and energy. Instead, what I yearned for were the numinous shadows hidden in the light of the gospels' words. The Church preached Main Street theology; by contrast I needed the back alleys, hidden piazzas, and deserted side streets filled with puddles, of a faith in crisis and confusion. The language of church doctrines was that of the garden and salvation, or order and degree, of certitude; my soul sought the harsh arid climate of the desert, the space of austerity and simplicity, the movement of lizards on hot stones, the slow ingestion of a little morsel, not the manic craving of a dizzy consumer. I felt crucified by clarity, rationality, and an absence of what my soul required, a sense of awe in mystery, laced with a shaky faith. I longed to feel the sharp sting of Christ's pierced side, not the comforting glory of resurrection and immortality. Not Christ's light-infused *risen-ness* but God's ineffable wounded darkness is what I thirsted after. Belief had become musty, even a bit moldy; it needed some dusting off, if not a thorough spring cleaning. I thought of packing a vacuum cleaner.

My story had become despondent; it needed to be prodded along in its sluggishness, even permitted a transfusion. I felt less compelled to save my soul, more interested in seeking its shadows. I asked myself one day, *What are you most alive to?* I sought aliveness, coming to life in this journey, some wise blood that would increase circulation to counter my spiritual anemia.

The one authentic desire I felt and believed in was to explore this spiritual life by retreating from as many distractions and comfortable impediments as possible in order to see what arises within a cauldron of scarcity, simplicity, and as well as I could cultivate it, serenity. If nothing came of these desires, then so be it; I would have seen a sizeable chunk of America on a grand road trip transforming Club Mystery into Club Med. One cannot know the feel of frigid mountain water until one steps into the stream. I simply wanted to get my toes wet in the flow of spirit because I felt some deep and intangible life spirit moving through me. Its time had come for a fuller expression, and I needed sustained motion to shake loose the meaning that lay dormant. Were my motives too excessive, too grandiose?

The year prior to my sabbatical my father died and I returned to Ohio for his funeral. As I planned my trip now, I began to feel that I was repeating not my father's acute alcoholism but his excess, his preoccupation with one thing to the exclusion of his family's needs. I didn't blame him, but I balked when I realized I might have simply mimicked his behavior, his addictive patterns of thought and action through a disease that disallowed a healthy and full life for any longer than a few days at a time. With a shock of recognition I discovered that, with his death, I felt the grief of his loss for the first time fully and knew that living with his disease throughout childhood and young adulthood now needed to be confronted and explored, if not outright forgiven. Little did I know how large a part the presence of his spirit would play in my upcoming pilgrimage.

I kept in mind that I was on sabbatical, a curious word with an engaging history. I read in Wayne Muller's book, *Sabbath*, that "sabbath time can become our refuge" (10) from the busyness of life, which can be "a kind of violence" (5) as he understands it. The practice of "Shabbat, or Sabbath," he writes, "is designed specifically to restore us, a gift of time in which we allow the cares and concerns of the marketplace to fall away" (31). Rest, refuge, restoration, renewal, retrieval. These five *R* words I wrote in my journal and kept them close the entire voyage. They encouraged me daily to remain focused on what a sabbatical should include.

I also read a classic work a colleague had recommended: Rabbi Abraham Joshua Heschel's *The Sabbath*. I used his words as a primer for my pilgrimage: "One of the most distinguished words in the bible," he writes, "is the word *qadosh*, holy; a word which more than any other is representative of the mystery and majesty of the divine" (*The Sabbath*, 9). Both of these books remained constant companions for the entire journey.

Several days before my departure date in mid-August, I began to load my Ford Ranger pickup. I had installed a fiberglass lid so I could fill the entire bed with gear and necessary equipment and lock it. What I took with me I thought at the time were the barest of essentials. I had bought a new tent and sleeping bag for occasions when I was between monasteries. I took far too many boxes of books—four—and a second-hand laptop that I bought for the journey but used only twice. I packed both light and heavy clothing because I knew that I was heading north into Oregon and Washington, then south toward Utah, Colorado, New Mexico and Arizona to outrun winter's insistent emergence. I stored notebooks, pads of paper, and a bag of pens, as if none of these things could be purchased on the road. For one instant I thought of packing my passport. I took a cooler, a butane stove, some plastic ware and cooking utensils, rain gear, two pairs of boots, tennis shoes, sandals, two cameras, binoculars, and two plastic containers of clothes.

When I left, the truck was filled in both the bed section and behind the seats. At the close of the first week of August I said good-bye to my wife and headed to Highway 101 North, just a short distance from our home, and drove toward San Luis Obispo and then on to majestic Big Sur and the New Camaldoli Hermitage, my first destination of the pilgrimage. I wondered if the cash and traveler's checks I had brought and hidden in my gear would last me, but decided that since I was going to receive a check each month while on sabbatical, I would not concern myself with financial matters. Best to be frugal to avoid debt.

These and other practical concerns, however, receded in importance with each mile I put between home and me; I was now on the road full of expectation, open to the future and free, for a time, of the exaggerated cares that often kept me distracted from living more consciously in the spirit of God and other people. I sensed I would be gone long enough for the Novocain of a numbing life to wear off. I called to God for protection, to reveal to me what He wanted me to understand about my own place in the cosmos. In William Blake's catalogue that he created for showing his own art in 1809, he suddenly exclaims: "The human mind cannot go beyond the gift of God, the Holy Ghost" (544). I prayed for this gift of God, the presence of the Holy Spirit, to guide me in these next few months toward who and what I was destined to meet and to become.

Such exhilaration heading into the unknown! I felt already both more alive and more anxious than I could remember. Now my days would be open, not full of schedules, and I wondered if I were capable of handling so much loose and wild reality at one time. But I knew that not trying would be the death of me.

4

The Road on No Map

New Camaldoli Hermitage, Big Sur, California

> If you have a true and proper will, you lack nothing, neither love nor humility nor any virtue. . . . The will is perfect and right when it is without all attachment, when it has gone out of itself and is shaped and formed after the will of God.
> —Meister Eckhart, *Sermons and Treatises*

SQUEAMISH AND GIDDY, I drove on mid-August afternoon up empty highways along the coast, then inland up Highway 1 out of San Luis Obispo to Big Sur, one of the most scenic landscapes in the United States and a robust rival to the Amalfi Drive in southern Italy, which I had driven during a trip from Rome to Sicily years previously. My thoughts were that this trip was right and the time was appropriate to begin it. Perhaps something in my own fatedness demanded it and so I decided to give myself over to the choices I had made and the schedule I had set, knowing full well that what I thought were choices made by me included some invisible hand making them for me. My blueprint for life for the next three and a half months would be: "Thy Will Be Done." What liberation I felt in saying those four words! With this resolve, I let dissolve my feelings of anxiety as well as all compulsion to control this journey in the shadow of constant uncertainty; instead, I began the slow process of shifting out of one schedule and into another, one life venue into another. What I sought on this initial leg of the pilgrimage was simplicity and slow time.

I drove the coiling two-mile driveway up to the Camaldoli Monastery sitting high above the ocean directly below. From the cool air at sea level, I entered the white, still heat of August. Above the fluffy marine layer, from the parking lot tucked into the side of the Santa Lucia Mountains, the ocean remained invisible under a white foam of clouds.

I parked my truck under a tree that shaded it from the hot sun and walked through the main entrance into an elegant and fragrant bookstore and gift shop. The monastery was founded in 1958 by Benedictines who traveled from the small village of Camaldoli, high in the mountains of central Italy (where I would later spend a week with my wife [*Sanctuaries*, 62]); the monks who live here each has his own hermitage. Most of the guests could stay where I was, or, for longer retreats of several weeks, could request one of the metal mobile trailers tucked down below in a parcel of secluded spots. I imagined that in this broiling heat they would be more like microwave or toaster ovens and preferred my little room, which the monk who checked me in graciously led me to. With a breeze off the mountain, and both doors open, I felt like I had a great natural fan running at mid-speed all day.

A man of austere speech but a very quick step, the monk showed me the kitchen where we retreatants would take our tray and plates from the room and serve ourselves, then return to our rooms to eat in silence. The setting is such that no communal dining area is available. The monks preferred we join in their life of solitude and silence as much as we could, so communal gatherings were reserved for our time together in chapel or in the bookstore, in which conversation was allowed.

The monk asked me as I was shown around why I have come here. I responded without even thinking, that I was still grieving over the death of my father the previous year. I was surprised by my response. He asked if my mother was alive and when he learned that she was, he told me matter-of-factly: "Oh, so you are now half an adult. When she dies you will enter adulthood completely." I was startled by his stark observation and could think of nothing to say. I thought about his questions and whether his insight was true as I finished unpacking: in my fifties and not yet an adult? This was shaping up to be a very revelatory journey! Not yet on the road two days, and already my status in the world was being questioned.

I did have to acknowledge that my father's death had made me feel more alone in the world, more vulnerable in my movements, my travels and my future. It also made me freer than I had ever been before. His death altered my destiny and the monk's observation brought this thought to the surface. My father's death brought both a stronger fear and a greater sense of freedom into my life, as if for the first time I could talk to myself honestly and openly about his alcoholism and fits of sustained rage every weekend and every holiday vacation throughout my childhood and adolescence. I knew and felt for the first time what living in a field of terror and trauma was like; the scars from such a battlefield were only now, at his death, coiling to the surface of my psychic and emotional skin. What is it, I thought, to be free of terror and trauma after several decades conditioning? Perhaps this retreat would give me the grace and the courage to confront such a release from incarceration to the emotions of shame and rage, which bubbled within me still.

I liked my room, which was only twenty feet from the kitchen and communal showers and had a front and a back door. The back door opened to a small grassy yard, very parched, with a few flowers struggling to stay alive. Then the land ended abruptly over a bramble-thick sheer cliff. A wooden fence about five feet tall divided my space from that of the next room and afforded me privacy where I could sit out back in the cooler part of the day when the shadows had overtaken it. I looked out the front door to the mountain that continued straight up, thick with foliage and dangerously dry. A warning posted in each room asked us to be very careful with matches and cigarettes if we smoked. A forest fire could swallow this entire hermitage in a matter of hours and the summer drought made it even more susceptible to a forest fire, which would not be this area's first. Beauty brings with it its own dangers.

My room was simple, spare, and carried powerful memories of the pleasurable simplicity of Gethsemani Monastery so many years earlier and the Cleveland Diocesan Retreat House before that. I enjoyed this austere uncluttered arrangement best. It was clean, with a small bed against the wall, a desk with a hard straight-back chair, a shelf across the back window for books, a bathroom by the front door that was also screened, and a simple framed saying by St. Romuald, founder of the Camaldolesi order in Italy. His profound directions for meditation hung on the wall just above the desk. Its simplicity summarized the monastic life:

St. Romuald's Brief Rule

Sit in your cell as in paradise. Put the whole world behind you and forget it. Watch your thoughts like a good fisherman watching for fish. The path you must follow is in the Psalms; never leave it. If you have just come to the monastery, and in spite of your good will you cannot accomplish what you want, then take every opportunity to sing the Psalms in your heart and to understand them with your mind. And if your mind wanders as you read, do not give up; hurry back and apply your mind to the words once more. Realize above all that you are in God's presence, and stand there with the attitude of one who stands before the Emperor. Empty yourself completely and sit waiting, content with the grace of God, like the chick that tastes nothing and eats nothing but what his mother gives him.

St. Romuald lived and worked in the late tenth and early eleventh centuries and followed the simple rule of St. Benedict, which stressed simplicity and solitude in the hermitage. These two words —simplicity and solitude—so muted in my own life, which was characterized more by complexity and frenzy, seemed foreign to me at this moment. I felt, however, a strong desire to emulate and to follow St. Romuald's guiding words and so tried without forcing it, to make his gentle instructions part of my spiritual vocabulary. This experience of consciously emptying myself became a core value, along with the ability to wait, let be, allow the future to come toward me rather than my heading toward it. None of these acts, however, could be approached without the sustained presence of silence.

After copying his words, I continued to sit on my bed in the heat of the afternoon, with its quiet breeze, and delight in my surroundings. I didn't feel alone but rather a part of some quiet universe enshrouding me. Some invisible resonance folded around me and I felt happy that I had dared to step back from my familiar world, to stand apart from it in order to view it with a clarity impossible when I was in it. I felt a supportive peace of mind, a calmness and the energy of a silent expectation, of what, I could not tell. Outside, no other retreatants could be heard, though there were three other vehicles parked close to the building.

My attention shifted to them, all still invisible but living near me; I wondered what had prompted them to come here? What was the thread of their stories that brought them to retreat as well? What draws each of us to retreat: to recover something lost, or to simply want to dwell within the gratitude of God's love? I felt a strong sense of wanting to bring things together, parts that had unraveled from one another, that needed to be re-stitched or resewn together to mend the fabric of a life loosely threaded. This place of calm, serene silence was the right site to begin the process, to let it be done *to me,* according to God's will.

I sat very still for a long time, then instinctively picked up my journal to write what I was hearing inside me, as from a voice unrecognized but familiar, gently urging me to remember what I heard. They were not my thoughts but seemed more delivered to me from outside myself to record:

- Perform every action as an offering to God.
- Do not desire the fruits of your work.
- Be even-tempered in success and failure.
- Be calm in self-surrender as you work.
- Do what is required of you and what you love but without attachment.
- Doing so will take you to the ultimate truth; work without anxiety regarding results.
- Deny entrance to negative thoughts and emotions for they will retard the entire pilgrimage.

When I finished transcribing these thoughts, I sensed a growing fullness within me, a fullness of the moment. Nothing else, I realized, was needed or desired. For the first time, sitting there on the bed in the quiet of a hot afternoon, with small flies clicking against the screen, I knew that one thing I desired to gain from this trip was the ability to pray. I did not know how to pray, or to pray with my entire heart. I don't mean just to recite prayers I learned as a child in mindless repetition and numbness; I wanted rather to feel through prayer a deeper presence of God's grace in the fullness of the moment, in the fullness of the deep, silent scarcity of the moment. St. Romuald's words were offered to me as a gift early in the journey to help me with this crucial part of the pilgrimage.

This is what I sought: the silence of God, the fullness of God, even the darkness of God and a fullness of silence opened through the corridor of prayer. Prayer as a path to God's presence seemed right at this moment, but I restrained my natural (and even neurotic tendency) to make it happen within the next twenty-four hours, or twenty-four minutes—so ambitious and eager are my innate inclinations. A small piece of what I was doing on this journey fell into place.

God help me learn to pray toward your presence. I kept my small black-covered book, *Twenty-Four Hours a Day* reader close by. Used by millions of Alcoholics Anonymous members, it is a daily prayer and meditation guide for staying sober. Surrounded by several alcoholics most of my life, I knew that I was prone less to drink than to carry the habits, tendencies, and attitudes of the alcoholic within me. I learned a term for this residual form of alcoholism: Para-alcoholics. Earlier in the day I had read: "We alcoholics are emotional people and we have gone to excess in almost everything we have done. We have not been moderate in many things" (September 7). Bingo. Moderation is not one of my virtues, so praying is as much a strategy to slow down, to follow the motto: "Easy Does It," as it is a means of asking for God's serenity and calm. I have been reading this little book daily for fifteen years and it continues to offer new insights into my own behavior.

The bell began to ring for Compline in the chapel, and I, along with a few other retreatants, who slowly appeared like apparitions out of the heat of the late afternoon, walked the gravel driveway to the chapel. Compline is a brief but necessary time for prayer at the end of the day and, as I learned, the word Compline means "complete." Here the day comes to a close in the gesture of completeness in prayer, reminding us all that the day had begun in prayer and now ends in worship to complete a spiritual and temporal circle, even a prayer cycle. The time of Compline, though brief, was important because the entire community gathered to mark the beginning of silence that should now pervade the monastery until the next morning. I could not remember when I was made so fully conscious of the end of the day, of its completeness. Prayer brought consciousness to a fuller awareness. Silence punctuated the sound of communal worship.

The prayers were simple and included parts of the Psalms, a book of poem prayers I grew to love deeply on my journey. So beautifully do the Psalms bring poetry and prayer together in a single utterance, expressed in song. The Buddhist tradition speaks of "the culture of the heart" (*Buddhist Meditation*, 76). The Psalter pays close attention to this culture in order to keep one rooted in the body and in feelings so the intellect does not assume command. The sounds of the words sung exacted a perfect marriage with the silence surrounding them. The rhythm created between silence and the cadence of Gregorian song could be felt palpably in the echoing chamber of the chapel.

We greeted one another with a nod and a smile as each entered the air-conditioned dim light of the chapel and found our seats; we sat in silence for a few minutes until two rows of monks, all wearing creamy-white robes, entered silently from the hall. The cool air was a gift, offered by both God and technology. I wondered for a moment if I could get away with slipping in here later, in the darkness, with my sleeping bag and enjoy the cooler atmosphere. The thought of the cool darkness in this empty space all night was a great temptation.

Next to the rows of pews facing one another was a large circular room with an altar in the center. A few chairs rested along the walls; it had a spacious emptiness about it, kept dark except for these times of silent meditation and the sacrifice of the Mass. I loved its spare openness, the harmonious emptiness of it, a space I planned to use for periods of silent meditation.

After Compline we remained seated until the monks filed out, shuffling their sandaled feet in two rows and disappearing into their cloistered enclosure until the next morning. Of the twenty or so men, most were elderly, interspersed with two or three young novices, the order's future. I began a habit of remaining seated as the rest of the retreatants and people who had driven to the monastery for this time of prayer left. I learned to linger, and to love the silence and solitude after the lights were turned out and only the last dim illumination of the sun's glow entered the west windows. I sat with eyes closed in the orange glow—the most sacred time of the day for me, next to the early morning hours of darkness. When I opened my eyes, I could see tiny specks of orange dust hovering in the air like fairy sparkles; a luminosity from the sun flooded the chapel in silence and created for me a supernatural setting. I considered lying down on the wooden bench and sleeping there all night.

I thought of my day here and wondered if I should just stay put and cancel the rest of the journey. *No, this time I will stay with my planned pilgrimage.* I would return on another trip to those places holding the most spiritual presence for me. With this decision made in the growing darkness of the chapel, I left to find some dinner in the galley.

Wonderful fresh food was in abundance. I helped myself to soup, bread, salad and rice, and took my tray back to my room to eat in silence by the window that opened out on the ocean below. I then cleaned my eating utensils and dried them by my desk, becoming conscious during this simple process of what I was doing and trying to move slowly and with full awareness in the simplicity of the action of washing and drying a plate and a cup. I felt a joy in the slowness and deliberateness of these actions, done in full consciousness. What a novel experience it gave back to me as a blessing. Slowing down in performing these simple, mundane tasks, I felt the rush of recognition that these movements could also be moments of praying, in the gestures themselves.

Praying as a growing consciousness of what I was doing and why brought forth a feeling of immense gratitude for being given life so I could perform these actions. I finished washing and straightening up my food wares, fully conscious of this gratitude. Such a simple and uncluttered way of eating, praying, and living; all of it invited gratitude that helped me work with the deepening feelings of the loss of my family, friends, and a communal life. If I thought that this journey was not going to have its own costs, that idea was dispelled at this moment of cleaning my eating instruments.

That night I read in *The Rule of St. Benedict* about "Silence After Compline." There he asserts, since the entire rule sounds like a series of harsh proclamations, that "monks should diligently cultivate silence at all times, but especially at night." He then lays out the arrangements under which monks should sit and eat their two meals a day. Of Compline he insists: "on leaving Compline, no one will be permitted to speak further. If anyone is found to transgress this rule of silence, he must be subjected to severe punishment except on occasion when guests require attention or the abbot wishes to give someone a command. . . ." Maybe part of the reason I was here was to save some chatty monk from a severe reprimand. I have heard that God can assert His enigmatic presence at any time; could this be one of those moments? Guests as buffers for the punishment of monks.

I rearranged the furniture in my room, lined up a dozen or so books from one of my boxes along a shelf that ran even with the window, and was about to settle in for a comfortable read before retiring around 8 p.m., when I noticed something stir in my little fence-enclosed back yard, a space of about twelve feet square and divided from the back yards of my neighbors by a worn set of benches and a small wooden fence. Two foxes lay lazily and with great familiarity beneath the gray weathered benches; they dozed lightly as they gazed indifferently at me now standing by the back door. Their large fluffed tails rivaled the size of their bodies. They lay very close together, apparently, like me, prepared to settle in for the night. I felt both delighted and honored that they had chosen my little hermitage green space to bed down in, and I felt strangely safer by their presence. I thought of these two foxes, which became permanent hermitage mascots of mine during my week's stay; I looked for them each night as I prepared to turn off the lights. Apparently they too enjoyed the arrangement, for they were present each day of my stay. Later I attempted to give them some poetic permanence:

A Fox Tail

Two slim foxes roam outside my
monastery door seeking to convert.
How many souls have they enjoyed watching
slip out of bed at 2 a.m. to snatch
the milky sky of stars and gather
them into the hungry cat's bowl next to
the kitchen's warped screen door?
The two foxes seek the shade cast by
a leaning fence in late afternoon.
Perhaps they will sleep through vespers
and dream instead of vegetarian
throwaways.
The church bell's clapper slips beneath
their sleep, bringing their tails to life
with a twitch and a dance.
I think they may be the fluffy shadows of
earlier monks, ancestors buried next to
the chapel engaged in mild penance
by visibly marking me as one who
should be wearing newer sandals and
seeking their large ballooning tails of
Redemption.
(*Casting the Shadows*, 58)

Next morning I rose at 4:30. At this dark blue hour even the flies
and pesky gnats still slumbered. Morning silence was different from
the silence of evening; this newborn silence had a whispering quality
to it here high above the Pacific Ocean on the western lip of the
United States, where I gazed down at the invisible soothing power of
the surf, which I could hear but not see below stretching to the black
horizon. Soon the bells would ring for Vigils at 5:45, but I was already
awake in my small room, putting things in order, gathering myself
up while feeling enshrouded around me the night's deep blackness,
interrupted only by my reading lamp pushing against it. I felt that in
this pilgrimage right now God was closest to me in the dark, silent
beginning of the day, more so even than in the evening. In the morning, God the Father; in the evening, God the Son; during the day's
actions and prayers, God the Holy Spirit. True? And mothered by all

three of these presences? I have no idea, but in my waking/dreamy state the simplicity of the thought had a great appeal at this hour.

If setting can influence one's thoughts and emotions, then I saw Benedict's wisdom in insisting on scarcity and austerity as part of the monk's life and their cells being enclosed, snug, and functional. A certain ascetic atmosphere began to pervade my feeling life. I wanted nothing, desired nothing, only now, the fullness of the silent moment in this small enclosure. The moment of the present was in complete accord with the snugness of the space. All appetites were silent, all dreams directed toward the future muted. This moment was the first instance of a deep harmony in myself and with God that I had experienced since I began the pilgrimage. I knew that a quiet and ascetic approach to each act I performed, each book I read, each person I spoke to was possible and could be cultivated. In this moment a strong impulse of human freedom moved through me. Some connection between liberation and austerity joined forces; the less encumbered, the freer I began to feel. The arrangement was profound. I felt liberated from so much toxicity, mostly of my own making. I stopped what I was doing and simply felt the presence of this absence of all desire. This is the feeling available to us when Grace confiscates the moment. Nothing more than this, nothing greater than this.

I washed my face in the bathroom sink. A paper sign on the wall warned me not to drink the water from the taps. Fresh water was as precious as prayer here, high above the inhabitants living at ocean level, so all water was recycled. Retreatants shared two showers off the kitchen, next to my room. They were dank and musty little cubes with a slatted wooden floor and a flimsy plastic curtain clinging heroically to a skinny round bar with thin metal hooks. I enjoyed the dark wood walls and the intimate space of these stalls; when I entered them I always felt like I was in a cottage or cabin in the woods. The musty, wet smell of wood soothed me as completely as the water refreshed me.

Liberated from phone, fax, radio, television, and computer, I enjoyed the feeling of neatness and order. I had shed all avenues of communicating with the outside world and felt a healing salve in the simplicity of life that the monastery cultivated. Silence replaced the continual noise of civilization. Everything seemed now to be moving at half speed, gaining in the trade off a simplicity I had not felt for years. Demands were for the most part minimal and self-imposed. No calendar book to follow, no series of meetings, teaching duties, paper grading, presentations to make, or obligations both personal and professional to perform. If only to escape these fatiguing but necessary demands, one might come to a retreat center, I thought, as I made my bed and folded the blankets at its foot. Just sensing the act of being was enough for the moment. Ordering my little room somehow ordered my interior life as well. No wonder Benedict encouraged work to accompany prayer. Work, he intuited, could in fact be an act of prayer. Making my bed was a small praise to God; sweeping my room and stacking my plastic ware was a mini-hymn of joy to being alive; hanging up my clothes was an expression of joy in creation.

I returned to enjoy once more the words of the anonymous Russian Christian whose classic, *The Way of a Pilgrim*, explores just this connection: "Many people reason quite the wrong way round about prayer, thinking that good actions . . . render us capable of prayer. But quite the reverse is the case; it is prayer which bears fruit in good works and all the virtues. . . . The work of prayer comes before everything else" (8). Prayer as work; it required an effort of the will to pray. What it required to pray well and truly is what I was slowly discovering in the mystery of communicating in this deep way. First, however, I had to make space for its presence.

I did not know at the time that I had also inadvertently entered into another of Benedict's beliefs, even a mandate from his inspired pen. He told his monks to go against the cultural norms, for the spirit of the monk must be aligned to the most famous and worshipped cultural rebel of his time: Christ. The monk's spirit should express the spirit of revolution: nonconformity, resistance to challenge the complacency of cultural acedia (*Benedict's Way*, 13). Practiced now for over fifteen hundred years and begun by a rebel, Benedict himself, this life was one of a disciplined rebellious austerity that heals. I read a page of his *Rule* each morning in order to enter into the spirit of the place; there I discovered that his simple regimen arose naturally in me, neither forced nor coerced.

The Road on No Map

I looked out over the cliff just outside my back screen door. A gray dawn began its birthing into light, to be born across the ocean beneath the puffy marine layer swaddling it below. A gentle breeze slipped through the screens, along with the morning singing of birds in the trees next to my room, then exited quietly out the front screen door. Even this early, my monastic foxes, who lived just over the edge of the cliff, but slept in my backyard, were already stirring. One of them peered, head bobbing and nose alert and twitching, through the back door to see if I was awake and perhaps even ready to feed them. The only nourishment they received from me was a silent salute and gratitude for their presence on my property.

Both of them gathered and began foraging along the building, searching for food and water. Perhaps other retreatants before me who had them as back yard campers fed them so they naturally assumed each of us would break out an early meal. In their early friskiness they leaped onto the wooden fence and began their ritual promenade back and forth, slowly gathering momentum, as if they literally wound themselves up in an accelerated dervish dance for the day's hunt. I knew they had been schooled by the order of life here and thus practiced a learned monkish patience. They did not press their claim for food too insistently.

I quietly slipped out the front door toward the kitchen to find a cup of early morning coffee. The monastery's resident tabby cat, plump and contented in her orange fur, was totally absorbed just outside the kitchen door; she looked up at me for only an instant, too covetous of a fresh bowl of milk laced with granola flakes to concern herself with my needs. Except for the tiny sounds of her rough, lapping tongue moving in a steady and serene rhythm just above the bowl, which I could hear even before I left my room, there was no other distraction except for the sharp, piercing, white light of the stars overhead. They were as thick and white as the cat's milk.

Two milky ways mirrored one another. Brilliant and still in their muted splendor, the stars gave off a faint vibration in their shining. From foxes and cats to a cosmic curtain across the sky, I could not doubt that this order in the world for me to witness and enjoy was no accident; the measured design of it was far too apparent and conscious. I reveled in God's mindfulness through these peaceful animals and the distant but mothering stars. I sensed in their natural simplicity the motion of grace itself.

Within this early morning silence, punctuated by the light of the stars, arrived a deep feeling of joy that had been missing in my life. It came to me slowly, but fully, in the silence, even in prayer. I began to imagine that I had been praying since I woke up, simply in being present to the back yard foxes and to the gently lapping cat. Prayer, I thought, may be no more, and no more profound, than an interior disposition toward the sacred in the ordinary events of the day. Silence and prayer had allowed me to strip away the world's distractions and my responsibilities, false promises, superficial and self-serving hopes, and droning desires for entertainment and diversion. Prayer allowed me to be present to what, in the busy rhythms of my daily life, I had forsaken. Prayer, in fact, was a way of envisioning the world in its newness each day. It was not so much about petition but about presence, about learning to be present, even to be present to presence.

The "order" of the Camolodese was a name for an entire ordering of life around a sacred sense of being. It gave my life order, like a poem can, or an authentic prayer, or a psalm. Poetry and prayer were more akin to ordering principles, so that the world took on a significant aura and shape. I liked the idea of this ordering presence and wondered if each "order" of religious life I hoped to visit would have a different (or at least a modified) ordering through the tenets of its religious roots. Each monastery may indeed have its own poetic and prayerful way of ordering and arranging the world, to disclose God for them in a particular way. I would be attentive to such divine disclosure.

The bell summoning us to Vigils suddenly sounded, cracking the monastery open to a new day. The coyotes in the mountains surrounding me on three sides and just behind the chapel responded with their own litany from the deep and brittle-dry forest thickets. They too waited to be called, if only to sing. Simplicity and repetition were the gifts that ruled life here today and every day. There existed in the life of the monks a fundamental paradox: a sense of abundance without excess in the spare quality of their practiced life. This spareness, I felt, coaxed me into an innate rhythm that seemed more fully a part of how the natural world redeemed and renewed itself each day, especially in the early morning hours. Present as I walked across the crunchy gravel to the chapel was a pervasive sense of love rather than desire, of abundance rather than need. I felt this through the way my appetites were curbed, yet neatly satisfied. In this repetition I could feel the faint presence of eternity assembled in the folds of the daily sameness of prayer, work, worship, eating, rest, prayer, work, and worship. It is a rhythm that, once felt, was a new gift I did not want to discard or take for granted. Some who visit monasteries might find it boring; I discovered in it a form of blessed fullness.

Basic needs were nourished, especially through the kitchen, where meals in large pots or in bowls covered with cellophane or tin foil and placed in the refrigerator like manna dropped from heaven by invisible hands. I waited until after prayer to return to help myself to the simple fare of granola and grain bread, which I toasted and waxed with butter and jam. Lunch, the large meal, often consisted of a casserole dish and fresh greens or potato salad, sweet corn, and asparagus. Dinner, a bit more austere, might consist of some combination of soup, salad, and bread. Abundance, I learned, has many faces and flavors.

Vigils, sung by the monks who invited us to join in, was followed each morning by Mass. Receiving the sacrament of the Eucharist was an important event in my daily life; I anticipated it as one of the most important central actions of the day. Attending Mass always carried with it the years in elementary school when I served as an altar boy, trained well by the order of Ursuline Sisters. I prided myself then in having mastered the entire service in Latin and reciting all the prayers in response to the priest with rapidity and efficiency, always anxious to please. Even that day, some of the Latin phrases came rushing back into memory as I heard their English equivalents. *Kyrie eleison*, Lord have mercy; *Christi eleison*, Christ have mercy; *Et introibo ad altare Dei*, I will go to the altar of God. These were powerful memories of my first encounter with a foreign language and my joy at learning the mysterious drama of the Mass through it. With their melodic ring, these strange phrases in a language now largely deceased made the mystery of the Mass even more potent to a boy of ten and offered sweet memories now as an adult.

The second most anticipated event for me in the day was Vespers and what followed. At the end of the day, at 6:00 p.m., we gathered in the chapel to sit quietly and wait for the monks to arrive. They entered singly or in groups of three or more, appearing just as the sun's light entered the west windows. Quiet, like silent sacred specters in white robes that whooshed gently in the dimly lit chapel, they appeared wrapped in silence. Yellow light filtered through the windows, casting a supernatural golden hue across the faces of those sitting facing the sun. When the monks entered, the chapel assumed a very different life; its atmosphere underwent an immediate metamorphosis almost immediately. Their singing of the Psalter for that day encouraged, actually evoked, a mystical presence. When sung, the Psalms carried with them a special grace that suffused the chapel. I had been here for only three days but felt the rhythm of the Psalms beginning to become part of my daily consciousness. Singing inspired a graceful presence that suffused all of us in prayerful attendance.

Immediately following the chanting, all who wished to could enter the large circular chapel for a thirty-minute silent meditation where we would spread out and sit on the floor or on a cushion we pulled from beneath one of several wooden benches placed around the circumference. After giving us a moment to settle in, one monk would emerge holding a gold container of the Eucharist and place it on the altar; another tapped a Tibetan bell with a wooden mallet and "OOOouum," the signal for meditation in silence, filled the space with a mysterious, otherworldly sound. Then, complete silence swallowed the metallic vibration.

I closed my eyes and was immediately confronted with the most unruly, restless mind revving at full throttle with a thousand thoughts, saying at the same time, *Try to shut me down.* Quieting the mind and allowing an openness to emerge was the hardest part of meditation, especially for a beginner like myself. I thought almost immediately of how much time had passed, as if that mattered. But for a mind wild in its motion and frenzied in its desire to control, like a skittish animal, it was urgently important. So was the matter of where a fly landed, or who just coughed, whose feet gave off a pungent odor, who took their shoes off—anything rather than settle down into the dark space of silence and solitude.

Like a bucking bronco, my mind kicked and spurted, jerked and bit the bridle with a gusto I found astonishing. I recognized with some horror that I had my hands full with this wild creature and that if on this pilgrimage I could learn even just to be quiet and calm, I would have grown considerably. Find God? The thought seemed farcical when here I was wrestling with something as rudimentary as trying to quiet my own head for a few minutes.

Oooummm! I was astonished that thirty minutes had passed! I stirred with the others, placed my cushion under the chair and walked in a daze back to my room. Is this the turmoil that civilization exacts from each of us and would prefer that we remain within? I thought that I had better begin, however slowly, to practice a time of meditation on my own and to move gently into the rhythm that meditation affords and into the discipline that it exacts. I did not have to sit in my room to accomplish this. I needed help. With a mind this frisky, I would spend any meditative time galloping through the trivial and mundane as a way to escape the quiet solitude I sought.

Benedict's *Rule* is very clear on prayer: not too many words. "God," he writes, "regards our purity of heart and tears of compunction, not our many words. Prayer should therefore be short and pure" (29). Fair enough. Then, "Lord, help me to quiet my mind. Thank you." Short enough. I made this mantra part of everyday. So over the remaining days, though my mind did not grow completely quiet, it did grow quieter, with less snickering. I had constructed my own prayer out of a real need. Doing so refreshed me and helped me enter the spirit of monasticism with a feeling of gratitude and a fullness of a simple life. It also taught me something about self-forgiveness and about not beating myself up for failing to accomplish in a few weeks or months what monks and others who meditate had worked on for years, even a whole lifetime.

Later that evening while leafing through my thirty-year-old copy of Thomas Merton's *Conjectures of a Guilty Bystander*, I found these words underlined with a shaky red pen: "Why can we not be content with an ordinary, secret, personal happiness that does not need to be explained or justified? We feel guilty if we are not happy in some publicly-approved way, if we do not imagine that we are meeting some standard of happiness that is recognized by all" (56). I underlined these words years earlier and discovered that I still struggled with realizing them in any significant way.

I sat outside on a bench in the cool evening of The Hermitage and thought of Merton's words—a private happiness he was calling for, known only by the person and God. No fanfare, just a deep contentment minus all publicity. Here was one of the hallmarks of the monastic life: to be happy privately with no need or desire for justification or recognition. What a liberating idea! Many thanks, Father Louis, for that insight.

The August heat had become oppressive after 11 a.m. All of us realized that any long walks should be taken in the early morning, so I set out one day to walk to Highway 1, about two miles below me down the snaking, rough driveway with its washed out portions and warped strips. I had learned, from shorter walks down and up the driveway, to take a small towel from my room with me to swat the tiny black mucus flies that attacked all walkers any time of day or evening. Walk and swat was the forced rhythm of meditation, where the towel was as handy and effective as a cow's tail to keep the gnats from entering ears, eyes, and nose. I walked down the path immediately after Mass and a bowl of cereal, with the quiet of the morning sun as my companion. I felt refreshed and strong, with the entire day ahead of me, unplanned, unstructured except for chapel and meals. Exhilarated, I sensed in my body a deep feeling of freedom that simplicity encouraged.

As I walked I thought of how people treated one another here. I discovered that there exists a devotional quality to human interactions. People spoke softly, even whispered to one another, especially in the kitchen where several of us might be portioning out our meal before taking it back to our rooms. No one raised a voice; absent were loud laughter and outbursts. The rhythms of human action changed markedly. All of us began to feel, as I did now walking in the morning sun and still, cool air, the rhythms of the day, from dawn through the heat of the afternoon to the cool of the evening, followed by the slow covering of night and darkness and a deepening silence and solitude. Embracing this rhythm was one of the most complete experiences at all of the monasteries. It always left me with a feeling of joy in simply being, as well as gratitude for life itself in its simple flows and eddies.

Even time had slowed to a palpable rhythm. Silence had a chance to blanket all activity, even the throaty gurgles early in the morning from the small three-cup percolator in my room. I loved moments early in the darkness when the smell of coffee would mingle with the sweet aromas of the mountain foliage outside my room and the foxes' slow stirring to the smells. It enlarged the sense of peace and tranquility and replenished the spirit while healing my wounded nature. My perspective began to alter as I walked: I was not retreating *from* as much as retreating *to* a source greater than I, which offered secure direction and serenity if I could bring myself to yield to it. I was not negating my family and professional life but rather affirming a life of the spirit that was neglected so often during the days that ticked by unconsciously in a monotony of sameness if I allowed it.

Already the day was heating up as I descended to the cooler air closer to the ocean. I saw that the wise path was to walk on the side of the road where shadows, while shortening, were still long enough to afford shade. At the bottom of the driveway I discovered a small bench close to Highway 1 to rest on with my journal and a book. I gave myself over to the natural scene and listened to the birds in the trees surrounding the entrance to the monastery and felt in that moment what might be called ecstasy wedded to contentment. I wanted for nothing and delighted in that feeling of having desires calmed and slumbering within. Prayer, or a state of prayer, might be just this sense of yielding to the moment and asking or wanting nothing of life but that it be felt and lived. Few cars passed by the road just a few yards from where I sat; the area's silence and the sun's warmth were gifts beyond measure.

I had brought with me Thomas Merton's *Life and Holiness*, a favorite that I had read and underlined decades ago but wanted to reread. Slowly reading passages that had attracted me in the early 1980s, I paused over these lines: "In fact, our seeking of God is not all a matter of our finding him by means of certain ascetic techniques. It is rather a quieting and ordering of our whole life by self-denial, prayer and good works so that God himself, who seeks us more than we seek him, can 'find us' and 'take possession of us'" (29). Is this the openness required of the monastic life, of giving oneself over to *the possibility*, and not *the inevitability*, that God will find me and take possession? If it were inevitable, then where would faith reside? In the uncertainty of all of this I found my faith weakest; the temptation to move to techniques for achieving is perhaps strongest when faith is frailest. I slowed the questioning and simply sat in the silence contemplating Merton's insight.

He goes on to attack a culture obsessed with technique and a management style of dealing with any difficulty, from weight loss to a "five-steps-to-wholeness" culture that can swallow us with rules and guidelines for improvement. The hyperbole of this tendency can be seen in the proliferation of the often-insidious series, *The Idiot's Guide to...* wrapped in bright, yellow, monotonous sameness that simplifies all forms of knowing, from computer formats to finding God. *The Idiot's Guide to Transcendence*. A fictitious title today that may be a bestseller tomorrow. Such an approach to understanding is a symptom of the abhorrence of mystery, uncertainty, and ambiguity, a form of *Monarch Notes* to life itself and to the opaqueness of divinity's presence. How might I have gotten caught in such a fiasco, where I sometimes mistook the map for the experience of the journey? All sorts of thoughts began to whirr in my head and I realized that I was losing the peace and serenity that the walk had invited me into.

Sitting in the coolness of the ocean's breeze and the shade of the live oak trees close to Highway 1 watching an occasional car or truck pass, I began to feel the sun's warmth on my neck as the air around me warmed. Time to ascend before the heat descends.

The heat of the day stirred me from my reverie. The road had become busy with late morning traffic and I realized as I rose to walk uphill that I brought a towel with which to swat flies but no water and no hat. Careless. Did I think it would stay cool all day? I knew better. I started up the winding road with some haste in my stride. All along each side were thick foliage and trees. I walked in the diminished and very foreshortened shade of the trees leading back to the Hermitage: chaparral, redwood, madrone, bay laurel, and oak forest. I felt the perspiration begin to run on my face and down my back and with it an awareness that the higher I hiked, the hotter and more demanding the air became. Stopping to rest often, standing now in the sun, I fought off the growing swarm of gnats attracted to my perspiration, hovering around me singing in my ears. A few landed by my nostrils and were inhaled. I coughed and swatted, coughed and swatted, and felt a dizziness overtake me. How easily I succumbed to the natural world when I entered it unprepared to adjust to its changing moods.

I finally reached the level ground of the Hermitage and slipped under the shade of trees bordering my room. The room's inside was no cooler than outside, so I went next door to an empty room and found a plastic wastebasket, a twin brother of the one in my room. I filled both halfway with cool water, took off my hiking boots and socks, placed both wastebaskets by my desk chair and planted a leg in each one. Miraculously, it helped to cool me while seriously curtailing my mobility, but it was the only air conditioning available and worked splendidly. I did not mind the immobility after hiking all morning. I wiggled my toes and the coolness shot right up and through my body. God does provide. I thought of how I could strap both baskets to my feet, perhaps with a little less water, and slosh my way around the monastery, cool in a Huck Finn kind of inventive way, but knew that the water's splashing up and out of the baskets would create far too much noise, so I contented myself with staying put and cool.

When I was younger, one of the only memories of my father playing with any of us as kids was when he would turn the garden hose on us on the front lawn and spray us as we ran past him in our bathing suits. He would pretend he did not see us until the last minute, and then would laugh while the hose soaked and cooled us in the thick August heat close to the shores of Lake Erie. It was joyous because he was both sober and playfully attending to us. These were rare moments and I recalled them with pleasure as my toes enjoyed the rubbery coolness of the plastic wastebaskets. I realized with a growing melancholy how infrequently were moments in my childhood when I had the sober attention of my father. Perhaps because it involved water, I have always been partial to swimming and water sports. He was afraid of swimming and whenever we went to the beach or out to a rented cottage in western Pennsylvania for a week, he shied away from it, even fearing to ride in our rented fishing boat. Someone had taught him to be afraid of it, so he never entered into our playing and splashing in the dark lake water. These moments alone in my room brought up these water memories, beginning with my cool feet and rising up into consciousness. They were embodied memories, where most originate from; I wondered if this trip was going to give me more remembrances that I would be forced to face and forgive? I decided that once again this was out of my hands and so welcomed them. It occurred to me in an oblique way that perhaps this was as important a part of my pilgrimage as anything else: the path of forgiveness as a pilgrimage of liberation.

My stay here was about complete. In the process of meeting several monks I had a promising talk with Father John about becoming an Oblate of the Order at Camaldoli. He informed me of the program and gave me all the information I needed to apply, including a copy of *Oblate Rule of the Camaldolese Benedictine Monks.*

The next morning, after making myself a light breakfast and then attending Mass, I returned to my room to say goodbye to the foxes, but they had already risen and begun their day. Disappointed, I loaded my truck in the cool shade of the morning, then walked up and said farewell to the monks working in the bookstore where I had spent a few hours each day reading books or learning about the Order. I felt very sad as I pointed the truck down the driveway to Highway 1 and the rest of the world. For a moment, in the quiet solitude of the morning air, I stopped the truck just before I lost sight of the buildings and paused, looking back through my rear view mirrors for a last double vision of this sacred place. What a grand site from which to initiate this pilgrimage! I had not anticipated the sorrow of leaving.

I then headed north on a quiet empty highway on a sleepy weekday morning in Big Sur, content to let this holy ground recede into my dual mirrors as I pointed the truck toward Oakville, California and the Carmelite House of Prayer in Napa Valley.

After several days with a close friend in Alameda, we parted and I drove north on Highway 29 to the Carmelite House of Prayer in Oakville. As I entered their driveway above San Francisco and into Napa Valley, I felt a terrible loneliness for my wife and sons, accompanied by an awareness that I must try to settle into this pilgrimage instead of fighting it. Otherwise I was in jeopardy of aborting it and heading home. Some force of destructiveness was at work here. What energy was this that continued, like a small voice that was only half-conscious, to derail my voyage, by trying to convince me the trip was self-indulgent and that I ought to return home?

I felt a loss of appetite, coupled with a vague emptiness that was more and beyond psychological explanations of simply being lonely or depressed. It was a nagging impulse, negatively-charged, trying to send me home by exorcising all joy from the trip. I felt within myself a renewed desire to resist it and push on. The tension was palpable and sometimes unnerving.

As I drove, I remembered something one of my Masters in Counseling Psychology students, Cynthia, had told me when she learned of my plans for this sabbatical. She had spent many months in meditation retreats and had also guided several groups. I trusted her judgement. "When you feel like leaving," Cynthia suggested, "give it another day or two. When the desire gets real keen to jettison it all and head home to safety, give it another day. You will be tempted often to pull the plug on your pilgrimage; those are the moments when you should not give in to despair."

I recalled her words and asked myself with astonishment: ok, but so soon? Just over two weeks old was this journey, and I planned to be gone for three and a half months. Will it only get worse? I continued driving and wrote her words in my journal to refer to as moral backup when I needed a life buoy to keep me from sinking into feelings of loss and loneliness. These feelings arose spontaneously and often acutely during my stays. I asked God to help me accept the loneliness and even despondency as part of the journey and not to surrender to their dark shadows. But these negative feelings were about to become much stronger before they abated. Something, I sensed, was after me, and I did not know if I carried the resources to counteract these calls to retreat and to resist all impulses to default on my plans. Instead I filled my being with the sense of calm simplicity and silence that grew deeper the farther into the pilgrimage I penetrated, always with a prayer as my partner.

5

An Isolato
Dogged by Divinity

The Carmelite House of Prayer, Oakville, California

The dimensions of prayer in solitude are those of man's ordinary anguish, his self-searching, his moments of nausea at his own vanity, falsity and capacity for betrayal.
—Thomas Merton, *Contemplative Prayer*

I DROVE NORTH OF San Francisco on Route 29, which runs up the spine of one of the most famous vineyard settings in the world, Napa Valley, and spotted the subtle sign to the Carmelite Center on my first pass. I was told that the sign marking the monastery on Oakville Grade road was not well marked. Nor was the sign earlier designating the entrance to Camaldoli. The geography of this world-famous vineyard valley overwhelmed me with its yellow and green beauty and I looked forward to learning more about it.

Along the road on both sides were lush vineyards groaning under the weight of huge grape clusters of deep purple and translucent green. Harvest and "the crush," I soon learned, was about to begin and the grapes seemed to know that their time of harvest was at hand. They hung heavy in the hot sun, waiting for the workers to cut them loose and transform them into some of the finest wines in the world. The driveway led into the cool shade of large eucalyptus trees. I snaked through the property to the front of a majestic three-story mansion, formerly owned by the Doak family and purchased by the Carmelite friars in 1955.

In front of the magnificent Georgian-style building sat a large fountain and a pond teeming with fish. To the left of the main house were a large one -story cottage building with six bedrooms, a communal living room, and a kitchen. All looked as if they had been recently refurbished. One of the brothers with a French accent greeted me at the door, showed me where the evening meal was to be served, the location of the chapel and the surprisingly ample library with thousands of volumes, and the cottage where I could park my truck under a large shade tree. He mentioned almost incidentally that I would be the only one staying there since this time in early autumn retreatants were scarce. After being around other people at Camaldoli, I was pleasantly taken aback to realize that I would inhabit this large cottage by myself. I envisioned sleeping in a different bed each night of my stay, a monastic Goldilocks, but finally settled on one just off the kitchen.

Since it was already late afternoon, Brother Pierre suggested I unpack, then join him and the other priests for dinner at 6:00 p.m. The cottage was very modern and clean. I unpacked my gear in the room that faced the back of the building and looked out to the large forest that spread itself darkly up the mountain. If I really sought solitude, I was being given it in terrifying abundance. The adage to "be careful what you ask or pray for" swept into my thoughts. Here I was in a building both spacious and empty; I needed to adjust to a depth of silence that would begin to unnerve me in a few days.

Since I did not enjoy changing the bed sheets after a stay, or even making it each morning, I devised a technique of laying my sleeping bag on top of the spread, pulling out the pillow from under it, and sleeping in the bag. When I left, I changed the pillowcase and I was out the door. I enjoyed the smell and feel of flannel inside my sleeping bag; the arrangement was also very efficient. Flannel's smell and texture were full of memories of camping out as a Boy Scout decades ago as well as camping with my wife on trips in our past. I enjoyed inhaling the heavy cloth smell and decided it served as a pacifier at night.

Brother Pierre and the priests at dinner were very cordial and social. They treated me more as an invited family guest than as a retreatant. We had wine along with a wonderful assortment of food served around a large oak table in a dining room that was elegant and spacious, with freshly waxed hardwood floors and paneled oak walls. Three of the priests were from Ireland and had been here for decades; one had returned recently from the doctor and was ailing. He spoke only briefly about it initially, but I sensed that he was in great pain and dying. All but one of the men were in their late sixties and early seventies. I felt that I had entered a period of history that was fading, and these were really the waning shadow days of this elegant monastery's once bustling and fully populated life. The grounds, though neat, were parched and ragged. The large swimming pool had been empty for years. A quiet integrity pervaded the setting, and I felt the deep peace that energized these grounds.

Father Pat told me that for decades this estate served as a novitiate for young men, but like everywhere else, there was a diminishing number of vocations, so the order decided to make it exclusively a retreat center. Once a year, exactly ten days from now, they would celebrate their annual fund-raising bazaar and carnival, when thousands of people from the area attended, bought crafts from the neighbors in the region, and donated their time, and help to keep the monastery solvent. Volunteers performed all of the labor, and each morning meetings took place to plan where the sites of the various food booths and game kiosks would be located. This annual event infused the place with enough money, coupled with retreatants' donations, for the institution to survive another year. I liked immediately the warmth and openness of the men and felt that I was being given very special treatment with my status of Sole Retreatant.

After dinner I walked out to sit by the pond and settled into the place as the light from the hot day began to soften and cool. Strangely, I felt once more, as I did at Camaldoli, the presence of my father again; I remembered his passing just two years ago. Was I here because of him? The pattern of his life at home slowly began to take form as I listened to the comforting sound of the water fountain in the middle of the pond and watched large gold fish swimming closer to the surface. Their slow emergence into visibility paralleled my father's image rising within me.

A mild man, not given to much conversation during the week, and a hard worker, he walked up to Holy Cross Church most mornings and attended 5:30 Mass; then he boarded the transit bus and rode it from our home in Euclid downtown to work in the personnel office of the Cleveland Electric Illuminating Company. He walked home from the bus stop every night, unless during heavy rain or snow my mother would drive to get him. In the evening he spoke little to us and practiced a tight regimen of early bed and early rising, a habit I seemed to have inherited. When I recalled these evenings, I always saw a reticent man sitting in a living room chair behind *The Cleveland Plain Dealer*. Almost no conversation passed between us.

On Friday nights he would not arrive home at the usual time but instead would swagger in at least two hours late because he would stop at Lokar's tavern at the end of our street. Then would begin a second ritual pattern of behavior reserved for the weekend, of drinking himself into a rage, followed by a Sunday stupor and an effort to sober up enough for work on Monday morning. That, in a nutshell, was the texture of our weekends during all my years of growing up. He led two lives, as most addictions demand. On the weekend the gloves came off and his raging alcoholism terrorized all of us until we would clear out, scattering like birds out of a startled nest, to relatives or inviting ourselves to sleep over at a friend's, or wandering the streets, going to a movie—anything to avoid the turmoil and trauma of the interior pandemonium. During the week he was both reticent and spiritual; on the weekend he was loud and full of spirits as he traumatized my mother, brothers, sister, and me through all our younger years.

Our school friends, from our traumatic perch, seemed to look forward with happy anticipation to the end of the school week because they or their families had plans to do things together; we, however, dreaded the end of the school week and the wild storms of Saturday and Sunday that we would be dropped into unless we had made plans to escape. We prayed for Monday morning to circulate back as quickly as possible. My father often did not make it to work on Monday because he was too hung over. How often, as I prepared for school, did I hear my mother on the phone to my father's boss telling him Roger had the flu and would not make it to work that day. I wondered now, in my monastery room, how many calls this manager received on Mondays at a time when alcoholism was the family secret across the nation.

I remembered priding myself on not drinking during high school when my classmates were all experimenting with alcohol. I abhorred the idea of becoming an alcoholic like my father, my uncles, and some of their cronies we met when we were taken with him to the Schindley Avenue tavern to spend part of our Saturday afternoon playing pin ball and drinking Nee-Hi grape soda. I vowed never to repeat his destructive patterns; but on this retreat I began to realize more fully, now that he was dead, that I had become only partly liberated from his influence and at the same time saw how much I resembled him emotionally.

This recognition was like a slap in the face, the afterglow bringing up years of shame. I thought that from his example I had also been drawn, without being aware of it, to a spiritual life. But instead of booze, I had taken up his rage without the alcohol. I seemed to be enraged often and about anything. Over time I realized that this rage was my way of expressing a profound depression and a deep shame that began partially to lift from me after his death. They were also signals of what I was to learn was part of the "para-alcoholic's" life, namely that when one suffers through life in a dysfunctional family, one inherits the traits, patterns, and propensities, without booze, of that behavior (*Adult Children of Alcoholics*, 335). Perhaps these powerful images of the distressed household had come to me now, in tranquility, to be exorcised, or at least accepted as a past that had shaped me in many positive ways. Out of the shadows of our souls can arise the treasures that are part of these dark recesses, but we must, I now understand, be willing to accept them both.

How wounded we all are, I glimpsed as I sat in the cool evening air watching the large goldfishes' curiosity bring them closer to me. I enjoyed listening to the splash of the fountain in the middle of the large pond. I didn't like being alone with these thoughts but knew that they were visiting me now as aggressive ghosts so that I could look at them with less emotional upset and more compassion. Vague feelings of exorcism crossed my awareness and I wondered if this too was going to be a crucial landscape of my interior journey. Part of me did not want to go back to the empty cottage, with all those vacant bedrooms and my imagination full of disturbing images from childhood, to face the silence of the place. I had cleared a space in my life for grace and instead ghastly ghosts tumbled into the silent silo of my soul. Then I recalled my promise to myself in planning this pilgrimage: look for nothing in particular. Move from place to place, settle in wherever you are, submit to who and what you find there, and take careful note of what emerges on its own for contemplation. Yield to everything in your path. God finds you when He needs to and visits you with what you need to hear and bear. However, it will not be more than your capacity for burden. Stay open and surrender.

I did not expect the presence of my alternatively enraged and reticent father to follow me on this journey, but there he was, beside me and there I was, mirroring him in attitude and design more than I had ever realized. What I thought I had avoided I had in essential ways become. This recognition stayed with me and brought me to consider who my two sons were becoming and whether this same pattern was also working itself out in them. Here was a part of parenting that I had never calculated—but needed to, now, in solitude. No wonder our noisy culture eschews the presence of solitude; it is too powerful a place for what was set in motion. This was going to be a pilgrimage that included facing demons by entering some infernal pockets of my past. The journey's energy had taken on its own life, its own motives and its own intensity. I had the choice to truncate this trip and leave, head home, to spend the rest of the sabbatical on chores around the house to keep me busy, distracted and unaffected by such visitations. But some feeling of destiny overrode and deleted my desire to choose retreating from the retreat. Resignation overpowered my restlessness.

I could stay and wrestle with what was put before me. My loneliness increased as I walked slowly back to the empty cottage in the gathering dark stillness of a lovely fall evening. I looked with hope to see if another retreatant had perhaps arrived and parked close to my truck, but there it sat by itself under the tree, appearing as solitary as I felt. I resolved to stay at least another day, to break the trip down into edible pieces to digest so as not to be overwhelmed with what had just entered my thoughts. I also knew that if I drove for two days

An Isolato Dogged by Divinity

I could be home. I was still in California; familiar territory was only a matter of hours south. Something deep within, however, resisted acting on this delicious, and yet a bit dispiriting temptation. Instead, I put my journey in God's hands and prayed that He show me the path. Doing so instantly calmed me considerably, and the ferocious rage of my father's uncontrollable behavior softened and temporarily receded. A feeling of relief crept over me and bequeathed me the courage to enjoy the solitude of a quiet and isolated night. But I did not relish this specter emerging from the deep again—yet I knew it would.

Mass the next morning was intimate and beautiful. Several people from the area came each morning; about nine of us attended regularly. It was a fine and deeply centering way to begin the day. I loved the kindness and openness of the priests who lived here in the mansion and seemed to enjoy our conversations as much as I did. I ate breakfast and decided to walk the road back to Route 29, flanked on either side by heavy grape vines anticipating the coming harvest. The mornings were sunny, calm, and cool. I took my small camera with me and instead of walking along the road I walked for the first time in my life between rows and rows of purple and white grape clusters through a vineyard that stretched the two miles to the highway. Grapeland was in full cluster.

The aromas from the grapevines were intoxicating. The vines were hung like ripened udders from a herd of cows in the morning, full of milk and lowing in discomfort to be relieved of their precious natural liquid. The grapes seemed to low softly, inviting me to empty them of their red juice, miniature swollen udders about to explode if the pressure of their abundance was not soon attended to.

I found myself thanking the earth for helping them to grow and the workers who would soon help the grapes be crushed and stored, ready for the slow process of being transformed into wine that would travel throughout the world. I sensed at the same time some analogy in me wanting to be transformed, to be relieved of pressures in my interior life. Was this the time of my own harvest, my own ripening wherein some fundamental change was preparing to occur? I found the sight of all these grapes calming and soothing as I walked between their rows, sinking a bit into the soft soil. They had an ancient atmosphere about them. Clusters hung patiently in silence, waiting. Their time had come; they were ready for the crush. The vines were exhausted from holding the grapes, but they did not let them fall. Their tough, gnarly texture held the heavy clusters in midair. An atmosphere of quiet expectancy hovered over the dusty green-gray leaves under a ripening sun.

I thought of the connection between their future wine and my own, sometimes excessive whining about life, about small niggling things and knew that if I became more conscious of such complaining and simply accepted them as part of life's rich texture, I might learn to tolerate them more graciously and hold them in suspension rather than cut them down. The grapes of my own whining needed transformation as well. They deserved their own crush(ing).

I stooped to pick a few of the most swollen, washed them with the water from my plastic water bottle, and enjoyed their bursting liquid in my mouth. My fingers turned a deep purple-red when I squeezed a grape and swallowed it. Christ had taught his followers: "I am the vine and you are the branches." In that simple but profound metaphor he spoke to common people who sought faith in the simple furrows of their own lives. Here in the vineyards of Napa Valley was the essence of connectedness in faith. Faith too was indeed fruitful. The particularities of the natural world melded into the world of spirit. Matter and spirit felt suddenly like the same substance, imagined from two different perspectives; one happened to be more visible than the other, but this did not slight the powerful reality of the latter.

The gap seemed suddenly to close between matter and spirit, between soil and soul, in these vineyards caressed daily and predictably by the California sun. In the dry, hot air the grapes ripened. They needed the intensity of the climate and its unwavering steadiness to fulfill the grapeness they were destined to become. Dryness evoked their ripening. Only then was their time ripe for the larger transformation into wine. This metaphor from nature found soil deep within me and took root. I felt the headiness of nature's matter infused with the spirit of the Creator. I felt the dryness, the scarcity of abundance, exactly what the grapes demanded in order to ferment properly.

An Isolato Dogged by Divinity

As I handled the purple clusters on the vine, I felt a ripening in me, one that could perhaps only happen in the intensity of this pilgrimage. Is this how God reveals Himself? I paid closer attention to the language of the natural order to see what nature reveals about spirit and divinity: we were all from the same stock, the same vine, grafted onto the main vine but branching out in our own uniquely trellised way. I thought of the fear of the apostles of Christ after he had been crucified. They fled and hid, too fearful, too drained of courage to be effective as ministers of the Word. I felt that same fear; I was being asked too much right now. Their fear resonated across space and time and infected me in the way a blight might afflict the clusters in the vineyard. In my journal later I tried to give this experience language.

Sacred Body
Cowering in a stenched room
its corners full of doubt and fear
faces turned inward
against the haze of non-belief.

The apostles, those still
left feeling the absence of light
reluctant, turn outward to gaze
in disbelief at

the subtle body of a wounded man
who abrupts into their
mist, blood dried and cracking
on wrists, forehead, feet.

Each senses in dream a more
intense and deeper flesh
than crucified nails would
ever submit to.
Faith enfleshed lifts
fear from frozen vision.
(*Casting the Shadows*, 33)

Later, in the library, I read the Cistercian monk Thomas Merton on contemplative prayer. He cites Abbe Monchanin, who reminded me of the vineyards I passed through earlier: "For us let it be enough to

97

know ourselves to be in the place where God wants us, and carry on our work, even though it be no more than the work of an ant, infinitesimally small, and with unforeseeable results" (*Contemplative Prayer*, 12). Faith required a certain humility about our life's work. It asked of me not to take my own achievements as signs of personal merit, but to rejoice in the belief that I was where I should be, contributing to the world what I was able. I had in my mind made too much of this pilgrimage; I needed now to twist it down to size, to squeeze it smaller and give up any desire to know its results. I sensed that this was the true path to liberation. I should remember it as well when I teach my classes and cease assessing them to death (and cease judging this pilgrimage). Yet, the paradox became ever clearer; this too was part of the journey so nothing should be left out, dismissed, or whittled down into irrelevance.

Acceptance of the common and the ordinary was such a monumental task for me, perhaps because I had not yet learned how to pray and to trust in total abnegation. Merton understood profoundly the soul of the monk: "The monk searches not only his own heart; he plunges deep into the heart of that world of which he remains a part although he seems to have 'left it'" (*Contemplative Prayer*, 18). He singled out the paradox of the monastic life by making clear that this seeming abandonment of the world is also a paradox; in truth, he or she was then "able to listen more intently to the deepest and most neglected voices that proceed from its inner depths" (25).

When I read this I thought of my father's voice, his actions, his tormented life as an alcoholic, a disease that had a thick core and a very populated line running throughout my family of Irish Catholics. He visited me powerfully and vividly at both retreat centers, wanting perhaps to be heard, or even noticed, by me. Withdrawal from the world was becoming too frightening; in fear and loneliness, but feebly, I had a wish to sustain it. I realized that such was the path to a deeper silence. Perhaps in this silence, the voice of my father, who was so reticent in his sober life, now wanted a conversation; I hoped that I could garner the forgiveness in me to oblige his insistent purpose.

If Christ is the logos, then God is the dark silence that precedes

Him, the origin of it all. Prayer is a human attempt to reach that deep silence. I reflected that the Holy Spirit may then be synonymous with the imagination itself, a way of apprehending, even dimly, this mysterious relationship between language and silence, logos and its echo that fades, eventually to be swallowed by silence. The emptiness of my cottage was full of nothing but silence and solitude; it grew less wearisome and less frightening the longer I stayed. Could I eventually adjust to this deeper form of monastic life? I had been brought here, at this time of empty rooms and vacant parking lots, to experience the deep emptiness of the heart, an evacuating, even a stripping away to the most austere level of myself, which is why I felt such a strong compulsion to flee. I could handle the silence only in small doses; solitude is a strong potion that needed to be taken in a little at a time, at intervals.

I knew that if I did not give myself some respite from it, I would eventually abort the trip for home. So I began taking short road trips north in the morning up Route 29 and visited for a few hours the lovely and unique towns that rested along its margins. They reminded me so much of the small hill towns that gathered in clusters in Italy, so in this Mediterranean landscape I began to experience great solace. I enjoyed being around people; I visited with shop owners, ate lunch at an intimate little restaurant, visited bookstores, sat in the towns' parks to read and called my wife to let her know I was doing well.

I knew that I must do this in order to return to the solitude and silence and be able not just to bear it but to learn from it. I grasped for the first time St. Romuald's words about the monk sitting in his cell: that small enclosure would teach one all he or she needed, yet I had not factored in the immense courage it would take to remain in that small space.

What I discovered, however, was that in touring in the morning I did not really leave the silence and solitude inherent in the monastic setting. These qualities were now no longer anchored to place, or to just that place. They had "grown legs," become portable, bringing with them a shift in the interior life of the heart. I sat in a park ten miles north of the Carmelite Center and read Merton's *Thoughts in Solitude*. I believed in his instruction to learn to forgive myself and then to forgive all those who had offended me, and to forgive myself similar offenses. How else could I learn to love and experience the love of Christ? In this forgiveness, when truly experienced, I felt a deep sense of gratitude coupled with an absence of desires and fears.

I looked about me in the park and witnessed tourists entering and exiting shops across the street. The weather was cool, the sun warm. The air smelled sweetly of the cultivated flowers growing beside me. Tiny hummingbirds wearing bright luminous feathers hovered over a cluster of pink flowers trying to decide which one to penetrate with their quick-darting beaks. I sensed the unbelievable gift of all of this, freely offered by a power much greater than that of the entire world. In the simplicity and abundance of this moment, I was given the strength and affirmation to continue the pilgrimage.

How could I take this world for granted, especially here in the delicious sights and smells of Napa Valley, surrounded by the lushness of the coming grape harvest and the kindness of the climate? I was alone but no longer lonely and reckless to head home. I felt secure in the solitude that surrounded me and realized the deep connectedness I had with all these people shuttling around me. I carried with me the sense of the sacred in ordinary things that I felt envelope me at the Carmelite cottage. Perhaps I was not yet strong enough to abide in the ground of the center, but needed instead to move in rhythm back and forth so as to get used to the sustained pilgrimage. Oscillation can be a good thing, if it kept the journey somewhere between rest and motion.

Yes, perhaps I was escaping a deeper silence and solitude promised on this journey; right now, however, I was not yet equipped for it and instead trusted that this pattern I adopted would unfurl in its own time. This too was part of the path; I should not force it but instead settle into it and have faith that it is leading me, without my knowing, to where I needed to pilgrimage next.

When I awoke in the morning, the Carmelite's resident dog, Rusty, was on my front porch waiting, as he did each morning. He was old and wise; I saw it in his eyes and in his majestically wrinkled forehead. He would accompany me to Mass, walking always just ahead, making sure I found my way by constantly slowing and glancing back at how far I was. When I came from the mansion after Mass and headed back to the cottage for breakfast, he was always outside waiting to escort me. If I sat for more than ten minutes on a bench beside the pond, which I had learned to love as my private meditation locale, he suddenly and silently materialized next to me and put his large black head on my lap. I loved to feel his warmth and his hospitable presence.

I thought more than once of dognapping him and taking him with me for the rest of the journey, then dropping him back here when I headed home. I, who had never liked dogs very much, wanted him to remain my sweet-tempered monastic guestmaster. He was a welcome companion. He liked me, I suppose, because I was the only retreatant in town. His choices for companionship these days were severely curtailed. Fine, because I selfishly enjoyed having him to myself. Far from breaking into my solitude, Rusty enhanced it. I have never owned a dog so I pretended on occasion that he and I had been together for years. We were easy and comfortable with one another and able to let many of our thoughts go unsaid as we sat together watching the large goldfish surface or the bullfrogs peer out of the water with their flat faces and black, blinking eyes breaking the surface. What a monastic mascot he was, schooled so well in the *Rules of Benedict.* I knew he would be a great loss to me when I departed.

Merton's observation in his book on solitude was like a tonic to my exhausting battle against the forces of loneliness: "Solitude is a great risk. There is no true living without it, for it allows us to love our own poverty" (11). This line threw a hard lesson my way—to love my own poverty and through it, to feel compassion for the millions of other souls suffering the same condition. I was indeed poor in spirit, but I desired to learn to accept this rather than push to change it. Just to think of my own poverty was humbling and freeing at the same moment. This kind of deflation was not demeaning or negative. In meditating on it, I sensed a greater space open in which to live; it was expansive and liberating to think of it and to accept that I was poor in so many ways. It rubbed right against the thick grain of my own desire to be a success, to have a reputation as a writer, a teacher, and as someone popular with students and colleagues. These desires really did define my own poverty, not my richness or worth.

Contemplating Merton's words *on* solitude *in* solitude was painful but not repellant. Recognizing my own poverty helped me to settle more into a life of contemplation and to accept with greater charity what intruded or emerged or presented itself as necessary to confront head-on in this place. If I had other retreatants to talk to, the experience would be dispersed, scattered in some way, made more diffuse and easy to avoid, so I would lose the strained intensity that being alone demanded. I knew that the powerful presence of solitude was a necessary part of the journey, and it needed to be excessive. Such an attitude sprouted directly from growing up in a house of scarcity, where there was never enough, even hardly enough, except for the weekends when excess was delivered first hand in my father's drunken rages.

Sitting by the pond, I recalled the days in my parents' home when food in cardboard boxes suddenly appeared on the back steps. No one spoke of its origin. One day, I asked my mother who was bringing this food and her quiet reply was Holy Cross parish. Apparently our family secret was out in the neighborhood now, and had reached the church folks who knew of our paucity and delivered the goods. My own sense of shame heightened considerably, and I prayed that my friends or any of the kids I went to school with would never discover the inner condition of my home. Given that our household had one modest income, with five children and the drinking habits of an alcoholic, the money dwindled well before basic needs were met.

I also remembered the patterns that grew in me as a result of this life of scarcity: becoming accustomed not to have new clothes but to wear the hand-me-downs of my older brother, Marty. When getting a glass of milk or Kool-Aid from the refrigerator, I poured only half a glass or less; learning to drink powdered milk mixed with whole milk and adjusting to the chalky nastiness of it; when I began to drive, I drove just at "empty" most of the time and never filled the tank more than a quarter. A full tank of gas was simply a testament to abhorrent excess. I continued this latter habit until my wife, years into our marriage, introduced me to the very extravagant ritual of filling the gas tank. Such abundance was initially unnerving. Grace does indeed appear in a variety of quantities and octanes.

I realized that I lived out this same kind of uncontrollable excess whenever I could as a way to balance those years of scarcity. But I had in the process missed the poverty of excess; Merton's words put me directly in touch with it. He had become one of many memorable and necessary guides on the pilgrimage to self-understanding.

My last morning at the Carmelite House of Prayer passed quickly, and I found myself packing my truck the next morning, after which I showered as usual around 5 a.m. and prepared to read in the living room before attending Mass. As I dried myself after showering, I felt a sudden sting in the middle of my back; I had either pulled a back muscle or pinched a nerve. The pain was a deep ache that immobilized me. I straightened up partially and shuffled to the bedroom and sat on the edge of the bed, my back stinging so keenly I could hardly move. I felt so helpless: no wife to call to, no neighbors around. I was immobilized, crippled and frozen to the spot, my body giving me no respite. From the window I saw Rusty sitting patiently on the porch waiting for me; I didn't tax his abilities by inviting him in to help me. I grabbed on to the dresser with both hands and lifted myself up, found the aspirin bottle and took several, hoping to alleviate at least some of the pain. I needed to dress slowly even if it took all morning. I very gingerly put on one, then another piece of clothing.

Moving about actually helped a little, but when I sat on the bed and leaned forward to put on socks and shoes, the pain sharpened. I could not negotiate the gravel road barefoot, I convinced myself, so I slipped into my untied sneakers, put my socks in my pocket and headed out the door to the chapel, led, of course by Brother Rusty. By now it was daylight and Mass was to begin within ten minutes. I needed to find someone to help me. With Rusty as my guide and looking back sympathetically to allow me to catch up, I shuffled up the hill, cautiously climbing the front steps of the main house and entered the large hall. Inside, one of the neighbors, a man who came to Mass every morning, was reading. I had no room or time for pride or feelings of self-sufficiency. I shuffled up to him slowly and told him my predicament and asked if he could put my socks on my feet and tie my sneakers.

He chuckled, knowing full well the delights of aging and pulling a back muscle. He took my arm and guided me over to a chair and helped me sit down. I handed him my socks as he knelt down and slid them on my feet. I remembered so many years ago, when I was very young and I would watch my mother's hands guide my socks on to my feet at a time when I was still learning to do so. I also remembered putting on my sons' socks and shoes when they were younger and always feeling very close to them at those moments, especially when they would scratch the back of my head as I stooped in front of them. Something about feet is very intimate.

My childhood and those of my sons returned to me in this simple generous gesture as I felt the socks gently moving up my feet, then each sneaker slipping on and tied. The man tapped the second shoe to signal that he had finished. "There you go," he said. "Take it easy today." I thanked him and felt a deep gratitude for this man's presence, a gift to me at a time when I was rendered helpless and felt the vulnerability that accompanied each of my days, like a shadow always present and sometimes felt.

Some impulse, perhaps the gesture of the body itself at this moment, brought up the figure of Christ washing the feet of his apostles in an act of humility, as well as the image of Mary Magdalene, in an act of selfless love, washing His feet, then drying them with her hair. It was a simple act of charity that embodied in its motion the words: "Do unto others as you would have them do unto you." Such a small act: a man helping another man finish dressing in the morning as both prepared to participate in the ritual of the Mass, which dramatizes each time the ultimate sacrifice of one man for all others in an act of grace.

Now I have to be careful about what I am about to say, so as not to overload the incident with the supernatural; yet it was present in a tangible way. After Mass, as I lifted myself so slowly from the kneeler after the final blessing and grimaced in anticipation of the expected pain, I realized that it had subsided, as if something that had slipped out of place had now found its way home again. I walked out of the chapel and down the steps to my cottage to make a simple breakfast and dared to stretch without feeling even a tingle of the previous ache. I thanked God for this quick recovery because I could not imagine trying to drive later that morning under these conditions. I thanked God for this man, whose name I never asked, who stooped in an act of generosity to help me when I could not help myself. Here was the presence of Christian love, I thought. Service to others is really the central action of this form of love, of doing for another joyfully without any desire for recompense. The image of this man stooping to put on my socks and sandals, and offering me words of support, stayed with me as a model to imitate.

Outside between the truck and the front porch Rusty had sat waiting for me, fully aware that I was another soul who had stopped for a short respite but was now departing. I spent a moment thanking him for his gracious hospitality, including listening with such attention as I shared with him personal things. I knew his head was packed with bits and pieces of many retreatants' stories collected over many years; he bore them all with grace and canine charity.

Patting him one last time, I buckled into the truck and retraced my initial drive back to Route 29 and the road that would take me into a very different spiritual habitation: Sonoma Mountain Zen Center outside of Santa Rosa, California. These "painful pull-aways," as I called them, were always difficult and nostalgic moments as each place that began in unfamiliarity always ended with my feeling as if I were abandoning a peaceful and familiar home. I treasured and wanted to avoid these moments, these rearview-mirror visions of a place that had become so intimately a part of my existence now growing smaller as I watched it moving away from me. But this was a necessary step in the slow process of finding its own home in a larger remembered narrative whose next chapter was down the road.

6

Meditations Out of Time

Sonoma Mountain Zen Center
Santa Rosa, California

When you are a truly happy Christian, you are also a Buddhist.
And vice versa.
>   —Thich Nhat Hanh, *Living Buddha, Living Christ*

I FELT A DEEP JOY steam up in me as I bought a hot cup of coffee at a store along Route 29 and drove through the morning mist of Napa Valley. I loved this part of the pilgrimage as much as arriving and settling into the rhythms of the retreat centers. A healthy oscillation, one I had not planned, seemed to have entered my trip, wherein the breaks from the retreat centers had become as joyful as my stays. The California weather and geography reminded me of our two years in Italy, of driving through the small towns of southern Italy from Rome to Sicily, full of open markets, fresh fruits and vegetables, whole roasted chickens and the mysterious yellow light of the Mediterranean. California had all these wonders and I felt the glow of a quiet joy descend on me in remembering the Italian geography and climate.

My meditations carried me farther north into the lush geography of northern California, to Santa Rosa. Back on Highway 101, I headed to Petaluma and found Petaluma Hill Road. I turned right onto Roberts Road and easily discovered Mountain Road, which took me to the Zen Center in a quiet stretch of road with neighbors in small farmhouses and even a few trailers surrounding the property.

Founded by Jakusho Kwong-roshi in 1973, the center offered private rooms in various cabins on the property as well as hermitages for more private, secluded meditations. Because I knew so little of this form of spiritual practice, I requested permission to be able to practice zazen meditation in the Zendo where all religious rituals took place. I wanted to become as much a part of the daily life of the community as possible, to let my Catholic familiarity with the monasteries recede into the background and to enter a tradition that I had no direct experience of. I simply promised myself to surrender to what presented itself for the next five days and to reflect on its value afterwards. I was not disappointed as the days unfolded. Something about the unfamiliar made me more alert, more conscious of the incidental events that sprouted each day.

I checked in and was assigned a room in the Kanzeon cabin about two hundred yards from the main house where meals were taken in community. Individuals rotated cooking, and everyone pitched in washing, drying dishes, and cleaning up. There were about nine other retreatants from diverse personal and professional backgrounds; we all met and warmed to one another's company quickly and with amazing ease. The bustle of a thriving and friendly community replaced the more solitary life of my last week.

I learned that there was no great fanfare to a new arrival's presence. People were flowing in and out of the center all the time. The trick was to find my assigned place to sleep, unpack the minimum number of things I needed, set up, learn the schedule, and fit in as quickly as possible. Within an hour I was nested in my room and reported for noon meal where I learned the schedule for that evening and the next day. No silence was specified while others and I were assigned our daily chores and gathered for meals. In the Zendo, however, silence was the key to it all and meditation in silence was insisted upon. Dress code and ritual entering and exiting the Zendo were important to the spirit of the place and closely monitored. Here people spoke softly to one another and everyone worked to keep a sense of calm and serenity in their behavior and speech. I felt that I had entered a strange but authentic and welcoming place for the next week.

Margaret, the gatekeeper and hostess for new arrivals, greeted me and handed over four sheets of instructions to study. She was a kind and thoughtful woman who, after visiting here for years, moved in as head resident and bookkeeper. I liked her immediately. She described the ritual practices when entering the Zendo to engage in silent meditation. I loved the ritual and took to it with a zest that surprised me. Margaret also assigned me the task of working each morning from 8:30 a.m. to noon in the garden under the tutelage of a young man, Sam, who with his new wife had signed on for a one-year resident training program. They had already completed half their year when I arrived. Most of the fruits and vegetables the community ate were grown in the garden, and I was pleased to be given this work area. I liked the ritual rhythm of worship and the sweaty work of digging the earth under the hot California sun, transplanting crops, and preparing the soil for new seeding; the balance, as I entered it more each day, created an atmosphere of harmony in me that offset my tendency to sink into a mild depression when alone too much.

I was also introduced, through the Zen center's spare but engaging library, to the writings of perhaps the most famous Vietnamese monk of our day, Thich Nhat Hanh, who wrote eloquently of work: "Work is life only when done in mindfulness. Otherwise, one becomes like the person 'who lives as though dead'" (*The Miracle of Mindfulness*, 60). Mindfulness in everything I did increased my awareness of simple tasks I would naturally perform, for the most part, unconsciously. Mindfulness is a way of thought that revealed the interconnectedness of all acts, thoughts, and persons. Working in the garden as well as being assigned other menial but important work tasks would, I hoped, allow me to become more conscious of this interconnection, what Buddhism refers to as "codependent arising." To learn to embody in action these ideas could take a lifetime, but I could begin here and now, in my assigned duties.

In the afternoon Margaret met me outside the communal house, handed me a rake, and instructed me to drag the gravel and dirt path that stretched from the house to the entrance of the Zendo; if done with dispatch and haste, this simple task might take fifteen minutes. Instead, I was invited to perform this work slowly, in a spirit of meditation. One of the staff members, Sally, illustrated how to create large circles with the rake in the gravel so that when I was finished, there would be a pattern of circles intersecting one another with fine lines created by the rake's steel strips. The deeper task was to imagine the process rather than race to achieve results.

I soon grew to live this exercise, which at first made me feel conspicuous and self-conscious as people came and went from the house and graciously stepped around my work, not wishing to disturb its design. It allowed a form of meditation in doing a simple task that made me realize that even the most menial or repetitious of chores harbored its own beauty if approached slowly and with mindfulness. I discovered that this activity too could be a way to pray and meditate. Creating these raked series of lines in the hard gravel surface allowed me to put my mark on my experience, to impress the place with my own contribution. I let go of worrying about "doing it right" and instead allowed the flow of the rake handle to guide me. Mindfulness began to be a way of paying attention to the designs made in the gravel from the rake, which left me more aware of my own presence in the simple gestures of raking than I would have been without this menial, yet meaningful task. Such a simple activity satisfied something deep within me. I rake; therefore, I am. Prayer, I began to sense, was as much in the body as in the soul or intellect. Not what I was doing but the attitude in which I approached it turned something menial into something deeply significant as I created a geometry of meaning in the interlocking circles.

While raking under the blue sky and thick, green maple trees, I recognized that one of the purposes of this trip was to learn something about calming the mind and moving into a quiet center, as well as to develop an attitude of greater awareness by slowing down my actions and thoughts. I had no desire to begin a serious study of Zen Buddhism, but I entertained a strong curiosity about its practices and path and desired some greater understanding of the Buddha and insight into a deeper reality that had the capacity to inform me of the life of spirit. I wished, as I formed the circular motions, that meditation practices had been part of my own training within the Catholic Church, but I never even heard the word spoken. This simple shift of attitude, to increase my ability to be present to the simplicity of life's task, provided immense joy. There was such a profound alteration of attitude in the simplicity of manual labor.

In the Genjo Ji Library off the kitchen of the main house, I discovered Nhat Hanh's book on breathing. His words marked for me the beginning of this exploration into meditation through the breath. The attraction of such a practice rested in its possibility of developing some intimate relationship between psychology and spiritual awareness; his language was principally about consciousness, about deepening one's awareness through cultivating being present to simple practices and their connection to a spiritual awareness. Surprisingly, I found in his book *Peace is Every Step* a discussion of anger that hit very close to home: "Anger and hatred are the materials from which hell is made. A mind without anger is cool, fresh and sane. The absence of anger is the basis of real happiness, the basis of love and compassion" (56–57).

Even hearing the word *anger* ignited a reverie in me of the anger that occupied our home on weekends when I prayed before going to bed on Saturday that we would all make it peacefully to Sunday morning. But rarely did that occur. Usually the drama of anger, shouting, drunken fits, and explosive outbursts would begin around midnight, often to the sound of plates, cups, anything breakable crashing to the kitchen floor. My father, now in an alcoholic rage, swore and cursed at my mother, his only available outlet for the shame he carried from his own mother's abusive attacks on him.

Booze allowed the underworld in my father to open its horrific maw, and out poured all the infernal rage and shame that a childhood and adulthood had so successfully ingrained in his soul. Sunday, sobering up, hung over and full of remorse, he would sit on the edge of my bed and, with head down, apologize profusely as he tried to muster a bleary-eyed resolve to make it to work the next morning.

What I did not recognize was that his shame and rage, as toxic temperaments, would fully enter me and my brothers and sister, making us all overflow with our own angry outbursts. How to calm the body and soul from rage? Nhat Hanh's writing proved very helpful.

I felt in his words that the serenity of calm which was nothing short of learning to live within love and compassion. I kept these words close to my heart while I was here, to let them assist me in becoming more conscious of both anger and shame in my youth, which I had as companions even now, and to feel the force of these destructive emotions that deterred me from moving out to others with selfless compassion. I wanted to feel more intensely the liberation that comes from quieting desires, quelling appetites, and muting ambition. Inside of Hanh's words I heard the "Prayer for Peace" attributed to St. Francis of Assisi:

> Lord, make me an instrument of your Peace.
> Where there is hatred
> Let me sow love;
> Where there is injury, pardon;
> Where there is doubt, faith;
> Where there is despair, hope;
> Where there is darkness, light;
> Where there is sadness, joy.
> Oh, Divine Master, grant that I may seek not so much to be consoled as to console; to be understood as to understand; to be loved as to love; for it is in giving that we receive; it is in pardoning that we are pardoned, and it is in dying that we are born to eternal life.

His words are not really different in spirit from Nhat Hanh's meditations. The latter writes eloquently in *The Miracle of Mindfulness* of the deep interdependence of all life: "we are the other" (45). Freed from anger, resentments, vengeance, and envy, one can sense the heart liberated as it moves—almost by its fundamental nature—toward compassion: "Look at all things with the eyes of compassion. That is the sacred call" (59). I found that the experience of non-attachment, of emptying, brushed up against my own soul's yearnings. I felt that the desire for non-attachment can also be another way of attaching, and I laughed at the yawning trap. Yet there was a healing quality in his language that I felt within me; I realized that the idea of quieting anger and resentments, of confronting the specter of shame as well, might be a good place to begin meditation the next morning in the Zendo.

I set the small alarm clock in my room for 4 a.m.; it seemed to jar me from sleep almost as soon as I lay down. I showered and dressed in the empty house, once again the only retreatant staying in this particular refuge. I waited for the bonsho bell that would ring across the expansive field and garden to call me to the Zendo for zazen (meditation prayer). The day began in an enveloping dark calmness, my favorite time. The roosters across the road at the farmhouse had not yet stirred into their morning shrieks.

I tidied up my room and then entered the living room to read for about half an hour in the comfort of the old sofa. As I sat on the couch, my eye caught some movement in the kitchen next to the stove. It moved as quickly as a thought or a shadow might appear and disappeared as I looked up and sat quietly. In a moment, a mouse darted out from under the stove and scurried a foot or two to a box of rodent poison sitting between the stove and the refrigerator. He stuck his little gray head in and ate a mouthful or two. Then, as if he suddenly realized he was on display, he snapped his head out of the opening in the poisoned food container, scattering the little pellets across the floor as he scooted under the stove. What a floorshow, so early in the morning!

Then the house mouse peered out and up from under the stove with his ears spread completely opened and pointing forward, like Japanese fans. His ears were as large as his head and looked comically like the Mickey Mouse club ears of the old Disney television show, or the ears of Dumbo who learns to fly by means of his floppy head wings. It looked directly at me, then scampered under the stove. After a moment he scurried out again over to the box of poisoned food and began eating again, repeating the entire escapade. What an elaborate way he had instantly developed by which to say "good morning." I watched him until the bell called me across to the Zendo.

In my week's stay the little critter devoured the entire box of poison food and appeared to thrive on its contents. I welcomed him as the official Kanzeon cabin's pet and fed him some table scraps after he had emptied the box of food that was supposed to encourage his demise. Never in my life had I seen so much personality in a house mouse. He deserved to remain there, in the kitchen, under the stove, living a happy life, perhaps enjoying his own form of mini-meditation and listening to the retreatants come and go. Certainly at night he had mastered better than I ever could the act of remaining silent. He became part of my morning meditation for the entire week and I thanked God for giving me yet another animal to help me through the retreat house's silence and solitude. God does indeed provide, even a mouse, when small is called for.

The rituals surrounding movement in the Zendo were mysterious and strange to my Western religious practice. I grew in time to love them and wanted to learn to practice them well, to feel the full ritual effect that palpably shifted my spirit. When the bell rang, I took my flashlight and followed its narrow band of light just in front of my feet as the strip of light penetrated the deep darkness and silence across the field along the footpath to the Zendo. How many have followed this path in the past, I wondered, wearing it down deep into the earth so that my feet felt the familiar grooves of hundreds of soles that had gone before me.

Others appeared from out of the shadows to meditate from 5:15 to 7:30 each morning. Because of an implanted prosthetic left hip I was not able to cross my legs in the sitting lotus position. Instead, I was given a chair to sit on as I faced the wall after settling in for zazen. The ritual for entering the Zendo was very precise, as I soon discovered all the rituals of motion were.

Gassho: hold palms together with tips of fingers at nose level. Thumbs should be closed against the adjacent fingers. Elbows were extended out at right angles, so that arms were parallel to the floor. When bowing, one bent at the waist at a 45-degree angle, moving the entire upper body as one unit. A proper bow contained presence, humility and reverence.

("Zendo Form and Practice Procedures," 1)

To enter the Zendo required a certain set of actions as well: "Cross the threshold with the left foot (foot farthest from the altar). Bow to the altar with hands in gassho. Then place one's hands in shassu, which is the position of the hands required when moving inside the Zendo or from the Zendo to the main house" ("Zendo Form," 2). In shassu, I closed my left hand gently around the thumb and placed it next to the sternum of the chest. I placed the right hand over the left and kept elbows slightly out from the body.

I then bowed in gassho facing the seat, followed by a bow to each person on either side of me, each of whom returned the bow. We all moved clockwise, bowing to one another. I then sat in my chair and turned clockwise to face the wall. The instructions suggested facing the wall with head erect and eyes wide open, then dropping them to the floor in front of me. Keep them open. I was to learn how closing them invites sleep, which tried to reclaim me almost instantly. We were not to breathe so others could hear us.

The lighting inside the Zendo was very dim, making the entire sacred space feel like a dream setting and brought on a temptation to relax back into sleep—just what one did not want to do. It was calm and serene; the silence suffused in soft yellow light made alert meditation a constant challenge. I settled into my chair facing the wall; I let my eyes drop to the floor and my body find its most comfortable position. For the number of people present, it was very quiet. Each person moved slowly and in silence. We had each left our shoes and socks outside on shelves, so all human movement was quiet enough not to shatter the deep silence. Of all my experiences at the Zen center, these periods of meditation were the most profound and lasting, perhaps because they were the most difficult part of my daily schedule. Silence began to fill the space of the room as a calm serenity enveloped each of us. I tried without force or will power to become part of the meditation.

After a few minutes my mind felt the new freedom and began, first like a frisky dog, to roam from thought to thought, sniffing at past events—anything to circumvent the present moment. My mind was also like a fly, lighting on various scraps of food, not content with any, always looking for a tastier morsel. I tried to think of God and almost laughed out loud. The image that arose was anything but sublime; I saw that energetic mouse under the stove with ears twice the size of normal mouse ears. Its comic silhouette peering out at me from under the stove, eating and thriving on the box of poison pellets entertained and distracted me further. God is a mouse with big ears who thrives on poison food. I tried to shake off this image of God, as the humor of my situation burst to the surface. How absurd this was! If the mouse was put in my cabin and now in my mind as an image of God, then I immediately felt better about God, who has a very subtle and disarming sense of humor. I tried again to meditate and to pray for some insight that would help me here in the dim light as I stared at the wooden wall in front of me. I wondered what others were thinking about and how successful they were in meditating. Competition began to replace contemplation. I realized then that I had a very long road to travel ahead of me. Stilling the mind's wildness would be, by itself, a sufficient achievement for the entire pilgrimage.

Settling down, I recalled Nhat Hanh's wonderful meditation on the Eucharist, which he believed was a profound way for one to practice awareness. When Jesus broke the bread and shared it with his disciples, he said, "Eat this. This is my flesh." He knew that "if his disciples would eat one piece of bread in mindfulness, they would have real life. In their daily lives, they may have eaten their bread in forgetfulness, so the bread was not bread at all; it was a ghost" (*Peace is Every Step*, 22).

Practicing mindfulness was one of the core practices of meditation. One way to gain a deeper sense of the feeling of mindfulness was by breathing every breath with awareness. I liked the simplicity of this practice and began now, in meditation, to pay closer attention to my breath. Simple small steps, I reminded myself, was all that was asked of me.

My eyes were almost closed as I felt the air slowly and gently entering my body; breathing out I said quietly to myself: *God, help me to sense your presence.* I felt something shifting in me, a peaceful calmness that was a new sensation. It was easy to lose attention to the breathing, so I remained with it, trying but not forcing myself, to remain aware of the breath and with it, a sense of my own incarnation. How peculiar this pilgrimage was. I was realizing more and more that something as simple as breathing with awareness was new. I had not even learned, in all these years, to breathe properly. Seeking God, or finding God, seemed so remote when I was still wrestling with the simple exercise of right breathing. I felt so naïve.

But instead of chastising myself, as was my habit, I let go of criticism and returned to my breathing. I would read later in his work: "By following your breath and combining the Full Awareness of Breathing with your daily activities, you can cut across the stream of disturbing thoughts and light the lamp of awakening" (*The Sutra on the Full Awareness of Breathing*, 45). I thought that if I learned nothing else in these mornings, it would be a new awareness of breath and the body as a means of praying.

As I meditated into the morning's gray light seeping into the Zendo, I saw an image of my father in his upstairs bedroom. On the dresser were two statues made of plastic: one of Christ, the other of the Virgin Mary. It was that kind of pale, yellow, ivory plastic that absorbed the light during the day, and then at night would suffuse a soft greenish glow. As I walked up the stairs I saw my father kiss the statue of the Virgin. I never thought that he might have been praying to her, but now I realized that he was. Had I inherited his devotion to a religious life, or at least an attempt at a spiritual one, from his examples that really never registered before? Was this afflicted, tortured alcoholic struggling with his demons actually the presence of grace that I only now grasped? This exquisite memory served to reveal something of my father that I had not, until now, gained consciousness of. I wondered if this was to be the first of many insights that his travelling with me would reveal?

At other times I would hear him mumbling in his room, asking for help, praying in earnest. I believe he was searching for a cure from his alcoholism in prayer to a higher power; he did not know that such prayer alone might be insufficient, as I learned later in my reading of the Big Book of AA. No, he needed the companionship and fellowship of other recovering alcoholics. But from shame and guilt, or his natural introversion, my father never admitted to us he had "a drinking problem," nor did he ever attend an AA meeting to get the communal help he so sorely needed. But his devotion to the Blessed Virgin, I realized now sitting in the Zendo, was his attempt to cure himself through prayer. It was real, but doomed to failure. In some ways I had inherited, as a spiritual legacy from him, a deep hunger for a spiritual life as well as a propensity to create chaos in my own life, a shadow energy that wanted to destroy what I had achieved. My father—my brother—indeed! To preserve her sanity, my mother joined Al-Anon and found in that support group the strength and understanding she needed to survive my father's illness.

I was gaining an awareness of many things about my past in these moments of silent meditation; I allowed feelings of striving and competition to dissolve and returned repeatedly to the breath for comfort and support. The thought came to me: even breathing could be a form of praying. The nineteenth-century American rebel and naturalist Henry David Thoreau wrote a thoughtful chapter in *Walden* called "Solitude." He was a mystic as profound as any recognized by the Church: "How vast and profound is the influence of the subtle powers of Heaven and Earth. We seek to perceive them and do not; we seek to hear them and do not. Identified with the substance of things, they cannot be separated from them" (111).

His words helped me grasp the added value of meditation, of zazen. There is a subtle power in Heaven and Earth and this power must be approached with nuance and humility. Breathing in and out mindfully opened a path to that subtle awareness because it focused without force or strain on the subtle nature of the body, and through it the spirit. I remembered Thoreau's thought as the gong sounded to end the sitting meditation and begin kinhin, or walking meditation.

We rose slowly from our places and stepped into the row in front of us. The idea was to keep an even space between ourselves as we moved slowly in a clockwise direction. I formed my hands in the shasshu position and raised my head, back straight, glad to be out of the stiff chair. I kept my mind on my breathing and took one-half step with each inhalation and exhalation. The dim yellow lighting illuminated my fellow retreatants in soft silhouettes moving through a dreamscape, specters shuffling slowly through sacred space.

We spaced ourselves and began a very slow movement without making any noise, in tiny steps, with great pauses between subtle movements. During the course of kinhin, which lasted thirty minutes, I might not travel even fifteen feet across the Zendo. Slowing down like this was almost uncanny; it felt more like a caricature of movement, for as the body slowed the mind slowed. As the breathing became central, I felt a heightened awareness of the smallest object or movement. The unnaturalness of these thirty minutes pointed out to me how fast-paced I really lived while considering such speed normal. Slowing down exposed the insanity of living a life in high gear, which cancelled out both reflection and prayer.

I looked forward to this slow motion and especially enjoyed walking down to the large pond below the buildings to meditate; then, if no one was around (I was still too self-conscious in this exercise), I softened my gaze, put my hands in their proper position and moved very slowly through the grass to the occasional encouragement of croaking bullfrogs in the marsh. My breathing became more even and conscious; I listened to the few early bullfrogs beginning their chant, to the flies I could hear in the still air, to the birds in the surrounding trees and to a small fish that suddenly breached the surface of the water. I let the soft air of a fall evening circle around me and touch my face, felt a fly land on top of my head, heard the tires of a pickup truck hiss down the asphalt farm road.

In paying attention to my breathing and being more attentive to my surroundings, I sensed a mysterious emptiness, as if something, some impediment, had been exorcised from my interior life. It was not a hollowness of no purpose or meaning in life but rather an emptiness that invited life in, a receptive emptying, or a solitary emptiness, the kind of emptiness that could mature in the rich soil of solitude. This kind of emptiness in solitude began to dissolve all transient distractions. Nothing else was necessary. It was a feeling of wholeness and oneness. It also bred in me a feeling of relationship; busyness softened. I was content in the joy I felt by the pond, or in the Zendo, or raking the gravel into circles, or following instructions from my young mentor in the garden. It was all I needed of God right now. It might *be* God. God may consist at least of this: a feeling of joy, consciousness and contentment in the moment. That was sufficient for me right now.

I memorized earlier and kept close to me the pilgrim Ishmael's mediation in Melville's *Moby-Dick*: "we live in an ocean of subtle intelligences" (243). Solitude and subtlety: two extraordinary qualities to contemplate, especially how one invited the other and even made room for the other. This feeling of the subtlety of life, of the natural world and the world of spirit, comforted and consoled me in a way I had never before experienced. Later that night I wrote the following in my journal:

Still Bowl

I wake to a worry and hear another crack in
the bowl of deep inner stillness. A voice suggests:
Put the bowl on the wheel and slather new clay
around its weary outside, its battered face to the world.
Seal the cracks so the water I pour in it
later may be still and remain clear.
The new clay dries on the bowl's outer face.
I place my own face just above the water's still
reflection. Along the temple above my left
eye scurries a new scar. The water is my solitude,
my silence and my wound.

Each morning I meditated in the Zendo for two and half hours in
a practice that never grew easier, but the time seemed to become
more valuable. I sensed the years it must take in such practice to
become fully centered and more completely aware. I contented
myself with reduced ambitions, to take what I could, as a novice,
from the experience and let the rest go. If I made this a complex set
of activities, I would move farther, not closer, to God and to my
own interior life by substituting the project of meditation for a
deeply personal, transformative one. Just learning to breathe in
mindfulness for the moment was a great step forward; I asked God
for help in such a precious exercise each time I took off my shoes
and socks to enter the Zendo. I paid more attention to my bare feet
contacting the cool wooden floor. How unconscious I had allowed
myself to become toward the sensual body's constant contacts with
the world. Meditating grew to be more and more a sensate activ-
ity.At the end of meditation we all turned to the front for a service
of singing and prayer. One particular prayer I enjoyed saying each
morning was called "The Four Vows":

> shu jo mu gen sei gan do
> bon no mu jim sei gan dan
> ho mon my ryo sei gan gaku
> butsu do mu jo sei gan jo
> Translation:
> Sentient beings are numberless; I vow to save them.

Meditations Out of Time

Desires are inexhaustible; I vow to put an end to them.
The Dharmas are boundless; I vow to master them.
The Buddha's Way is unsurpassable; I vow to attain it.

What appealed to me as much as meditating in the Zendo, however, was working in the garden with Sam after breakfast and mingling in the kitchen each morning with other retreatants working and praying here. Speech was not chatter; it was more measured. Our social time together had a calming, contemplative rhythm. There was ample time for prayer and meditation, reading, physical labor, and social gatherings around meals. Frenzy was absent, as was running, talking fast, shouting, making noise, and drawing attention to one's self. I realized almost by accident how much I loved this place and already resisted thoughts of leaving.

However, there are always exceptions to any rule and here was one. Each morning I anticipated seeing and talking with a woman who had come for a week to live by herself in a hermitage. Her goal, she informed us during her first meal with the group, was to say a single mantra one million times. She kept a log of the number and when she arrived in the kitchen for lunches only, I would see her as a prizefighter that had just suffered through and survived another round with a formidable opponent. She looked increasingly worn thin with each day's passing; yet she carried herself in self-delight because of the number of times she had that day repeated the mantra. She chattered without ceasing through breakfast; then, after helping us with the dishes, she scooted out the back door to her hermitage, her words trailing her: "Back to meditation and chanting until tomorrow. See you." Sometimes she would resurface for dinner with us. I admired her fortitude and her breezy babble when she joined us. She seemed supremely happy with her task and I had no doubt she would one day hit a million strokes on her mantra. Then perhaps we would all join her in celebrating her victory with a "million mantra meal."

Growing up, I remembered that when I could sleep in my older brother's room when he was away with friends for the night, or when he was out for the evening, and I would sneak in to listen to his stereo, there was on the mirror above his dresser a sticker with the words: "Idle hands are the devil's workshop." I knew he was not responsible for putting such an admonition there. I thought of this sentence so many times in my life and discovered not long ago that its source was *Benedict's Rule*. On the nature of manual labor, he prefaces his discussion with: "Idleness is the enemy of the soul" *(Rule,* 47). To counter such idleness, Benedict believed that monks should have specified times for manual labor as well as for prayerful reading.

I liked Benedict's measured attitude; it sounded a bit dated in its austere and chiseled exactness regarding monastic work and leisure. I discerned, however, a note of compassion in his voice, as in the case where he addressed work and poverty: "They must not become distressed if local conditions or their poverty should force them to do the harvesting themselves. When they live by the labor of their hands, as our father and the apostles did, then they are really monks." And then, as I imagine it, Benedict paused in his writing and reflected for a moment. He thought of the kinds of men who might enter the monastery, carrying their own limitations: "Yet, all things are to be done with moderation on account of the faint-hearted" (48).

Severity laced with compassion is how I imagined this rebel for Christ and the spirit. In reading his *Rules* during my pilgrimage, I grew very fond of his often eccentric but always clear vision of the monastic life. I was grateful that he spoke so emphatically about work as one way to ripen the human spirit. His words helped to give my menial tasks a deeper significance, especially my digging in the garden.

In the garden Sam and I worked daily before the sun climbed to the center of the sky. I was instructed to dig a trench so that we could replant some of the melons growing at another level of the terraced hill. The earth was soft, having been well tilled and organically fertilized from the neighbors' barns. The trenches were about thirty feet long, so a full morning was needed for me to dig down one row and part of another. We also needed to clean out high weeds in order to reclaim part of the land for future planting. I loved the smell of the damp earth rising up, drawn by the warming sun. Feeling the sun warming my back as I dug instilled in me a sweet-tempered joy; the simplicity and repetition of the task allowed me to meditate and to feel a deep gratitude for a healthy body, for this day alone and for the companionship of my fellow gardener and mentor, who was about the age of my older son. Talking was allowed but it was to be moderate and focused on the task before us. Sam and I stepped over this boundary often to exchange stories of our pasts. He and his wife were in their sixth month and at the end of the year he believed he would be ready to move on. After, they would travel to Germany to live for a year or two.

When thirsty, we drank from the hose or nearby water fountain. I asked many questions of my mentor, and he was patient in responding. He knew an astonishing amount about conserving the soil, replenishing and rotating crops, and harvesting them. He worked slowly, talking to the earth and to the vegetables and fruits that were ready to harvest. He had a naturally meditative disposition in movement and speech and made a fine example for me to follow. In the Zendo each morning, Sam was the drummer and leader of the chants; he exhibited a zeal for prayer that was contagious.

As I worked, I wanted to keep in mind the breathing and the mindfulness outlined in Hanh's writing. He emphasized repeatedly in his works that to sit or work with mindfulness allowed "for a serene encounter with reality" (*Miracle*, 60) that promoted in our souls "the pure peace of the present moment" (87). But such mindfulness, his writing reminded me, is not exclusively in the service of our lives. The purpose of this attitude was "to help to lessen the suffering of those around us and to make their lives happier" (76).

Mindfulness struck me as a calling, even a vocation in its own right: to assist others by emptying myself of my own desires, or at least to mute them enough to allow the needs of others to be recognized and served. I found this simple awareness difficult to keep in mind, harder still to practice regularly as part of my daily life.

Working in the garden, I was in the service of those who would eventually eat the food I was for a short time helping to bring to the table. I was also in the service of the earth in a small way, for she was relying on me to care for her so that she could be of service to us as well. Sam served me in responding patiently to what I asked him about farming so that I might perform my own chores with greater consciousness. It was both elaborate and simple, this series of relationships, and perhaps in such interconnectedness God existed most emphatically.

In another one of his writings, Hanh refers to this awareness as "interbeing," a word that captured for him the state "where barriers between things, persons dissolve" (*Living Buddha*, 11). Just inhabiting this word generated a new feeling in me that I wanted to incorporate into my daily life at the Zen Center, and to take it with me. I sensed how all the distinctions, boundaries, definitions, and divisions we draw are finally illusory. Interbeing breaks them down and coaxes us to think of the relational quality of the human, natural, and spiritual orders and their intimate likenesses. Fear keeps these divisions in place to create a false sense of insulation from what I earlier refused to consider as part of myself.

His words were also a powerful testament to the fact that distinctions between Buddha and Christ are made mostly of papier-mâché. Mindfulness, for example, he compared to the Holy Spirit: "Both are agents of healing.... Mindfulness is a way to heal the wounds in my own mind" (14), a way of salving the lesions that develop when we isolate ourselves from one another by creating false divisions that lead to disagreements, dissensions, war, as well as national and global violence. As a seed in us, Nhat Hanh believed that the Holy Spirit was the force of healing wounds brought on by divisions, both internal and external. Meditation was simply a means "for surveying our own territory to see what is going on inside" (*Living Buddha*, 19).

How far I had drifted from work as a means of grace and prayer. What a changed workforce might emerge if work became less about earning a wage and more a form of prayer. Not to pray while working but the work itself as a way of praying. Leisure too would assume an entirely different quality by being more integrated into one's entire life. Work may be a sign of the Holy Spirit's presence in everyday life. What an idea to contemplate further!

The Holy Spirit, as an energy that helped me be truly alive by pervading my whole being, was very similar to the Buddha, a word whose root, "Buddha," means "to wake up" (22), to gain and practice mindfulness. In his simple but profound prose, Nhat Hanh helped me grasp something essential about the Buddha as well as revealed to me the interbeingness of Christ and this holy figure. Grasping these similar qualities allowed me to see in both traditions a common root of compassion and service to others. My time in the garden gave me both physical work and a meditative field in which to contemplate how this might be so. I felt a kind of garden consciousness pervading my arid landscape and offering a more fruitful way to cultivate a life of prayerful compassion. A former feeling of futility grew into one of fertility.

I felt a fullness in the simplicity of life at the retreat center and had misgivings that when I left I would lose its serenity as well. I was tempted once again to simply remain here for the duration of my pilgrimage, but I resolved at least for the present to honor the original intention of travelling, journeying, and dwelling in those places that had emerged during the planning of this trip. After all, had I stayed with Rusty and the Carmelite priests in Napa Valley, I would have missed the abundance this Zen Center offered me. I felt both fear and excitement at what might lie ahead. Staying at the Zen center would perhaps be too comfortable now, and time was now calling me to head out.

On the second-to-last day I was invited to participate in the oryoki ritual, an ancient practice "that came from the wandering Buddhist monks in India" as I read in one of the handout sheets I received when I arrived. Its intention was to show gratitude for food, as did the monks who wandered the countryside and relied on the generosity of the area's inhabitants for sustenance. I had never even seen this ritual performed, much less participated in it, so I eagerly assented to the invitation to participate.

Margaret asked if I had been shown the ritual process for the oryoki. She pulled a bowl, napkin, and utensils from the shelf and asked me to sit with her at the table where she illustrated the complex process of unfolding the napkin and placing the eating utensils in a precise pattern. The first bowl, she instructed, was the Buddha bowl and symbolized the Buddha's teachings. I would hold this bowl with two hands when I am served in the Zendo. The server will put food into it until I signal with a palms-upward gesture: enough. The second two bowls I will hold up so that the servers can put food into them.

I was told not to get flustered if I forgot the order of the ritual but to keep calm and enter into the practice as best I could with such little preparation. I was not to look around at how others were doing it but to improvise if I forgot what to do next. I was to bow to the server with each portion served. When finished eating from the second bowls, I would clean them with my spatula and then wait, composed and erect, for tea to be served in the first bowl. The instructions were to clean the first bowl after pouring the tea from it to the second bowl. I would wipe the first bowl clean, pour the tea from the second into the third bowl and clean the second. I was then to drink the tea from the third bowl and dry it, and then to fold up my oroyoki set and return it, when the ritual was completed, to the Sanga House where we take our meals. I knew there would be nothing leisurely about this repast.

When the time came for the actual ritual and attention was on me, I clutched under the pressure and went blank with panic. After beginning the process with some signs of competence, I forgot the signal to stop the serving in the first bowl. The server, with a bit of a quizzical look, continued to put a yogurt-looking tapioca pudding into it. I finally said, forgetting the sign, "that's enough." He smiled and moved on. I tasted it and did not like its taste or texture. But since there was no ritual for disposing of it except by eating, I took a deep breath and dug in with my spatula. The level of the pudding, however, seemed not to diminish. "Offer it up," I said to myself. There was no way out but down and so down it must go. I ate it, breathing through my mouth so as not to taste it.

Mercifully, another server came along with more solid food for my second bowl, and I remembered the gesture and took only a little. A third server followed with vegetables, and I thanked the Buddha for the variety of food that I was invited to eat in order to empty all three bowls. I thought that after this meal I would fast for the rest of my stay. I broke protocol and glanced to my left at a young man who seemed to know the ritual well; I simply followed his lead and thus, in a clumsy and jerky fashion, I completed the ritual. I had to congratulate myself for not dropping any of the bowls, full or empty, and recorded the meal as another first-time experience, to be savored afterward as part of what gave texture and new tastes to the pilgrimage. I knew that over time I would love this and all the rituals that shaped worship at the Zen Center and felt a deep gratitude to all who tolerated my clumsy and imperfect attempts to worship. Their spirit was one of unconditional kindness, if not forgiveness. I sensed their compassion for a beginner.

As I said goodbye to everyone at the dinner table that evening, I felt already a sharp sting of loss. Familiarity had bred a certain security in my surroundings and I felt once more the push-pull of settling into a place, integrating its rituals and rhythms, but then almost at once loading the truck for the next station on the journey. The world here was so different from anything I had ever discovered before that I knew I would return. I packed that night in the cabin and loaded the truck with everything except for the clothes I would wear the next morning. I planned, as always, to leave very early and wanted to have everything ready for a quick departure.

After fixing breakfast, I looked down at the box of mouse poison. It was empty. Back in my bedroom I found a small box of Junior mints that I had bought. I took one of the chocolate-covered mints, broke it and placed it in the box by the stove. "A treat for you, my friend," I said to big ears under the stove. I knew he was listening. I hoped the frisky house pet enjoyed the snack and that he would entertain other guests there with the same comic gusto he showed me.

Before sunup I headed through the darkness toward Highway 101 and two nights of camping before my reservation date at the Russian Monastery of Mount Tabor in Redwood Valley. I welcomed the time out, time when I would camp in a state park close to the ocean, cook meals outside, and hike along the ocean's enchanted beaches in the cooler climate of northern California. The loneliness had worn me down and I needed to see my wife, to spend a few days hiking around Portland as a simple tourist with her. I felt that if I did not concede to this enormous feeling of loneliness that I would soon be heading home. Determined to stay the course, I was not beyond compromise and accepted fully my human limitations. I knew that I was neither offending nor compromising God nor myself. Planning this rendezvous with my best friend, I felt lighthearted and settled into the newness with a calm and grateful anticipation of what awaited me down the highway. How simple and gracious and joyful life could actually be, I thought.

I also learned in my readings during this time that, unbeknownst to me, I had entered into what Geoffrey Moorehouse describes as a long Irish tradition called "'*peregrinatio pro Dei amore*,' wandering for the love of God," linked closely, it turns out, "to the notion of exile" (*Sun Dancing*, 122). While having an itinerary, I felt this sense of a wandering soul seeking solace and some deeper sense of spiritual life, a life of wholeness and simplicity. Strange, but I drew great strength from just thinking of the long tradition of Irish monasticism and that in some small way, driving a Ford pickup through northern California toward a Russian monastery, I was part of my heritage's ancient pilgrimage.

7

Loneliness Does Not Retreat

Holy Transfiguration Monastery
Redwood Valley, California

> The imprint of my smallest motion
> remains visible in the silken silence;
> indestructibly the least excitement
> is stamped into the distance's taut curtain.
> —Rilke, *The Book of Images*

M Y RESERVATION AT THE Monastery of Mount Tabor, known also as Holy Transfiguration Russian Orthodox Monastery, did not begin for two days. I had purposely built in some time away from retreat centers, thinking I would welcome an interval from the intensity and strangeness of each place. I was glad I had such foresight. I drove north on Highway 101 to Route 128, which I took over to the ocean close to Navarro Head and Little River. There I found a state campground; part of it was located on the ocean side in open terrain while the other was nestled in the deep piney woods just across the highway. I chose the piney woods because the individual sites promised more privacy and protection from the cool wind off the water. I could easily walk to the ocean in less than half an hour.

It was Sunday afternoon when I pulled into the campsite, registered and pitched my tent in a private site surrounded by lush, tall, silent pines and redwoods. A few campers had fires blazing in a lazy smoky afternoon. I waved to them as I set up camp and felt the coolness of the air already descending from the treetops. The trees embraced and sheltered me from above.

At dusk I called Sandy from a pay phone and we arranged some dates for her to meet me in Portland ten days hence. My loneliness for her had become too great, so I chose to break with my original plans of solitude and spend three days with her in Portland. When I hung up and walked back to my campsite, I sensed that the sting of loneliness had abated; a bit jauntily, and whistling low to myself, I prepared a simple meal on my Coleman stove.

As the late afternoon bent the sunlight through the trees, first one camper, then another, as if on some cue I had missed, packed up, waved to me and drove off. The campground became quieter by the hour. As I walked the winding paved road at 5:00 p.m. and noticed deserted smoldering fires, I realized that, once again, God had placed me in a wilderness alone. My modest tent was the only one left standing in the entire park, which had assumed a silent and darkening gloom. Everyone had cleared out for home or other campsites. The silence emanating from the trees surrounded me completely. I realized I would feel better if even one other camper was in the park, but not one remained. I settled in a bit anxiously and thought about lighting my lantern, but instead I began to walk to neighboring sites to scavenge abandoned firewood. Two had several small logs, so I gratefully gathered them and walked them back to my site, and not a minute too soon.

Just as I returned with my second load of wood, a ragged, noisy, and oil-burning Ford pickup scrambled down the road with three men in the bed. They drove slowly past each site and when one of them spotted any extra wood, the men jumped down, scooped it up, scavenging in the process any rope, twine—anything of value left by campers—then hurriedly pushed on. They never even looked in my direction. Campsite birds-of-prey, I thought, cleaning up some of the detritus of the weekend campers. I felt uneasy about their noticing I was the only camper in the entire park this side of the road. As it was, I apprised myself an easy target for the deranged and the detoured and wished for just a moment that I had a weapon hidden in my pack. All my fantasies of self-protection roiled up to circle me like a black bird flying high above as I tried to ease my mind by cooking some dinner on the stove, whose flames grew brilliant against the darkening air.

Night fell quickly. I lit a fire and prepared a simple meal, followed by dessert of instant coffee laced with honey. I began reading in the deep solitude of nature by my companion, the steady flames that illuminated my book. I felt very at home in its quiet peaceful growing. The trees especially, with their 60-foot stature surrounding my miniscule tent and small fire emanating warmth from the salvaged wood in the still night air calmed me. I began to think of legacies, of how we take in both the best and worst features of our parents, become them in our own way, and then pass them along to our own children.

As I sat in the chair enjoying the heat of the fire, I realized I was not alone. My father had once more decided to pay me a visit. Apparently he still had other things to say to me or to show me. This time he brought with him my two sons, Matt and Steve, so that he could highlight my own fathering.

His remembered presence was so much stronger than his thin physical shape late in his life, when he had stopped drinking but carried with him the same alcoholic personality that had driven him for decades, minus the raging episodes. Those were gone. His wounds to all of us, most especially my mother, were irreparable; now, he wanted to show me how I had been a harmful father to my sons in ways that I was unconscious of. Harm from the father on to the sons seemed as old as humanity itself and I was to relive some of the wounds inflicted throughout my childhood and adolescence. My father, sitting by me close to the campfire, revealed how his deep depression was passed on to me, along with the shame and anger that were its constant cohorts. Yet there was also something devotional to the life of the spirit that my father also passed on to me and which, with its negative features, I had passed as a paternal package, on to my sons. Violence and the sacred—were these inevitable partners? Whenever I returned home on Saturday night from working at a supermarket packing groceries for twelve hours, my father, enraged and at times howling rather than speaking words, would accuse me of being worthless. I tried to escape him and the house as soon as I could shower and dress. The violence terrified me. Most of my family had already left the house hours ago. I had no plans to be the only victim in his neighborhood.

Then, during the week, each workday morning, my father would quietly enter my room and take from the top-drawer coins that were my tip money for carrying groceries to customers' cars. Since he was broke, my stash became his bus fare which he would rifle daily. By the end of the week, little was left. Strange, but even those mornings when I would awake and see him pilfering my money, I did not have the heart or the courage to tell him to leave it alone; I simply let him take what he needed and in the process realized that I was now paying rent for living in the house. My tip money was my rent payment, which I paid for many years in this way.

What a revelation, sitting by the fire as it spit out hot embers against the stones that encircled it, to recognize that as parents we often unconsciously repeat, modify, and exaggerate both the sins and the sanctities of our parents. We might think we are liberated from their influences as we mature. Then one morning we discover we have been repeating them in our own style, that style can often hide the bare reality of the repetition.

"Father," as one writer calls it, has "many sinister, even murderous aspects. . . . The destructive, murderous father is perhaps as fundamental as the kind, loving father" (*From the Wrong Side*, 24). I was forced then to reflect on what destructive, even murderous qualities I had passed on to my sons in conscious and unconscious ways. Startled by all of this while sitting by my peaceful glowing fire, I questioned: is this one of the central reasons that I am on this pilgrimage? To be alone long enough for my father to be able to have his say? It unnerved me to think that these divinely designed pockets of solitude, which seemed to be part of the majority of retreat centers I visited, were there for sustained reflections on the ghostly remembrances of childhood traumas. The conversation and memories seemed to lose, in this recognition, much of their sting.

As the embers in the fire began to settle into a simmering and heated glow, I realized how the shame and anger, two emotions connected to the same color as the fire, that I had felt throughout most of my childhood and adult life, were present in different intensities in my sons' behaviors. I also saw that their curiosity, their reflective and even philosophical nature as they described events and experiences to me, was a part of my disposition. Their fastidiousness in clothing and personal appearance, in keeping their cars cleaned, including frequent oil changes and new tires as well as their love of motorcycles, were all parts of a heritage they gained from me. Their generous nature, their fundamentally caring dispositions, their desire to serve others, their acute sensitivity, were also reflections of both their mother and me.

Perhaps these trees surrounding me in their dark shadowy trunks to the sky had fathered these insights and offered them to me in the quiet of the forest amid the dimming light of the fire. Like the fire turning wood into itself, I felt that the flames of my own father's presence had turned me toward his presence in my sons and me. Now, I thought, let the softer glow of memory work this insight into the warmth of forgiveness, for that is what is needed now: forgiveness of my own father and forgiveness of myself. Fatherhood as a site of forgiveness, I thought. Let my sons father me into forgiveness. God may indeed use the natural order to elicit such responses from us, that his monastery included these trees, this fire, the enveloping darkening sky.

I rose from my chair in the darkness and placed my hand on a friendly-looking pine tree on the periphery of my campsite. Its thick, spongy bark was still warm to the touch, like human skin, from the sun's heat still clinging to it in the cooling night air. I felt the energy of this old redwood pass right through my pores and enter me. I leaned my whole body against it in the isolated silence of this expansive darkness and followed its massive trunk as far as I could in the darkness up to the cluster of branches and needles that disappeared into the night sky. Fireflies flickered against the black backdrop of night.

Never before had I felt such a connection and affection for the life forms in nature. What had changed in me? Some opening, some aperture, had been unlocked and the tree was now present as a living being rather than a static silent object. I leaned up against it in the deep solitude of darkness and stillness and felt a great desire to weep and embrace its warmth. My astonishment grew when I gazed at a dark sky so lit with stars that their mass rivaled the darkness between them. At this moment I felt the same joy of liberation, of a deep sense of freedom, that I imagined the pilgrim Dante felt when he and Virgil, having suffered the brutish and violent world of inferno, finally gained the clean air of the dark dewy earth as they made their escape through an opening in the ground:

> We climbed, he first and I behind, until,
> Through a small round opening ahead of us
> I saw the lovely things the heavens hold,
> And we came out to see once more the stars.
> (*Inferno* xxxiv: 136–39)

Such a serene and supreme moment did I share with these two pilgrims at that moment. I felt something of the loving father in His creation. This was a profound moment of grace's presence in my life, coming to me now as a gift. Grace, I suddenly understood to be a gift of freedom, of a full liberation from one's self. It did not ask that I or anyone deny himself; instead, grace became a way of moving closer to who one was, but by a route that did not depend on one's own will but on the will of God. It visited me in love, liberated in its gentle but powerful force.

As I thought about prayer, I realized that this encounter with a tree in a forest was also a form of praying; through the natural order I sensed the clear and loving presence of a God whose fathering and mothering nature was both harsh and benevolent, shattering and healing, life-giving and death-dealing, cool and warm. Meeting the natural order of things in their particularity was prayer itself, even a way in which nature's creatures prayed to God. All distinctions between natural and spiritual worlds suddenly collapsed. Alone by the glowing fire in the silence and solitude of a magnificent redwood forest, I experienced the ancient, profound nature of fathering itself. Past midway in my own life's journey, I felt the call, even the invitation to death, to a descent and to a deepening of the ordinary through remembering my violent past.

I felt fathered, held, and accepted intimately by this silent tree, a giant in the forest but with a soft, fibrous texture. Fatherhood was a way of being parented by and connected to everything in the natural order. I felt at this moment a divine Fatherhood present in these reflections, a sense of being a father that connected me with a divine principle through the particular qualities of this tree that did not bend away from my advances.

I returned to my fire and sat in my campsite chair for a moment. I glanced back into the darkness where the tree stood, still and friendly and welcoming; its silence evoked images which bubbled up of their own volition.

Tree Skin

Listen then deeply into the tree's skin
below the cragged black bark and deep patient
rhythm of age rough-hewn and weathered from
ten thousand sunrises, and
deeper still into the whorls of sandy-colored
shy moist pulp
the deep place where slowly in time its rings
move out to find the light and mark its time.

If you must wound the tree, first
touch its skin with your own palm face out.
Pause for a moment with the iron axe blade or steel saw
resting quietly by your side;
try with eyes gently closed to discover where
your flesh ends and its skin begins.

Imagine the moist pulp hidden deep within
holding water from another age.
You may then sense in that instant that you are
now a branch full of leaves of what you wish
to bring down.
Your feet and toes have already begun
to bud themselves
into the loam beneath you.
(*Casting the Shadows*, 71)

Reading these words in my journal, I grasped why the Psalms had gained greater attraction during this trip. Perhaps the difference between poetry and prayer was a thin membrane. Poetry was a way of praying, and prayer was one way of poetically experiencing God in His holy presence in things of the world, but especially in the natural order, for indeed it had its own order of being. Thomas Merton, a fine poet in his own right, saw a connection between the Psalms and poetry: "The Psalms are poems, and poems have a meaning— although the poet has no obligation to make his meaning immediately clear to anyone who does not want to make an effort to discover it ("Poetry, Symbolism, Typology," 53). Making the effort is at the heart of any pilgrimage.

This entire campsite offered yet another experience through which I could learn to pray, to be intimate with a God who seemed to be, like my own father, at intervals very distant and coated with negative criticism in a world that had grown cynical about traditional beliefs. By the light of my campfire I found in Psalm 64 an ancient affirmation of God and nature:

> You uphold the mountains with your strength,
> you are girded with power.
> You still the roaring of the seas,
> (the roaring of their waves)
> and the tumult of the peoples.
> The ends of the earth stand in awe
> at the sight of your wonders.
> The lands of sunrise and sunset
> you fill with your joy.
> You care for the earth, give it water,
> you fill it with riches.
> Your river in heaven brims over
> to provide its grain.
> (*The Psalms*, 116)

I discovered great solace in my solitude at the campsite through these images of God's relation to His creation. It was a wonder, a wonder of abundance. I felt this largesse fully in the moment, in the darkening of the day, which revealed as much as it concealed. How could I have not seen before now that the joy emerging from hiking or camping or visiting nature was a joy from God over His creation that, when I entered it, I could participate in that same joy? It may also be the joy of creation for its creator as well. I was struck by the marvel of this world in a way not felt or acknowledged before. I never expected such power or such sympathy to surface from nature's presence; it stood as one of the sublimest moments of the entire pilgrimage and repeated itself on more occasions.

My fire dwindled to a fading glow; the trees all but disappeared into the deep darkness and silence of the night. The only sound, now that the birds too were nested for the night, was the distant thump of the waves washing ashore below me and the occasional crackling of a frisky twig or branch that wanted to speak from the fire. My breathing eased, and all fear of being alone evaporated in the radiance of the burning wood. I solitary, as if I were inhabiting the present moment in an ancient and timeless way. I did not know at the time how important these discoveries of the natural world and the connection of poetry to prayer were to become in my future work. They resolved themselves into major points of meditation for the remainder of the pilgrimage.

I thanked my father for his presence, and I could think of no better way to have these conversations that would lead to forgiveness of him than in the deep woods, alone. Here he was, asking me to remember his soul, his anguish, and his despair over alcohol and revealing to me what legacy I was passing on to my sons. That night in my tent I slept without stirring until I heard birds singing in the trees above me next morning.

Breaking camp early, I drove up Route 1 to Highway 20 into Willits and then back down Highway 101 to Redwood Valley and West Road. I climbed back into the mountains several miles before the entrance to the monastery appeared on my right. The road afforded a steep climb up to this Eastern rite community of a dozen or so monks who live in hermitages scattered around the wooden onion-domed church and building across from it, where all meals are taken. It is a Byzantine monastery of the Ukrainian Catholic Church.

The weather had heated up considerably; when I arrived the sun was scorching. Not a soul could be found outside in the suffocating heat. I thought for a moment: my solitude here was going to be complete if I now learned that the monastery was empty of inhabitants. I found the kitchen, where a monk greeted me and directed me without conversation to the bookstore, where I registered and was directed to drive my truck up the steep narrow road behind the church. There I found a retreat building with a large living room, a galley kitchen, and a hallway leading to a series of dorm rooms, with bathrooms at both ends.

The monk instructed me to unpack later since it was now time for lunch and if I wished to eat, I should immediately walk down to the dining room. I had learned that at monasteries little time is given to meals and little fanfare to one's arrival. Kindly but distant, the monk encouraged me to settle in as soon as possible. I walked down toward the kitchen but could not resist climbing the wooden steps to the chapel's entrance as I passed, which was surrounded by a wraparound porch. It was built entirely of wood from its roof beams to the steep stairs leading up to its main entrance. In the dryness of the climate, a fire would turn it immediately to cinders.

I was astonished when I entered this cooler dark space. In the dim light were votive candles burning below dozens of icons on the plain wooden walls. They were the only source of light in the chapel. The iconostasis, where the priest stood behind a screen to say Mass, was covered with arresting iconic images of saints and Christ in Byzantine style. Their flat, one dimensional, brightly colored beauty stunned me. The smell of incense was deep in the woodwork and in the air, for one of the three daily worship and prayer services that comprised about five hours of each day had just concluded, and the monks filed out, talking to one another animatedly like a group of fraternity brothers as they headed to the dining area for lunch. The entire interior had an old world feel to it. I could hardly believe that hidden deep in the mountains of northern California was a community that could exist just as well on the Russian steppes or in a Ukrainian village.

Below me the dining room was astir with lunch conversation between the monks, who only glanced over to regard me casually for an instant at the table where I sat alone. I had come to expect that I would be the only retreatant and the place once again did not disappoint. "No visitors or roommates for this fellow, please," God seemed to have ordered. This soul needed to be alone. The lone retreatant, I nonetheless knew that I must pay close attention to how things operated here, and to what the atmosphere was so I could adjust to it in short order.

Among themselves, the monks were a lively and robust group. When they got up to fetch their food they were all business. I studied them right back with a strong curiosity. Salt rings stained their heavy black robes tied with a black leather belt. The white rings appeared across their shoulders and in big scooped-circles under the arms;

around the top were jagged white salt lines. Above and below their belts were salt stripes, as if I were looking at a photographic negative of a zebra. Across the black caps they wore, which were similar to baseball caps but without the bills, were crowns of salt. Across the backs of some of them, where perhaps they carried sacks of things— could it be bags of salt?—appeared circles of salt, markers that sweated themselves to the surface. Tonight, I imagined, they would read and delight at looking at one another, as one of them reads Matthew's quote of Christ: "You are the salt of the earth" (5:13).

The monks appeared to be of all ages, from late twenties to early seventies. I was certain, as I sat waiting to be signaled to serve myself, that they took their lives as monks with more than just a tiny grain of salt. They wore sandals without socks and their heavy feet kicked up the dust, which was considerable, from the wooden floor. The dust hung in the air and grew more restless with their movement. After they served themselves, one of the monks nodded to me to get my food after a brief communal prayer of thanksgiving. I followed suit, bowed when they bowed, and then served myself. The food was simple but fresh and I was very hungry: soups, bread, peanut butter, some vegetables, cold lemonade, coffee, water, and tea. Things moved very quickly and I sensed that the best plan was to sit and eat, for my mouthfuls were numbered. I chuckled to myself as I asked one of the monks at the next table to pass me the salt.

As I began to eat with some haste, a young man who appeared to be about fifteen entered and eyed me as if he knew me. He sat at the table next to mine after serving himself and watched me closely throughout the meal. I nodded to him and he returned a greeting. We had established a community right here among the monks who were all busy conversing spiritedly with one another. After the meal each retired to his own hermitage or continued work until supper at 4:30, followed by Vespers and Compline at six. They would rise for 5:30 Matins followed by Divine Liturgy, then a quick breakfast and work; on Sunday, the monks' day began at 3 a.m. for Vigils, followed by Matins. A certain austerity permeated the place and gave it a quiet and serene atmosphere, high on this hill absent any neighbors. Complete isolation enveloped this sacred temenos space and gave its foreign architecture and habits of worship a peculiar poignancy.

I was in another world: exotic, hot, unfamiliar, yet as friendly as it was reserved.

I ate quickly and then found a well-worn path deepened by hundreds of retreatants over the years that served as a shortcut through the thick, cool woods to the backside of the retreat house. I entered the living area with some of my things from the truck and surveyed the living room more closely. It was old, a bit threadbare, with old tattered couches and broken chairs. The lamps were flimsy; two of them were missing bulbs. The carpet, pathetic and worn thin, had lost all its color and wilted in wrinkles in the hot still air of the afternoon sun. The sunlight showed a haze of dust that hovered in the dingy space, giving the entire scene a feeling of exhaustion. I felt the same dreariness tug on me. I put my things down and slumped with a groan into one of the chairs. Dust, now excited from slumber, rose up when I reclined and then turned its arch to settle on me, a perfect coating to the despondency engulfing me. The heat was now ferocious at two in the afternoon. The only place that enjoyed air-conditioning, I was to discover, was the bookstore in the cellar of the church. I would soon make it a regular station on my walks on the grounds and up the mountain trails. But for the moment I was stifled in dust and heat and arrested by my disappointment. *Return me to the clear, clean atmosphere of my campsite,* I pleaded with God.

Sitting in the gloom of harsh light filtering through the windows and the dust that permeated the air, I realized how different was my image of this place when I had read of it. I had idealized its exotic description, which now fell dismally below my expectations. The dust, the drab furniture, and the emptiness all huddled together for a moment, and then attacked me from three sides. I sat back in the chair and began to weep, feeling a deep loneliness and isolation descend and begin with great success to smother me. What a shabby wreck of a place, I thought. This was a poor, threadbare hermitage. Was this really the best they could do? No wonder no one else was staying here. I remembered passing some motels just off 101 in Redwood Valley and considered seriously just replacing the few items back in the truck and canceling out of this dismal place. No, I was not looking for a Best Western, I thought, as I sat for a long time in the dusty silence and sweated in the sun as it moved across the floor and settled on my legs like a monastery pet. The silence, the solitude and the stillness were oppressive. A powerful nostalgia for home began to rise up out of the dust to coax me out of here.

I took out my wallet and gazed at pictures of my two sons who lived in San Antonio. I missed them intensely at this moment and began to calculate how long it would take me to drive from this shabby solitary space to San Antonio if I left within the next fifteen minutes. Such a thought gave me hope and hope is what I needed right now. Why, I wondered, would God place me here? It comprised such a wilderness of poverty conducive to nothing but depression. I knew that I could stay but instead began calculating what to do to escape its oppressive confines. Its emptiness and austere décor, though, was exactly what I needed, but I didn't yet realize it. Some force in me was fighting to leave; it was beneath me to stay here, it said. This was no way to spend your first sabbatical. Shove off, drive along the coast, stay in comfortable motels and treat yourself. On its argument went as I continued to compare it to the wonderful retreat centers I had already occupied.

Before I knew what is happening, I found myself out by the truck parked under the shade of a large tree in the back, unloading my suitcase and asking myself, *Why, why would I want to stay here?* I had no answer, but my bodily response was to move into my tiny room at the far end of the hall (past the other twelve empty rooms and open doors on one side of the hall), unpack and settle in, faced by my restless quest to leave. Choosing to stay or leave was taken from me. I yielded.

The room's small size and intimacy held a comforting appeal because it signaled something positive entering the dusty depression that had for a time taken me hostage. Could holiness be, in one of its many forms, a hostage-taker? I wondered. In it was a single bed, a tiny table and chair, a little reading chair, a lamp, and a blessed plastic fan that actually worked. Feeling depressed and isolated, I walked back to the truck to fetch a small clock radio I packed so I could hear another voice, even some music. Cheating was permissible tonight as I made the concession to music as a way to deflect simply abandoning the place.

I plugged the radio in, sat on my bed, and listened to music for a while. Even the voice of the weatherman helped to slow me down. The humor here was not lost on me: at any time on this voyage, just when I thought I was gaining something important, I was thrown back on my own weak, vulnerable, and whining nature because the world was not cooperating with my image of how it should behave. Did I blame God for a vicious sense of humor or choose to thank Him for his blatant and austere honesty? Was God friend or foe at this moment? I could not decide. But hope had reentered my life, and with hope I could survive. The thought of seeing my wife the following week also fortified me and replenished my meager reservoir of hope. I resolved to stay at least through the next day. When I broke the stay into digestible fragments this way, I felt my spirits lift, so I rose and set up house. No noisy retreatant neighbors here, I was happy to confess. Only the silence of the still air was my companion. What, I tried to imagine, was it to live without hope? It was to be in hell.

I thanked God for sending me sufficient grace, in the form of hope, to persevere. My response to this grace was the ability to say *yes* to the wilderness surroundings in which I had been cast. The wilderness adjoining the hermitage had entered deeply into the quality of my retreat. It called me back to the luxurious fullness of the forest and my cozy tent, the fire glowing, trees gathering closer for protection. By contrast, this hot and dusty room was hard to bear as another form of wilderness, a desert of sorts, that sapped all my resolves. It had also put me smack in the face of my own wilderness-driven soul, so the sacred circuit was complete.

I gazed out the back window of my room to the darkening forest and felt an immediate love for its cooling silence. I could see a footpath meandering along its slope and resolved tomorrow to head up the mountain, to hike to the top or as far as the path would allow. Planning pleased me immensely and gave tomorrow a bit of color. After dinner I settled into my room, leaving my door opened, and played the radio softly. A jazz station's music sent me into a deep sleep.

My alarm shuddered at 4:45. I showered, dressed, took my flashlight, and headed for the driveway, a steep and narrow road, down to the chapel. Through the calm and serene black air of morning I could hear the monks already singing. The service had begun and I was already late. I loved the dark, cool stillness around me, broken only by my beam of white light. When I entered the church, the monks were singing in the most lovely *a cappella* voices I had ever heard, so different and even more otherworldly than the Gregorian chants I had grown with in parish churches and other monastic settings.

They were singing the Psalms, but the quality of their voices belied the rough-and-tumble salty images I had received the previous day. The lighting was a dim yellow and suffused the room where a dozen or so people from the surrounding area had driven up to participate at Mass. Benches along the wall accommodated those who arrived to worship. I had a choice either to sit up straight, on an angle so I could face forward, or lean back against the wall and look across the room at other participants.

Father Abbot Boniface, founder of the monastery in 1972, officiated. A short, thick man with a magnificent white beard that cascaded down and gushed out across his upper chest, he carried the authority of a patriarch. His position was distinctive in that he was elected by a council of bishops to oversee this monastery and the surrounding territory of worshippers. He received the monastic habit in 1954 in Belgium and years later came to the United States to build a contemplative monastic center. As the patriarch of Mount Tabor, he commanded and received loving respect from his hermits. I followed his movements and tried to join the community in prayer by shifting and sifting through three prayer and hymnbooks, but it proved too much. I finally set them all down and simply listened to the singing, which was ethereal, silky, and beautiful. Incense began to fill the space of the chapel, which had the atmosphere of a small but ornate redwood lodge.

During the liturgy, at the kiss of peace, we were all invited into the sanctuary where each of us responded to a prayer said by each monk; then we formed a line to embrace each monk by turn. They stood to receive the dozen or so of us; some of them shifted their feet awkwardly in this sudden social arrangement. The more relaxed connection seemed to be too much for some of them, but they stood their ground gracefully and received each of us. Some of them looked away, avoiding any eye contact. Others were very stiff and held us at a distance, just touching our shoulders in a kind but awkward embrace. Still others were more extroverted and enfolded each of us with gusto and a warm smile. The spirit in the room was very joyful and friendly.

But many wore their years of solitude on their faces, preferring perhaps to be alone in work or prayer or with their brothers and so shied away from so much worldly contact. I grew fond of all of them at this meeting and felt their warm humanity outshine their shyness. Standing there in line, with bare feet in sandals and salty black robes, they appeared infused with a simple sanctity that was as mysterious and attractive as the lighting and the incense.

After Mass, at breakfast, I viewed these men quite differently. More of their personalities emerged at Mass to create a bond between all of us, monks and worshippers alike. This feeling of community seemed to be so central to God's presence and dissolved all differences between us. These men were solid, frail, flawed, and devoted to a life of hardship and austere obedience; yet a real joy suffused the room. They laughed and joked with one another. A couple of them might be called class clowns. They would say repeatedly, "I *swear*," to underline a point made. "Yesterday I cut enough wood to last me two weeks, I *swear*." Or "I can't remember it being so hot and dry, I *swear*."

I liked being around them. They exuded a pure gentleness of spirit, were full of vitality, yet were not pushy or overbearing. In time I would speak to several of them individually and found them to be wonderfully kind men. In their presence I began to realize something: give life, Providence, the Holy Spirit a chance to unfold, to be heard, to help you. Don't be too rigorous, too deadly stiff about what's coming up. Keep a sense of humor about you, and enjoy the mere presence of life itself, for in life is the spirit of grace that pervades all things. In the initial dismal dust and depression that grew from it, I found a flowering of warmth and generosity that I would have missed had I bolted when I felt an initial repellence toward the surroundings. Grace does not always present itself in shining foil. In late evening I sat out on the porch and listened to the birds and wrote in my journal or simply enjoyed gazing at the natural world to feel deeply the joy it brought me.

On the second evening, the young man I saw at meals, but who disappeared immediately thereafter, walked up the steep road to my building, accompanied by a large and energetic German shepherd who pushed his muzzle into my hand as I sat on the chair. The young man told me his name was Ernesto and that he lived in his own little cabin down below the dining room.

One of his several duties at the monastery was to walk the dog, Gustav, every night after dinner. The brother who had become Ernesto's mentor and guardian had trained the dog using commands in German, so Ernesto had to learn a handful of German phrases for Gustav to respond without confusion. The young man stood in front of me in the fading light of evening while Gustav wandered close by, sniffing out two groundhog holes. He told me that he was at the monastery in a last attempt at rehabilitation. He had been in trouble for years and the juvenile justice system, frustrated with his violations, was ready to lock him up. The monastery agreed to take him into their spiritual setting and impose an order of strict discipline on him. Every morning a car pulled up to take him to a special class for at-risk youth in the nearby town. He seemed to be doing well in this guarded way of attending classes and strict regimen at the monastery.

Ernesto's conversation turned after a few minutes to a more personal level. I sensed that he did not have many people to talk to here and he welcomed the ears of a sole retreatant. I was a stranger— safe, temporary and appeared interested. He told me that for three years he had operated a drug-selling ring with eleven people working under him. At one point he had made mountains of cash. By the age of fifteen he had already fathered two sons by two different young women; he missed seeing both of his children.

He then admitted that the purpose for his being at this isolated hermitage was part of a larger plan to extricate himself from a gang that had threatened his life if he tried to leave its membership. To be initiated into this gang, he had had to accompany two other gang members when they ambushed and executed a rival gang member.

Then Ernesto's voice grew very quiet. The fading evening light made him almost invisible now as he stood not three feet in front of me. "You know," he observed, "there is very little blood when the bullet enters the back of the neck. I had to witness a young boy my age forced to kneel down and put his head forward, exposing his neck. The gang member shot him at the base of the skull. What I was surprised about was that almost no blood came out of the wound. It hardly bled at all." He spoke of this horrid initiation in a soft steady voice, as if he were reliving the moment. It was the blood's absence that fascinated him as he witnessed this gruesome violence. I asked him, imagining what he saw, what he thought of having to witness it.

"Well, the reason they wanted me to witness it is that they told me that is what would happen to me if I ever tried to get out of the gang. So right now I have to be guarded wherever I go. At the school I attend, we have to be searched for weapons before we are allowed in. I don't know who might try to kill me on any school day?"

I could no longer see Ernesto because of the darkness. His voice had grown progressively disembodied. I felt fear creep over me as I listened to him. He seemed to have little emotional involvement in what he had witnessed. I asked him what he thought of the boy who was killed and of the gang member who killed him. His response was terrifying in its matter-of-fact tone: "When you mess with a gang, going either in or out, certain bad things are going to happen. I just don't want to be killed because one day I want to care for my sons." Realizing how dark it had become, he turned in the cooling air and called to Gustav. He said goodnight as the two of them made their way down the road in complete darkness; both of them knew so well their way around here that they did not need a flashlight. I told Ernesto as he left that he was welcome to come by and visit any time. He thanked me and said he would be in school until four the next day, but that he would bring Gustav for a walk up this way tomorrow evening.

The next morning I talked at length with the monk who sponsored Ernesto. He filled in more of Ernesto's history. "Yes, Ernesto walks around fearing that someone will try to kill him. He has had little discipline in his life so we are trying to salvage him so he can begin a new life outside of violence and drugs." After this conversation, I began to notice Ernesto at early Mass, always sitting in the back, looking around, very distracted and uninterested in the liturgy. He was ordered to show up for Mass each morning. On the fourth morning he was not present and the monk I had spoken to about him left his place in worship and hurried out the back door. Within minutes he returned, followed in a matter of seconds by a tired, yawning, and disheveled Ernesto, who had just been awakened. I greatly admired what the order and Ernesto's guardian were doing to save one young man from an early death or a life of crime. I befriended Ernesto and we spoke every day for the remainder of my stay. He was a good soul, very smart, and knew precisely what he must do to begin a new life; he understood the value of prayer and of a disciplined life. I grew fond of him and we became friends for a short time. When I eventually packed to leave, he came to say goodbye and promised to write me. I never heard from him again after I nosed the truck down the driveway and headed north to Oregon.

After the first night I put my radio away. In only a couple of days I had grown to love this austere place; in fact, I saw more clearly the beneficial grace of austerity itself as a way of living. I anticipated with joy each day simply walking down in the darkness of the early morning and listening to the monks sing the liturgy in the mystical dim yellow light of the rustic church. Each morning I felt I was entering an altered reality when I pulled on the creaky wooden chapel door and stepped into a musical world of deep worship. A great sanctity and joy pervaded the lives of the monks; it flowed into the liturgy in an atmosphere that was mystical, unworldly yet very much in the world. I was drawn to the mystics and returned to reading the fourteenth-century German writer, Meister Eckhart. His sermons evoked sustained meditations in me. The spirit of a place has this uncanny power to create in one a certain disposition; I understood more deeply how the many paths to God are infinite, full of varied atmospheres and diverse conditions. Eckhart writes: "But the person who is not accustomed to inward things does not know what God is. Like a man who has wine in his cellar, but has not drunk it or tasted it, such a person does not know that it is good" (*Breakthrough*, 131). I knew from his words that I needed to develop more openness to inwardness if I wanted to see more fully the diverse range of God's workings.

The monks' singing each morning opened something up in me, a force so strong that I felt compelled to weep for the whole world's suffering, not just my own. My response was involuntary, uncontrollable, and intense. I wept for the sufferings of my immediate family, my sons and wife; I wept for the suffering of my parents, brothers, and sister; I wept for the suffering that suffocated individuals all over the world, those suffering from addiction, disease, and loneliness, for those with too much and those with not enough. I began to sit well to the back of the benches because I was made very self-conscious by this rush of emotion that descended on me each morning, and only during this early chanting. It was a powerful force "that through the green fuse drives the flower/Drives my green age; that blasts the roots of trees/Is my destroyer" (*Norton Anthology of Poetry*, 1176), in the lush poetic language of Dylan Thomas's poem. I touched the green fuse and it was hot to the hand. It was the heat of the burning bush that does not consume, but it does transform the ingot into something more valuable.

I did not seek an answer to this emotional effusiveness, content instead to let it pass through me. But when reading Meister Eckhart in the afternoon, I loitered next to his insight in Sermon 9: "It is not because of God's righteousness or strength that he asks a lot of human beings. It is because of his great joy in giving when he wants a soul to be enlarged. God enables the soul to receive much so that God himself has the opportunity to give much" (140).

This enlargement of soul was a blessing; Matthew Fox's commentary on Sermon 9 added that Eckhart's creation theology is a blessing theology. "All of life is a gift, a blessing from the Creator." For God, deliverance and blessing were one: "Blessing is the basic power of life itself" (*Breakthrough*, 147). Such a large idea to grasp, but my own sense was that part of my feelings of dissolution into the suffering of the world and weeping during the liturgy might just be a response to this enlargement. How quickly had this initially dreary place taken on such magnificent splendor!

I asked myself how anyone prepared him/herself to receive this gift, to be ready for it, to be open to receive it and even before that, to first recognize it as a gift. Should one accept everything as a gift, with no discrimination? That seemed naïve. And yet, was that brand of naiveté needed to be open to whatever form God's gifts might wrap themselves in?

In the next, Sermon 10, Eckhart writes of the soul's powers, which he believes are threefold: "The first power always seeks what is sweetest. The second power always seeks what is highest. The third power always seeks what is best" (153). His faith was that the nature of the soul was so noble that it could "rest nowhere but in the source from which trickles forth whatever goodness accomplishes" (153). God's consolation was always sweet, he concluded.

A basic goodness permeated the soul's nature, but how easy it was for this impulse to the sweetest, the highest, and the best to be suffocated or muted. I took to heart Eckhart's insights into the soul's seeking as I walked after Mass every morning up the mountain trail that expanded out to magnificent vistas and a deep delicious moist silence. The trees that thickly covered the valley and mountains gave the impression of a lush shaded green carpet over the earth. Along the path at strategic points the monks had placed benches for anyone to sit and enjoy the deep green landscape that stretched over several mountain ranges before disappearing into a mist in the sunlight. I haunted these woods alone and with great joy, feeling each time blessed to be so close to the force passing through the green fuse, one that infused me with the joys of the natural order simply as they were.

As I sat in the morning's cool stillness, broken only by the melodious birds that filled the trees above me, I smelled the damp earth and decaying leaves lying everywhere. My solitude was suddenly broken by sounds behind me, the racket of someone or something moving very quickly along the path. I turned and even prepared to defend myself when I saw down from the top of the mountain a monk running. He glided past me with a slight nod and continued, almost as if he were continually falling forward on a deep descent toward the monastery. A priest running a-monk, I thought, in startled recognition. I knew this priest even in his shorts and tee shirt as the one who managed the bookstore. Later, he would tell me that he runs to the top of the mountain and back every morning. His devotion to running is also his way of praying. He meditated on his run and entered through it to a serene space, which he felt was as much a part of his spiritual life as any other activity of his day. Since he and I had fallen into the same exercise schedule, I saw him every morning at about the same time; when he passed me his face indeed had a trance-like quality suffusing it.

When I returned to the retreat house, there was a young monk named Robert cleaning the hallway and washing down two of the vacant rooms. He paused when I entered and wanted to talk. I asked him about his vocation and how he chose this form of monastic life. He too had made a retreat in the eastern United States and one of the retreat masters was from this Byzantine order. He liked what he saw and became a novice a few years later. We talked of the kinds of people who made retreats. He laughed and related how a group of parishioners from a neighboring parish recently rented ten of the rooms for a weekend. When they arrived together on Friday evening they immediately called out for Dominos pizzas to be delivered, cranked up a stereo system they had brought with them, and in no time had transformed the silence of the retreat house into a mountain Club Med.

The monks were unsettled by the reckless attitude of these "retreatants" who really wanted to party at a secluded spot and so chose the monastery as the best site for their card-playing, pizza-munching festival. After we laughed about them, he grew very sober: "What are we to do? We need the income from this retreat house and don't want to turn people away, but if they are going to ruin the solitude the hermits came here for, then we are destroying ourselves in trying to survive." I appreciated him greatly for his candor and for the few moments of companionship. Then, realizing that perhaps he had been too social and talkative, he put his rubber gloves back on and continued cleaning the rooms in silence as I straightened up the living room and washed down the kitchen area.

How important it was, I thought, to choose carefully the right setting, to select surroundings both exterior and interior that would nourish my desire to develop a deeper prayer life within a period of sustained solitude. I recalled Thich Nhat Hanh's advice on practicing meditation gently, steadily, and everyday throughout one's life. He reminded me not to miss any opportunity to see deeply into the true nature of my everyday existence, including my problems, frustrations, fears, and points of angry upset. To be in communion with life and with the sacred presence of God in His silence was crucial; it was accomplished in large measure through the breath. "As your breath becomes peaceful and gentle, so will you, for it will unify body and mind" (*Peace*, 12). In my journal I wrote at the top of a page:

> Everything hangs brutally limp facing
> The sun—
> No energy—only gravity.
> A leaf turns pale grey. Nothing
> Moves in the limpid garden.
> Seeds underground are called to full alert.

I liked the spare quality of these words and wondered if this sacred and silent place had subtly shifted me toward what I call an austere abundance.

My days here had discovered a rhythm of deepening solitude; I practiced silence as I hiked the mountains surrounding this enclosure, content often to just sit on a bench made for hikers in the mountains and look out over the panorama of spruce and fir trees that thickened the land. I was beginning to feel comfortable with my inner solace as well. This feeling brought with it a pungent clarity of the austere beauty of a monk's daily life. Simply watching and listening to the wind move the trees in a delightful rhythm as enough of a gift.

As my departure drew near, I did not want to leave. Ernesto came to visit me for the last time and asked if we could continue our friendship. He had taught me so much of gang life—more than I needed—but I knew that he had a strong desire to talk to someone outside the monastery. He asked if I would be returning anytime soon and I told him no, but if I passed this way driving home I would stop in to visit. He smiled and shook my hand as Gustavo's eighty-five pounds jumped up on me to say goodbye.

That night after dinner I packed the truck and thanked a few of the monks who showed me warm hospitality. The next morning before daybreak I cleaned my room, straightened the bed coverings under my sleeping bag, and gathered my few remaining belongings into the truck. For a moment I stood outside in the dark stillness and said a prayer of thanks to God for transforming me through the tattered and dusty retreat house so that I learned to love what I had first despised—so that I found a spirit of abundance when initially I could see only a tawdry scarcity.

As I drove slowly down the steep driveway, I paused by the wooden church with its onion domes just visible against the starlight. A glow of yellow light leaked through the windows to illuminate the wooden porch. The liturgy had begun, and the monks were singing in exquisite harmony. I turned off the engine and sat there in the darkness. Animals moved in the silence of the woods. Light from inside filtered through the windows on my side. I could see the monks in their vestments singing as they did every morning of the week, each week of the year, every year of their lives.

Sadness wrapped around me as I sat under the stars and joined the liturgy from a distance. I wept when I first entered what appeared to be a scruffy and uninviting center; now I sat in my truck at five in the morning and wept for its loss. How strange was the way of the world. What repulsed me when I arrived had turned into a gift I must now relinquish. I had learned much from these quiet, then boisterous, sometimes eccentric, and wild men of the hermitage, who spent much of their lives alone, in their huts, praying. I would miss them as I headed to Highway 101 and pointed the truck toward Lafayette, Oregon, south of Portland. There I would stay for a week at Our Lady of Guadalupe, a Trappist Abbey. I knew its world would be very different from the onion-domed world of the Eastern monastics I had grown so attached to. Such a salty and sacred bunch! I anticipated the excitement of experiencing many new and unknown events on this trip. What I had not calculated was the grief over leaving so many of both that had shifted my own life—I *swear*. Grieving over the gifts of Mt. Tabor I must now relinquish, I turned the ignition key and drove down the driveway and north onto the deserted highway. These salty monks had seasoned my pilgrimage with the gift of grace and a sense of humor that had developed from a life of serving God.

8

Nature's Mystical Muse

Our Lady of Guadalupe, Lafayette, Oregon

Content you with the *quia*, sons of Eve: / For had you power to see
the whole truth plain / No need had been for Mary to conceive.
—Dante, *Purgatorio* 3, 37–39

WO DAYS' TRAVEL culminated at the driveway to the monastery. My route had taken me on Highway 101 along the coast of some of the most magnificent geography in America. This journey into the northwest was as much a part of the monastic pilgrimage as the places themselves. I found a campsite the first night, a private one run by two older women from New Jersey who settled here, bought the place, and now spend their lives maintaining it. I was given a key to the shower and bathroom and shown what site was mine, across the grass under two large pine trees at the foot of a massive hill that marked the back boundary of their property.

A few other campers pulled in as evening settled and heavy grey clouds began to form in the dusky sky. About midnight, rain clicking against the nylon tent woke me up. I checked it for leaks; finding none with my flashlight, I fell back to sleep. Dreams this night were disturbing as my father appeared fixing me a bottle of milk when I was about three years old. It was more a dream memory than a fantasy. I remembered taking the bottle from his hands, a beer bottle, filled with warm milk and with a rubber nipple on it. I had forgotten that for most of my early years, I drank milk from a beer bottle and while sucking on the nipple would gaze in through the dark brown glass to the white fluid within. I saw myself lying on the living room floor of our three-room Cleveland apartment, sun streaming in from the windows facing the gravel and cinder parking lot; just beyond stood a row of houses in an industrial district and the New York Central railway tracks. I also dreamed that my father was often lying on the same floor with a few empty beer bottles around him. This confluence of the two of us occupying the same floor sleeping after drinking from the same brand of beer bottles unsettled me and I woke with the vivid and disturbing memory. Yet I could not repress the humor of the situation as well.

In the morning everything was saturated. A short lull in the downpour allowed me to scoot to the showers. I cleaned up and then packed everything, including one soggy tent, and headed out. The day cleared at midmorning and the next night, finding no campsites, I stayed in a motel in Lincoln City, then cut across Highway 18 into Lafayette and found the monastery midmorning just off 99W, about one hour east of the Pacific Ocean.

Construction workers were already at their task of building new units for retreatants, so the racket was of a full-throated construction site, which the volunteers who took my reservation had warned me about. I decided to come anyway. The housing arrangement was ingenious.

Several small condo-looking buildings with a downstairs and an upstairs accommodated two retreatants on each of two floors, with a shared bathroom on the lower floor. I instantly liked these "retreat pods," and hauled my belongings from the parking lot into my assigned bedroom. Beautifully designed wooden walkways and stairs connected all of them in a boardwalk grid. I was assigned a spacious room upstairs with a closet, a reading lamp, a single bed, a comfortable rocking chair, a desk, and modern carpet and drapes. The feel was more that of a modest remodeled motel than a monastery. Obviously the retreat section was enjoying an expensive upgrade. From the gritty surroundings of mountainous Mount Tabor to the more glittery Trappist retreat center was a quantum leap. I found myself, not surprisingly, missing the dusty space of my former austere and hot dwelling and thanked God for the contrast.

After settling, I explored the grounds and visited the warm and inviting chapel with its wooden beam ceiling. Some forty monks made up this community, which relocated here from New Mexico in 1955 "seeking greater seclusion." The order hired a nationally-famous architect to help them design the buildings. The main conference building sat low and showed markings of a Chinese influence as well as bits of the sleek design of Frank Lloyd Wright. The entire monastery was recessed more than a quarter of a mile from the highway and much of its front property was farmed. In all, it encompassed just under a thousand acres, buttressed by vineyards along the sides, and promised a wonderful solitude and seclusion— qualities that, as I continued my pilgrimage, had become ever less negotiable.

I had learned to love the silence and solitude of these centers but it was proving more difficult here (and across the country) to preserve an atmosphere of tranquility from encroaching developers— the natural predators of solitude and monastic life. Not here more than thirty minutes, I was approached by a friendly and gregarious monk dressed in the traditional Cistercian white robe with a black covering and spanking new white sneakers bound with Velcro strips. He was smart and stylish and I confessed as much to him. Father Jerome was eighty and preparing to celebrate his fiftieth year in the order, a golden jubilee; he was very excited. We gravitated to the subject of body breakdown and used parts. He told me that he had a recent surgery that had inserted a urinary tract prosthesis which was now causing him great discomfort. After listening with some squeamish writhing to a very vivid description of his prosthetic urinary plumbing, I shared with him my own surgery to install a prosthetic left hip two years earlier in San Antonio.

Father was eighty to my fifty some years and as we talked our bodies checked one another out. My titanium hip clicked once to greet the gurgling rubber bag below his cassock. Two warriors felled on different fields of battle, we compared wounds and breakdowns. Now I know why, when he rose from his chair during Mass that he slid ever so slowly from it as I in turn torqued my prosthetic hip smoothly toward the altar for communion. Dear Lord, I prayed, keep us both intact at least through Matins. I liked Father Jerome and visited with him frequently, always sure to admire his stylish

Velcro-snug sneakers. He encouraged me to watch when I hiked back to the mountain section of the grounds; on a clear day I would be able to scan the frosty head of Mt. Hood in the distance.

The foyer to the monastery, where retreatants registered, was packed with books, medals, and icons for sale. I was immediately attracted to the atmosphere of the entire monastery and discovered in its people a welcoming regard for all of us. At dinner that night I met the other retreatants. A man named Joe informed me his father had studied with Swiss psychiatrist C.G. Jung in Zurich so I immediately took great interest in him. My pod mate was Charlie, a medical doctor. A man named Mac and his daughter, Christina, about twenty-three years old, drove down from Vancouver to stay for a week. They resided in the pod adjacent to mine.

I realized at this first meal in the dining room that there was too much chattering for my tastes, but I was uncertain if I should confess it to the others. On the wall hung a "Silence" sign that someone had turned to face the wall. I casually asked the group about it and one of them rushed to the retreatants' defense: "If we don't socialize at meals how else will we get to know one another? We took a vote this morning and the majority agreed that we should be able to talk." I thought that perhaps I had entered a smaller version of Club Med. Relatives of the pizza-popping crew from Mount Tabor had apparently caught up with me! I enjoyed taking meals in silence but knew that I could not fight the group's consensus, so I vowed to devote minimal time to meals. Conversation about who I was and what I did was actually painful; it pulled me out of a place of quiet solitude that I did not know I had entered so deeply until confronted with this social demand to expose my history to the chatty group.

Then I laughed to myself. From what I had observed in the places I retreated up until now, there existed in each locale a rhythmic balance between solitude and community. Each group of monks or lay people worked it out for themselves as to how much of each best fulfilled the mission of the place and the needs of the group. I decided not to be so hard on these folks. Some were called here to solitude and others to a sense of community. I needed to back off and enter into the communal part without rancor or disrespect. Who knows the reasons for which God had called each of us to choose just this abbey at this time so that just this particular group of people suddenly appeared together at just this table? Perhaps God had a place and role for me in the midst of this community of chattering good-natured souls. Best enjoy them rather than judge them. The next morning I noticed that the "Silence" sign had been turned back to stare at us in mild rebuke during our quiet meal. No one touched it from that time forward. One of God's messengers had spoken.

After Vespers that night, where the prayers and singing refreshed me, I walked out with my journal to the large pond and nestled close to the living pods and parked on one of the benches to listen to the frogs along the bank and to the birds circling in the trees. The first thought to cross my mind was of my father, dead now just two years. I had been avoiding mourning his loss but continued receiving visits from him. The words that came to me in the solitude of the pond were: "You are your father, with all his rage and shame and with his deeply spiritual loving nature when he was sober." He had an enduring constitution, going to work each morning on the bus after Mass at Holy Cross Church. Suffering his addiction to alcohol to camouflage his own pain, he took to his grave. I thought that perhaps now I could truly grieve his loss. Part of his wrestling with alcohol within the landscape of his spiritual life had a strong influence on my even making this pilgrimage. Intelligent, a product of Jesuit training at John Carroll University in Cleveland Heights, Ohio, he majored in philosophy, played on the tennis team, and revealed a promising future.

His alcoholism, however, stopped him in his tracks and he never recovered or even admitted he had a problem, much less an illness. I felt now, in remembering him, how much pain he was in everyday but kept it cocooned in himself until he drank; then the rage of pain would pour from him, with us as his victims as he sought relief through his affliction. His remorse after a drinking bout was as anguishing as his violence was unsettling. This entire retreat pilgrimage seemed to take on as one of its layers confronting and conversing with the wounds inflicted on me and other family members as well as the deep wound of his own addiction that haunted him to his death.

I wrote freely in my journal without thought and let surface what sought expression. The anger and resentment and fear and desire for approval all of us felt toward our father carried into all pockets of our lives. Every member of our family was deeply traumatized by his weekend rants; now that he was dead, it was time to speak of it with one another. I realized that so much of the anger we each harbored was actually directed at ourselves, my brothers and sister and mother, and its toxic power to rupture our lives out of a peace that we intuited and desired but only rarely achieved. Had God led me on this journey in order to present to me, alone and away from those I loved, an opportunity to realize the lasting influence of my father's addiction and his spiritual desires in my own life? This growing suspicion continued until I finally assented to it.

I had spent my life studying psychology and literature in order to learn something of the deep pathology of which the human spirit is capable and how it often existed in an uneasy concert with the most lyric and even mystical impulses in one's search for God. But perhaps these studies had also kept me from thinking of him and his shaping of my own life until now. He was very much alive in me as I was very much alive in my own sons in ways that time continues to affirm.

Darkness began to fall on the pond. The slow and gradual descent of it quieted the birds; the fish kicked their tails to the surface less often. I realized that I had been lost in thought and in writing for some time. I walked slowly back to my cottage feeling that I had just been given some deep insight into my own destiny being intertwined with my father's, since he had appeared to me once more while I meditated by the pond. I thanked God for allowing me to enter the wilderness of my own past, with Him as my guide. Memory can be a frightening and revelatory place to be abducted into. It can take on the landscape of the underworld itself and must be entered with a guide who can retrieve one if necessary.

Christ's words at the Last Supper with his apostles, as he broke the bread before his suffering was to begin and instructed them as he distributed it, were: "Do this in memory of me." At the end of his public ministry he called on them to remember, for he knew that if they kept his image and his words foremost in their reflections, they would be given the grace to suffer their own hardships in his service. In his image and actions was the source of grace and courage. These images included the painful suffering and brutality of beatings as well as the unimaginable horror of being crucified. So these memories of my father's pain and disease were as necessary to remember as were the images of the suffering Christ for his apostles. These wounded memories were themselves a form of crucifixion; if I hid from them or diluted them in myself, I would not be true to the power or the purpose of this pilgrimage. They were part of my quest.

I dressed for Mass the next morning and noticed that my belt cinched one notch tighter. I studied myself closely in the mirror and discerned that the hiking I had been doing for over a month, the simple meals, often vegetarian, the lack of deserts, sweets, wine and beer at meals, had all contributed to a thinner pilgrim. Now here was an ad campaign that could fill retreat centers across the country! "Stay with us for a week and return home a thinner, holier thou." Every monastery could double its occupancy with a campaign that carried such a promise. "Faith is thin—pray within" could be a logo over the door of each retreat center. "Retreat and reduce." I envisioned a cottage industry growing out of such a waist-shrinking campaign.

I was attracted more intensely to the mystical tradition in Christian spirituality and continued to meditate on Meister Eckhart's *Sermons*, especially his insights into God's suffering and joy. "God suffers with man," he writes, but God also "is fully verdant and flowering in all the joy and all the honor that he is in himself" (*Breakthrough*, 156–57). They were both conditions I resolved to remain open to.

I also began to contemplate more fully the connection of poetry to prayer and wondered if there was really such a great divide between them. In the library I discovered *The Literary Essays of Thomas Merton* and in it a chapter entitled "Poetry and Contemplation: A Reappraisal," with this passage: "The contemplative is one who seeks to know the meaning of life not only with his head but with his whole being by living it in depth and purity and thus uniting himself to the very source of life" (340). Contemplation as an attitude was all-consuming, permeating everything one thought, remembered, and did, within and without the monastic life.

Merton's essay stretched my understanding of what the poets have to do with a mystical way of seeing the world in its particulars. Merton believed that contemplation "is related to art, to worship, to charity. All these reach out by intuition and self-dedication into realms that transcend the material conduct of everyday life. Or rather in the midst of ordinary life itself they seek and find a new and transcendent meaning" (341). Poetry as a means for contemplation to seek the transcendent aspect implicit in ordinary life made sense; it led me further into recognizing that poetry was at its origin actually a contemplative experience, in either the making or the reading of it. Both poetry and prayer served as corridors into this more mystical presence.

He developed then the experience of grace as the principle of active contemplation, but not as an end in itself. Rather, "it prepares us for a more passive or mystical contemplation. Christian contemplation is simply the experience of God that is given to a soul *purified by humility* and *faith*" (343). Poetic inspiration was one of the central forms by which the Christian's "vision of the world ought, by its very nature, to have in it." How far from Merton's insights had the study of poetry been sundered. He called for more writers and poets to live more as contemplatives rather "than as citizens of a materialistic world," to raise to fuller consciousness "the essential dignity of aesthetic experience" (343). My thoughts on this pilgrimage toward my own teaching were beginning to shift; I thought of how poetry could be taught from a more contemplative stance—not analysis but active contemplation; not explanation but musing over the metaphors so to steer the soul toward a fuller acknowledgment of itself in relation to God.

Toward the end of his chapter Merton reveals how in Christian mystical theology there are two souls: the inferior soul in its everyday, acting, decision-making disposition and the superior soul, really the same soul, which is "strictly the image of God within us" (347). Shifting from the first to the second signals a transference in knowing from one that is objective to one that is "knowledge by intuition and connaturality," a knowing-with in a complete embrace of the other. His thoughts helped me to bridge a gap that kept separate my love of poetry from a desire to deepen my own spiritual life. Here, in one of the most affirming guides on my pilgrimage, Merton stepped forward to help me transition and to link two worlds that I had known should be joined more closely but lacked the language to see it.

One of Merton's favorite poets was Octavio Paz, whose insight into the creative process the monk cherished: "The real ideas of a poem are not those which occur to the poet before writing the poem, but rather those which, with or without the poet's intention, are inferred naturally from the work itself" (345). Like poetry, prayer too had within its nature both a process and a discovery, perhaps even a recovery. And as with poetry, so too with prayer, sometimes in praying, the best gift came in the form of a sense of peace through abdicating my own will and desires to His will for me.

The property of the monastery was vast and thickly wooded. I hiked every morning before the heat of the parched Oregon fall built up to the top of the trees. The forest and the hiking paths invited both meandering and meditation. Walking in the woods had become my favorite form of contemplation. I loved to head out early in the morning with a bottle of water and a few energy bars in my backpack to hike into the silence of the forest's dark silence. I was as joyful in nature as I was attending the prayer services and Mass at the monastery. I relished my time hiking under the cedars that canopied above me. Another bridge I felt building in me was the intimate connection between the natural order, which I embraced with every walk, and the spiritual sense of the presence of God in all things. I sensed His presence with every solitary outing in the woods and secretly hoped that I would come across no other retreatants (who I selfishly felt, would spoil my solitude). I would read of Merton's own love for the natural world. He believed that monks should "work in the fields, in the rain, in the sun, in the mud, in the clay, in the wind: these are our spiritual directors and our novice masters" (*When the Trees Say Nothing*, 43).

Walking in solitude through the mountains filled me with a pervasive joy as I watched the orange, yellow, and green leaves, all in various stages of turning colors in their rocking descent. I loved walking in this technicolor terrain where nature delighted in her own transformation. Along the road in one particular stretch heading back to the monastery were large clusters of blackberries hanging heavy like small gatherings of grapes on their thorny vines. One of the monks told me that the monastery could not find a buyer for them this season, so they decided not to harvest them at all but simply let them ripen and become food for the animals. Or for strolling retreatants.

I put down my pack and stepped into the bushes still wet from the morning dew. The aroma from the berries was itself delicious. When I gently grabbed a cluster, their ripeness crushed in my hand, leaving only blue-black juice running down my wrist. I tried to pull them off the vine more gingerly, one at a time, and realized how labor-intensive it would be to harvest these large patches of soft fruit.

I reached toward another cluster as thorns cut across my bare leg, which began to bleed. I pulled a small cluster of berries off the bush and they buckled into mush under my fingers just as I was lifting them to my mouth. They had a sweet, soft, succulent juice and delicate, ephemeral texture. I delighted in the sweet blackberry pulp; my fingers were stained purple when I gathered several more clusters of their soft tissue. They were sugary and syrupy and instantly released the fragrant heavy sweetness of their flavor. Grace in matter, in the gifts of the earth. Such simplicity, picking berries; yet it reminded me of some secret sacred element in all the earth's creations.

I reached down to inspect the scratch on my leg and the purple juice from my fingers mingled with the thick red coagulating blood. Both purple stain and red blood were two vital life juices. I couldn't help but marvel at how the blackberry bushes carried their own protection in the thorns that framed their ripened clusters. They had marked me and taken some of my own juice in exchange for the plucked berries. A fair trade-off, I admitted, and felt that I had gotten the richer part of the exchange. I thought of these ripe blackberries as poems themselves, written by God for the world to consume and enjoy if only one paused long enough to recognize their purple poetics.

A shift in perspective toward the material world had occurred in me; in these sweet blue-black bodies I sensed some numinous presence, some divine energy emanating from them. What would it be like, I wondered, to squeeze this dark purple juice into a fountain pen and use it to write in my journal? Would my thoughts grow riper under such ink? I sat down on a nearby fallen tree trunk and clustered my words in my journal:

Blackberry Writing

Were I to go blackberry picking
in the woods that coat the backside
of the mountains behind our fence
And
were I to stomp them down in
a brown oak barrel ringed with
rusted steel belts, slightly leaking
And
were I to drain off the deep
ink of purple and fill my fountain
pen with it,
would I then gain the courage to
write my memoirs smelling of
summer sunshine afternoons
and punctuate my blackberry sentences
with the juicy ooze of memories
opulent and wet,
sticky like the tattoo ink of a
blackberry plot from the purple
clot of fruit?

I'd rather just eat the whole bulbous
lot of them, stain my lips
and teeth rather than the stinging
yellow jacket paper beneath me.

Let the past ferment behind
my back a bit longer.
(*Casting the Shadows*, 88)

This was my poem-prayer of gratitude for both the wound and the opulence of the blackberry feast.

I sat in the chapel early in the morning as Christina entered. She was the lovely woman in her mid-twenties who had accompanied her father on retreat. She wore black loose-fitting shorts and had beautiful legs and a firm young body. I gazed over at her and found myself as aroused by her presence as any hard-pressed sixteen-year-old. A bit embarrassed, I nonetheless could not suppress these erotic feelings that suddenly stung me. We were the only two in the chapel before Matins. My eyes continued to drift over to watch her; I both wished she were not so attractive to me and grateful that she was.

Is this another of God's displays of a seductive sense of humor? How wonderful the human body is; what a creation without equal! My attempts to pray quietly were thrown to the wind in Christina's presence. I felt a quickening of the blood, but it was not directed at God or my salvation. No wonder Dante's deep love of the young Florentine, Beatrice Portinari, was so strong that it inspired the entire *Divine Comedy*, with her as a central guide to his salvation through her beautiful presence. The love of God, Agape, was not separate from the love of another, Eros.

I was beginning to feel a little ashamed at my furtive looks and fantasies directed toward this young woman. Far from shutting itself out from the world, the monastic life brought the world's beauty intensely into its enclosure, often through a quickening of the senses. Here was a very real and delicious part of the world sitting across the aisle from me. She had brought the world palpably into the chapel this morning. I gave up any attempt to pray. I read in the *Song of Songs* some of the finest and most erotic poetry ever created; that it appeared in the Bible revealed how the body and spirit were not to be separated but united in a common joy.

> How beautiful are your feet in their sandals,
> O prince's daughter!
> The curve of your thighs
> is like the curve of a necklace,
> Work of a master hand.
> Your navel is a bowl well rounded
> With no lack of wine,
> Your belly a heap of wheat
> Surrounded with lilies.
> Your two breasts are two fawns,

Twins of a gazelle. . . .
How beautiful you are, how charming,
My love, my delight!
(*The Jerusalem Bible*, 7:3–12)

I savored like ripe berries this language of eros and desire and wondered about the human body in relation to contemplation. The poem in the *Song of Songs* praised the flesh's beauty and power and the potency of desire for the beloved. Poetry's words below brought together the pleasures of the flesh with the desire of Israel for God. The bride in the poem is no less aggressive than the bridegroom; their charged atmosphere was provocative:

> We will spend the night in the villages,
> And in the morning we will go to the vineyards.
> We will see if the vines are budding,
> If the blossoms are opening,
> If the pomegranate trees are in flower.
> Then I shall give you
> The gift of my love.
> The mandrakes yield their fragrance
> The rarest fruits are at our doors;
> The new as well as the old,
> I have stored them for you, my Beloved. (7:15–25)

Christina's presence both in church and when I saw her at meals or walking in the woods, reminded me that when the life of the spirit separated from the incarnated world, distortions and perversions were inevitable. She reminded me, in her natural and unconscious beauty and in my own frisky nature, that the spiritual life was not distinct or divorced from the body; if it became so, it lost sight of the creation we found ourselves in as God's witness to his love for human beings. Love need not be abstract. I was glad she was here in her own delightful manifestation; she was to be celebrated. I calmed down and began to enjoy her as a person in her own right and as a presence that should not be forsaken. Her name, Christina, is the perfect word for Christ and the flesh.

Mary Magdalene followed Christ with absolute fidelity; she carried in her character the place of eros, of human incarnated love within Christ's mission. Years later I read the Portuguese novelist,

Jose Saramago's, *The Gospel According to Jesus Christ*, a witty, poignant, skeptical and eccentric rendering of Christ's life and his subsequent marriage to Mary Magdalene up to the time he was crucified. His novel, along with the Greek writer Nikos Kazantzakis' *Last Temptation of Christ*, reveal something of the eros of Christ through the figure of Magdalene, making him most fully human. Faith was organic, not ethereal. It was also erotic, life-animating, and overflowing with desire and longing.

Far from stirring the waters of blasphemy and heresy in me, I found that Christ's words offered images on which to meditate about the Son of God, who each of us will finally imagine according to her or his own values and beliefs. The humanity of Christ could not be overemphasized. Saramago's novel reveals Christ as a rebellious, lusty, feisty young man who argues with God and asks Him why he should believe he is God's son. The central action of the novel is Christ's coming to a full awareness of who he is, as well as his unique destiny within a full acceptance of its truth. I sensed in Saramago's novel and in the gospels generally that to "become like Christ" suggests I not become Christ but *myself*, in the full reflective awareness that Christ fulfilled his own nature and completed his own destiny. The task is no less difficult for having recognized such a demand.

Word had gone out among the retreatants that a new shopping mall nearby housed a bookstore selling hardcover copies of *The Journals of Thomas Merton* for five dollars a volume. The mall was only twenty minutes from the monastery. After breakfast I headed out in search of this treasure. I enjoyed driving down the long road to the main street that would take me to the shopping mall. I felt like a young kid out for a bike ride after being in the house for a week. It was exhilarating to be out mingling with the rest of humanity in their ordinary pursuits. I arrived just when the store opened.

When I asked them about the volumes, they showed me to a table where, sure enough, there they sat hardback, each with a different photograph of Merton on the dustjacket. I was able to find volumes two, three, four, and seven. I could not believe my good fortune as I handed the clerk twenty dollars plus tax and walked out with an armload of hardback Merton and a skip in my step, and enlarged gratitude to Joe, another retreatant, for sharing his treasured find with the rest of us.

I found the journals more interesting than many autobiographies or biographies because they hosted a kind of writing that was closer to the bone of where the person lived; it was as if the reader were overhearing or eavesdropping on another's most intimate thoughts and feelings. Journals as literature resided somewhere between autobiography and memoir, between poetry and confession. I was drawn first to volume four, which spanned the years 1960–1963, years in which I was in high school and the year I made my first retreat as a senior.

I took great consolation reading the first fifty or so pages of this volume, for as a monk, Merton struggled with many of the same life situations I felt confronting me on this pilgrimage and learning, like him, how little I really understood of the human heart's desires and insecurities. I shared his wrestling with faith, questioning what it was, really, this struggle to believe as well as to question those beliefs. I found my own belief in God to be sloppy, slippery, contrary, messy, and muddy, with no neat or fixed or clean surface. My struggles with belief in God and allowing myself to let go and let His will be done left me feeling polluted, dirty, and completely inadequate. At age forty-five as a monk, Merton made a rare assertion: "Of one thing I am certain. My life must have meaning. This meaning springs from a creative and intelligent harmony between my will and the will of God—a clarification by right action. But what is right action? What is the will of God?" (*Turning Toward the World*, 46). His question consoled me; it allowed me to continue to pursue what may ultimately prove permanently evasive, but this was an insufficient reason not to engage the pursuit. Perhaps the true journey was in the pursuit of this deep questioning that Merton wrestled with his entire life. It was the most important question, in my mind, for one who seeks some healing redemption outside one's self.

If this most famous monk questioned what the will of God was and continued to pray in seeking it, then there was hope for anyone willing to be called to the question and not to some easily gained answer. I did not see his question as a despondent response but rather a hopeful call to search out this most mysterious of relationships. Was there a danger in becoming too certain of God's will, or was the struggle of faith to remain always in uncertainty, continually questing for it? Do I learn to settle into the doubt and uncertainty and allow space and time for faith to grow in me, slowly, in God's time? Prayer may then be closer to a questioning and a plea to know the will of God than it is to affirming His will. I read in Merton's journals the acute anger he often felt toward others in the monastery, his self-absorption, his struggle with his own narcissism and his desire to write and be published, along with an equally imposing desire to be a solitary.

No, I thought, the monastic life was far from a retreat or an escape from the world. It was rather where the world's problems coagulate and congregate in great and often intense numbers, in a puree of difficult motives and decisions, to be dealt with in the desert of one's cell and in the wilderness of one's own heart. I feared my room in the daytime hours and avoided it as often as I could. St. Romuald's advice was to sit in one's cell, where all one needed would be given. I needed instead to be roaming in the woods, feeling the freedom of movement, not the condensed anguish of self-doubt and the pressing walls of my room. Solitude bred its own terror in me, and I still lacked the courage to face it head-on.

I also read Merton the poet because in so many of his works he concentrates on the poetic voice, poetic expression, and on crafting subtle and implicit connections to prayer. Both of these areas aroused a keen interest in me. I told myself early on that I would follow on this pilgrimage the contours of ideas that presented themselves, both the painful and joyful ones, without resistance.

One of his favorite poets is Octavio Paz who he read in the original Spanish. On August 22, 1960, Merton focused on Paz's insight that "The real ideas of a poem are not those which occur to the poet before writing the poem, but rather those which, with or without the poet's intention, are inferred naturally from the work itself" (*Turning Toward the World*, 35). I thought of this idea in relation to prayer; something of its nature involves both a process and a discovery, perhaps even a recovery. When I made feeble attempts to pray, something was always given to me as a gift, some feeling or revelation that was unarticulated, some joy, some expansiveness unplanned and unexpected, some fuller grasping of a presence that gathered willingly in God's deep silence.

I had been on my pilgrimage for six weeks and if I originally thought this travel and contemplative life would clarify or reveal to me some neat packet of beliefs or limned contours of myself to me, I laughed at how distant that idea now was. Instead, I found myself swimming in a sea of ideas, thoughts, feelings, memories, desires, impulses, compulsive behaviors, goals, objectives, opinions, hopes, regrets, pleasures, fears, paradoxes, shame, and assumptions. My thoughts were crowded with how dependent I was on others, how I tended to sink down into myself often with no lifejacket or buoy to keep me on the surface. Yes, I realized, we each have our own infernos and purgatories to negotiate, but will we be as fortunate as Dante to have a Virgil or a Beatrice, or as lucky as Ishmael to have Queequeg, or as blessed as Odysseus to have Athena? Clearly, this voyage must not be taken alone. Right now Merton, several poets, and the sacred life of nature were my most secure lifelines.

I also began to wonder how much I could face and tolerate of my past? It continued to move up from behind me into the present with a force greater than I remembered was part of the original experience. Then I wondered if I was on this journey to gain some superficial sense of self-improvement; the thought made me want to pack up and head home. How self-deceived I would be if it were true. I resolved to continue to pray, to let God be my guide in all of this slippery mess of life and to remain firm but realistic about my goals—in fact, to make my goal giving up goals so that the real reason for my travels could be heard and felt. I knew at the time that reconciling the wounds inflicted by my father, and more recently, by me, had grown to impressive proportions since I left home.

One afternoon I discovered a path through the cornstalks, down to a shady bottom where an empty hermitage rested quietly in the cool shade of the afternoon. It was quiet under the September sun; dragonflies and other insects stirred in the air. The shadowy space of the hermitage offered me a delicious hour of respite where I did little else but enjoy the company of the crude hut, the well-used workbench under a tree, a shed for storing farm utensils, and a canopy protecting a picnic table. I sat there and prayed in thanksgiving for such abundant simplicity.

Looking up to the path I had followed down into this cool and shaded pocket, I saw it soaked in the hot sun, while down here, only a dozen or so yards away, the temperature was cool, the air dark and welcoming. I loved the darkness, which contrasted powerfully with the stillness of the brilliant sun. Here the air was moist and dark; it invited leisurely reverie.

Prayer was a way into such darkness and silence. I felt at this moment a deep revelation, not an idea of God but a presence of God that was new. God was less a figure or a voice than He was a silent, vast, and still darkness. As I sat on the bench next to the tiny hermitage, I felt an increased presence of God's infinite darkness and silence begin to emanate from this shady glen. It was a powerful moment in part because it splintered the notion of God as a figure or an image. Rather, God was more akin to Dark Matter, the darkness in matter, and the matter of darkness itself. I felt this darkness in the sustained solitude, along with a desire to be quiet and to be open, and to listen brought such awareness to the surface. I felt not awe or wonder only at this moment, but a deep courage and a trust that this courage emanated from the dark matter. Alone on a hot afternoon in the Oregon woods, I felt my entire experience of God shift.

I looked up into the field toward the path and realized that the light had begun to bend and soften. I rose and headed toward my cottage nurturing this revelation. Perhaps this was why morning darkness held such an attraction for me: it marked the time when God was most fully present in the world. If Christ was the light of the world, then God's other dimension was His unfathomable darkness. I wrote spontaneously in my journal before heading into the softening sunlight: "sink to the root, to the taproot, for that is where you need to abide." There was such a presence as holy darkness; I felt its healing properties enter my soul to comfort any restlessness I still embraced.

I packed my truck the evening before I was to depart this holy and generous abbey. I would miss it terribly. My farewells to everyone at dinner included my plans to leave early for Portland. Hiking the wooded mountain peaks had been a joy. Praying quietly, reading, and visiting the neighboring town of McMinville had renewed me; I felt more rested than I had in years and most comfortable with the dark reality of divinity than ever before. I was now ready to head down the driveway in the morning in search of further insights into the holiness of God and me.

9

Sisters Who
Make Much of Time

*Shalom Prayer Center, Queen of Angels
Monastery, Mount Angel, Oregon*

> Suddenly I saw the red blood running down from under the
> crown, hot and flowing freely and copiously, a living stream, just as
> it was at the time when the crown of thorns was pressed on his
> blessed head.　　　　　—Julian of Norwich, *Showings*

A T THE PORTLAND AIRPORT I picked up Sandy. Being away
from her had revealed to me what a treasure she is in my
life. We drove to the city of Mount Hood, found a fine bed-
and-breakfast, unpacked, then headed out to hike the woods and
enjoy the waterfalls for three days. The time out of the monastic
atmosphere revealed that God was as much other people as He was
darkness and solitude. I was grateful for this delicious interlude that
gave me time to reconsider the important elements and people in
my life.

After taking her back to the Portland Airport, I headed south
through the rich farm country surrounding Interstate 5 to the Silverton exit and found County Highway 214 to Mount Angel and the
Shalom Prayer Center, Queen of Angels Monastery. I was one day
early, so I drove in search of a bed-and-breakfast a mile from the
Shalom Prayer Center and rented a room upstairs of the house of
Chris and Betty Roehmer. Their home was immaculate, full of
home-made dolls, animals, and other crafty things on the walls and
tables. I enjoyed watching television in the evening. At breakfast,

Chris related how he could not work the fifteen acre farm anymore because of surgery to both knees, both shoulders, followed soon after by a heart attack. Social security would not compensate him; instead, they found him a position as a receptionist in another city and insisted he move to the new job. He refused their nonnegotiable offer because he would not move off the farm. Now he and his wife took in travelers for income. We spent the morning talking about his and his wife's future. When I left I told them I would return for another stay. I headed to the Prayer Center.

Shalom is an old college for women, converted years ago into a prayer center operated by Benedictine sisters. About twenty of the sisters from the order were making a retreat at the same time as my stay; I welcomed having others there in prayer and silence with me. The only men in the dormitory setting were Steve, a Presbyterian minister, and me. We immediately struck up a friendship. Sister Dorothy Jean was the guest mistress (and would in a year become director of the center). She arrived as a freshman to the school, literally walking across the street from her parents' home, and never left. She told me her work with God and her vocation were no farther than out the front window of her home and a walk across the two-lane highway. Her destiny was literally across the street from her birthplace. She laughed about how she never even needed a car to travel to search out her life's work.

My room was upstairs of the old school. Small, it was nonetheless very comfortable and opened out, as did all the others rooms lining it, to a large living room with couches, lamps, and tables. The sofas had Afghans on them, and the chairs had Irish linen doilies on their arms. I loved these small details made by the sisters. The entire room had a very different feel to it. The hands of women in creating this space were pronounced and welcoming. I chose a favorite Afghan and kept it close anytime I read in this welcoming space. A faint smell of mothballs wafted up when I covered myself with it.

The kitchen was immediately off the living room, next to the pantry, where we helped ourselves to breakfast. A coffeepot was always full, as was another kettle with hot water. Cookies or rolls or some snacks were always out for anyone who wanted to nibble between meals. Other meals were taken in the basement of the recently renovated chapel two buildings across from us. The refrigerator was available at all hours; a feeling of plenitude, even of modest abundance, was a conscious part of their mission. From the world of monastic men I had inhabited for so many weeks, this feminine, woman-centered space a welcome change; immersed within it, I felt very much at home and even pampered. The contrast between a masculine and a feminine structure of retreating was very evident, and I liked the balance between them, considering my current residence an unexpected gift. I had begun learning to accept abundance whenever it appeared suddenly.

The Benedictine sisters arrived here in 1882 and began building the main part of the monastery, finishing it in 1888. Women retreatants were welcome to stay in this building; men and other women lodged in the building across the driveway. Many workshops and lectures took place here every week, especially on the subject of the Enneagram, a personal growth tool that combines an ancient system of personality types from Middle Eastern traditions with Western practices of meditation (*The Enneagram*, 46). The presentations often involved a Jungian slant, which appealed to me. I planned to attend several to see how their workshops were conducted. I learned as well that many of the sisters were highly active in the immediate community; several of them worked at the Benedictine Nursing Center in town. I felt very comfortable around the sisters and the women retreatants, having spent eight years under the tutelage of Ursuline nuns in Ohio, where one of my aunts and a cousin were members of the same congregation.

Sister Joan operated the bookstore, and I was immediately drawn to her no-nonsense feisty personality. She taught elementary school for thirty-eight years in Florida and now at the retreat center had created a versatile and welcoming place for books, cards, and other stationary items. I visited with her almost every day. While here, I was attracted in my reading and meditation to women mystics of the church, especially Julian of Norwich, Hildegard of Bingen, and Teresa of Avila. I had felt spiritually lopsided in my reading and wanted to use this center to begin shifting to women writers of the church. Their embodied sense of spirituality often felt less heady, more engaged with the fleshy particulars of the world. I was especially fascinated and attracted to Julian of Norwich, an anchoress and a solitary who lived in Norwich, England, in the fourteenth century. She wished and prayed for a bodily sickness so she could enter more fully into Christ's passion. She sought afflictions by God's power, and by the time she was thirty God had, she believed, visited her with a chronic illness. To this disease she added three wounds: "of contrition, of loving compassion, and of a longing with my will for God" (*Showings*, 17).

Her belief was that the wounds of the spirit have their analogue in afflictions of the body. God is woundedness. What I remembered most, however, was her description of Christ's wounds and afflictions, through which she recognized God's compassion. Writing vividly of the mutilated flesh, she opened up a very different way of meditating on God's incarnate nature when it was incarnated in Christ's woundedness. Of a vision she experienced, she wrote: "Suddenly I saw the red blood running down from under the crown, hot and flowing freely and copiously, a living stream, just as it was at the time when the crown of thorns was pressed on his blessed head" (181). She was grateful because she believed this vivid and horrific image was shown to her "without any intermediary" (181). She sensed she was being gifted with a direct revelation of God's suffering and felt the experience directly.

I thought about her own affliction, her disease, and how it allowed her to see more deeply into the wounds of Christ, which I thought of as wounds of compassion. A wound as a way of *seeing*, of an alternative way to understand the suffering of others, was an idea that had become a major part of my journey.

What is this condition of being wounded? How does our own woundedness allow any of us to see more clearly the wounds of another? Julian's afflicted imagination arrested me. It was "so bloody real" and made me think of the power of a wound to alter vision, to let one see what otherwise might remain veiled, an idea I struggled to give voice to in one of my earlier books, *The Wounded Body: Remembering the Markings of Flesh*. I remembered reading a physicist's observation that only 4 percent of the world is visible, while 96 percent remains invisible. Could wounding be another way, even a sacred opportunity, of envisioning what was invisible? Does being wounded offer us a perceptual acuity to see what is unavailable to the unwounded? Julian's imagery recalling the power of the five wounds of Christ evoked in me compassion for others through one's own infirmities. Rather than allowing my wounds to embitter and even defeat me, they could also expose an empathy toward others I had not realized or felt before.

I loved Julian's unadulterated honesty about the body and found her a source of profound meditation. In meditating on the wounds Julian revealed, I sensed that wounds graced my life and grace at the same time had the power to wound that same life. Wounding might be understood as an initiation into mystery, into the incarnate mystery of divine presence, enfleshed, suffering, yet finally able to allow me to use this pain as an avenue to a deeper awareness of our afflicted and impermanent condition. What emerged was a more authentic feeling of compassion for others.

The five wounds of Christ were openings to the world from all parts of the body. How did the flesh allow an aperture into something beyond the human, into the realm of the transcendent? Wounds seemed to break open the surface of the familiar to reveal in their darkness or discoloration, a break in the normal flow of things, an interruption pointing to something beyond it. I thought of the 14th century poet Dante's own journey through the gashes of inferno where he confronted shades still wounding themselves and others with their resentments, angers, unfulfilled lives, hatred, and envy of others before he climbed out of the wounded pit of hell to begin the climb up Mount Purgatory. The wounds were openings into a fuller awareness of human weakness and grace that God offered in the form of afflictions.

No less was it true of Hildegard of Bingen, writing in 12th century Germany at the same time as Julian. Both women exposed a gutsy theology, rooted in the fragility of the flesh. Both of them allowed me to see that where and how I am wounded may be a gift because it allowed me to open to the wounds of another. Her range of subjects she wrote about was greater than anyone I had read or heard in recent memory. In a series of books she labeled "Scivias," which literally means "Know the Ways," Hildegard unites the spirit with the body in writing of John's "And the word was made flesh, and dwelt among us" (John 1:14). Like Julian, she directed my thinking to the matter of spirit and how the spirit mattered. God assumed flesh in the womb, she writes, "through the fervor of the Holy Spirit. And he put it on in the same way that the veins, which are the fabric of the flesh and carry blood, are not themselves blood. God created humanity so all Creation might serve it" (*Secrets of God*, 71).

I also enjoyed Hildegard's earthiness, her simplicity of expression, and her interest in the many permutations of the natural order. For example, she writes on grains—hemp, fennel, and yarrow. This last one she describes as the best poultice for healing wounds: "After the wound has been washed in wine, cook the yarrow in a little water [and then] bind it lightly, still warm, over the cloth that is placed on the wound. In this way it will draw the pus and foulness and heal the wound" (91). Her concern with the body, nature, and our fragile wounded flesh drew me to her spirituality of healing as one of my favorite guides. She writes of fish, minerals, rocks, trees, animals, and insects; nothing escaped her notice. The simpler and more unadorned her subject, the greater the mystery of creation revealed itself to her.

Her style and manner reminded me of a more contemporary mystic. Annie Dillard's *Pilgrim at Tinker Creek* is an engaging sequel to Hildegard's writing. Both women grasp in a deeply visionary way the spirit of God and the Holy Spirit in the world's particular matter; they write with a fluency that allowed me to feel a similar sensation, a sensate presence of God in things. Even the mythical unicorn received two pages in her observations: "and regularly, once a year, the unicorn goes to the land that has the milk of paradise, where he seeks out the finest plants and digs them up with his hoof and eats them" (*Secrets of God*, 95). This wonderful mythic beast is also, for Hildegard, a great source of healing, especially its liver. "Take the liver of a unicorn and grind it up and add the powder to fat prepared from the yolk of an egg and so make an ointment. There is no form of skin disease that if often smeared with this ointment will not be cured" (97). Her imagination of the world stated in such a matter-of-fact way gave me joy. I carried for days an image of a unicorn liver, meditated on it and found through it a deeper sense of being as an image of divine understanding.

I realized at the same time how important the wounds of Christ were to a life of faith. Hildegard's words recalled the many times that Christ healed the wounded, the blind, the diseased, the lame, and even the dead. Perhaps there was much more to meditate on regarding body woundedness and the vibrant life of the spirit in what Julian and Hildegard exposed. As I thought about this, I recalled the figure of "doubting Thomas," the disciple who insisted we consider the mysterious union of woundedness, uncertainty, and resurrection together. I returned to the gospels to read of his skeptical attitude toward Christ's resurrection. I imagined that Thomas felt some trickery astir in the air in the appearance of this man who claimed to be their teacher. Jesus had his own simple and direct answer for Thomas: "Touch my wounds. The reality of my resurrection is in my mutilated hands, feet, and side." My thoughts on Thomas and Christ assembled their own poetic shape:

Fingering Disbelief

Thomas who doubts points his
finger at the wound that gapes
in wonder at his disbelief
in a small room packed with fear.
Belief lies in the history of the affliction
that a mere mortal would never wake
to gaze upon.
The centurion, uncertain of
Christ's death, slides the sharp
steel point of his sword into the flesh
of Him hanging in solid belief,
but crying "Eloi, Eloi," as bones
bend and sag on the tree, the crux where
eternity and history hammer
into a fine marriage.
The wound in the room is still raw, dirty
too from Arimathea's tomb;
still open as if the one risen carries
on his flesh a second mouth for
a second coming—a gaping myth

seeking the ears of his disciples'
trembling ears to speak of what
cannot be
did not happen
will not be believed.

Yet the wound from the wood
Is a witness that death has been
entombed. The flesh open,
unzipped, waits to be known—
He calls now to Thomas to approach
the wound—a shrine of sorts—that
can make us gape, ourselves, in awe—
the relic of living flesh.
What lies here in the horizontal slice
of skin that shows without shame the
deepening layers of incarnation?

Thomas' finger moves to greet the gap;
his own eyes stare straight ahead,
to the eyes serene and clear, full of
liquid life—two wounds to the world
that gaze through disbelief to a finer
doubt, a thicker mist of unknowing.

Almost touching, almost closed, a finger of
Doubt
and witnessing wound not to the
unspoken pain of the other.
Only Jesus speaks: "Thomas…"
only now, early, does the sun, sleeping
for days, suddenly rise and send His
only begotten light through the open window
into the grey yawning room.

Writing this poem, then recopying it in this manuscript, I became
more aware of the intimacy between poetry and prayer. The poem
that imagined Christ and Thomas gathering their attention around
the resurrected man's wounds is, like prayer, a form of meditation.

The grounds of the Shalom Center were far too public. Traffic
hummed and hissed out front in the busyness of commerce. I

missed the deep quiet and naturalness of the forests and mountains, but I accepted it and sought solitude where I could. If I cannot learn to find solitude in the noise and motions of daily life, then I will not have progressed very far into a life of praying simply and daily.

Behind the building lay an expanse of land and a large apple orchard, which I strolled back into after Mass and dinner. I felt that I was always walking on the periphery of true belief. I identified much more with doubting Thomas than with the other disciples; he carried my struggle to give myself completely, in faith and submission, to Christ's suffering and resurrection. Part of me was always seeking the wound of faith through the penetrating sting of doubt. At moments I too felt the skepticism of doubting Thomas.

The apples in the orchard were ripe, and many had already fallen from the trees. As I picked one and ate the McIntosh's delicious but very tart white meat, I noticed I stood on the edge of a cemetery of sisters who had lived here over the past century. Cemeteries have a soothing finality to them; they are sublime places for moments of solitude and prayer. Something worth paying attention to was affirmed in cemeteries that I didn't find elsewhere. The souls buried here know something I do not, but wish to.

The Founder of this center died at age fifty-three in 1846. I did the math over one tombstone to discover that one of the sisters lived to be 102. Row upon row of old gravesites cut through the middle of the orchard. I sat on a bench under an old apple tree and gazed out at the stones marking the sisters' presence. Each of them in turn served God in nurturing this beautiful place. I imagined that when it was built it enjoyed open country with only a few farmhouses dotting its edges. Now it sat on the cusp of downtown. I admired these women whose courage created something lasting. "Rest in God." This is the refrain the sisters say at Mass each morning.

"Mother-Father" was their common address to God. They were all searching for a full spiritual and embodied life while practicing deep compassion for others. To include both genders seemed to ground God in the fullness of the world. RIG: Rest in God. All of these sisters, to whom I was drawn in the cemetery each evening, were now resting in God. They were silent affirmations of this phrase, which I repeated to myself at each visitation.

Sitting on a wooden bench in the orchard surrounded by the sisters, I realized I was marking the halfway point of my pilgrimage; week seven began tomorrow. Was I able to rest in God? Had I stilled my restlessness enough to feel that these sisters were, in spirit, *my* sisters? Their presence calmed me with their invitation into their silence.

Two days later I confessed to Sister Dorothy that I felt stir-crazy. Rain and a cold front had kept us indoors for days. She did not tell me to be patient or to pray more, but instead to get in my truck and drive to the woods. Her directions guided me to Silver Falls State Forest, about thirty minutes from Shalom Center. I thanked her, packed a sandwich, fetched some apples from the orchard, and grabbed two bottles of water, my small camera, and headed south. I passed through the beautiful little town of Silverton and continued fifteen miles south on Route 214. My drive took me through a half-dozen Christmas tree farms where the small spruce and firs reached heights of four to six feet.

After parking, I realized that I was one of only two cars in the lot. A little brown wooden box sold maps for $1.00. The weather promised to be sunny and eighty degrees after the rains. I felt a great rush of ecstasy and joy at the prospect of hiking, meditating, enjoying the natural order, and eating my lunch in the forest by a waterfall and praying. My soul sensed the great expanse of these deep woods and seemed to expand inside me in accord with it. I wished nostalgically that I could share these moments with my sons and wife. I knew I would return with them one day to hike these woods, which I returned to every day for the rest of my time at the Center.

What a discovery was this forest! Paths of various lengths branched out in many directions. One's stamina and ambition were the only limits to choosing one. The day was cool and sunny. I felt like a colt that has just broken out of the fenced corral and sees in front of it only a long meadow with no boundaries. I chose a six-mile path that would take me by seven magnificent waterfalls, full and noisy from the recent heavy rains. As I walked, large yellow and orange maple leaves fell from the trees, pulling me forward. Some were almost as large as my face. The trees were warm and welcoming; they stood as silent sentinels along the path—Douglas and

Noble firs as tall as the California redwoods. The woody, musty smell of the leaves and plants decaying into winter sated the calm air. Looking ahead, I witnessed the dappled lighting of the morning's white sunlight creating a spotted bower of trees as far as the path would let me see. I entered it as a Hobbit might stroll through the woods of Middle Earth, an enchanted forest in a fairy tale full of the ticking sounds of the water droplets on leaves and soft, trammeled earth spongy to the sole.

Some of the trees had fallen recently, others years ago. I could smell their decaying trunks, the intoxicating aroma issuing from their carcasses. I stooped to touch one, a great massive fir. Its decomposing quality was as grand and majestic in death as it was in life, when it stood tall in the forest. The horizontally dead lie down with the vertically alive. Yet some of the trees, still vertical, were also dead. On some of the decaying moist remains, new trees had already found a roothold and were busy growing, as if from the bellies of the rotting ones. How life and death were perfectly at home here in the forest. How some trees that were positioned as if alive, were in fact lifeless. Why do we separate with such fury life from death in the human order? Was there not something the living can learn from the dead when we observe new life growing naturally and directly from the dead in this forest? This wonderful cycle before me was muted in the human order; we deny this cyclical quality of life and death, of life emerging from death and even nourished by it. Life nourished by death: a powerful (de)composition.

As I walked and paid more attention to the simple movement of nature, I was aware that all we need to know metaphysically and spiritually we have access to in observing the natural order. I gazed at and was grateful for the river running parallel to the path in graceful symmetry. I saw what respect the water showed to the rocks that it divided fluidly around, allowing them to exist in their space in the river.

I heard ahead of me the sounds of a quiet sustained roar that signaled how closely the first of seven waterfalls was. I moved slowly along the path where I passed only a few hikers because I did not want this morning or this path to end anytime soon. A bench by the river afforded me a chance to relax and more thoroughly enjoy the waterfall, a perpendicular white gash in the green surroundings. The water spilled from eighty feet up in a thick foamy flow falling past a fern-covered rock face. I felt a sensation of deep gratitude in accord with an absence of all desire. I could only pray in gratitude to God for this creation. Miraculous in its simplicity, the entire scene was a gift wrapped in multi-colored beauty and offered unconditionally.

Coated with moss, laden with lichen life and roots, the trees here had a furry skin. I enjoyed stroking the trunks, like petting a large mammal that stood patiently and enjoyed being touched. They told me their tight secrets, old and crusted with words, in the lighted dark shadows of forest grown heavy with quiet. Silence became a canopy that covered all of this below the sky. A Douglas fir deep in meditation, seeking with its deep roots the secret of things, confessed to the sunlight that the birds were the voices of trees, where deep soul-stirrings could be heard. God's voice may at times be thunderous, but here God was no more vocal than the groan of a branch in the wind high up or the sound of a bird clicking and chirruping as it built its nest in the branches of the giant.

The trees themselves remained quiet, stiff or bending along the seasons. Several species of birds rested on their branches in exchange for singing their souls of the firs' deep darkness. All that had ever been thought or known was now slumbering in the lumber of them; I listened closely, paying attention to the rhythmic sounds of the birds' songs. They would give me what knowledge the trees wanted me to have. Receptive to every nuance of sound and motion, I became aware that at least for the present the trees had no desire to speak except to the wind and to God. Receptive, open, grateful, content, without desire, and loving: these were the qualities of the sacred and I think that if I approached no closer to God than this, it would do nicely.

While I loved the liturgy, the singing of the Psalms, the Mass and the sacraments, I also realized deep in my nature that sitting here by the waterfall in solitude was as sacramental in its own naturalness as any ritual of the church. God was a deep silence. Christ was the Logos of this silence. Could I learn to pray between the silence and the sound? I did not yet comprehend how deeply important darkness and silence were subtly becoming in my development, but as I remembered these moments in the woods, I sensed a deep compassion emanate from nature, and a palpable grief for all the species of animals and plants that had been extinguished by mortals' overexerting what Nature's abundance could accommodate.

The trees and this waterfall were my most profound and immediate guides through the forest, steering me through what I loved, the natural order, to a sensed presence of God and the sacred. Dante must have felt something like this same connection to nature when he acknowledged, in a sonnet of *La Vita Nuova* to his beloved Beatrice: "Love and the noble heart are but one thing, / Even as the wise man tells us in his rhyme, / the one without the other venturing / As well as reason from a reasoning mind. / Nature, disposed to love, creates Love king" (59). Love itself is as natural and divine an act as the presence of these loving trees.

His poem is a prayer to nature, to God and to his lady; how could I separate out the multiple loves he feels? What an idea he puts before us: Nature loves. That is what I felt while walking this forest at every opportunity. The forest itself loved; each tree, fern, spring, waterfall, bush, bird, fox, decaying matter, was an expression of God's love. I felt very quiet as this thought passed through me.

God is a poet, a truth often lost in the fundamentals of church doctrine. Without this poetic sense, which God is often denied, the life of the spirit is flattened to prescriptive practices. How poetic is the natural world in all of its particulars! I needed Walt Whitman's poetry over dogma, Henry David Thoreau's lyric insights before prescriptive beliefs. God's creation was a finely thought-through poiesis, God's own *itinerarium mentis*. I sat at the waterfall enjoying the program of God's mind manifestly incarnated in things. I began to walk the path again with the sense that I was in God's imagination as I moved; God possessed an itinerant imagination, an imagination of movement; what I observed enveloping me was His movement, at times appearing in the slowness of a plant's exuberant unfurling or the violent upsurge of a crashing tree.

Silver Falls State Park

The ancient mossy forest
between great noble firs
the white splashed sunlight
on the maidenhead ferns, so still
in glorious presence, asks me to
pray.

So still and full of its own presence
is the sun's soft light dappled
helping every live thing grow fully
into itself.
The dark shadows become more
of who they are in the late morning
light.

Green, white, darkness—the life of
new ferns gathering around the husky
carcasses of fallen trees.
Death as a form of growth imagines
Life, its half-sister. Life is promised and
delivered in the still fullness of decay.

Around a rotting old stump of fir the roots
gain and rise from the trunk's soft pulp,
insisting skyward, gathering their energies
to form a new tree, supported by old
growth that feeds its rising, like a persistent
memory, an old habit, an aroma that
opens a world forgotten
to find its place in the sun a hundred
feet from death's delicious smell.

Is this the mystery of the resurrection? At once the death of Christ
and His rising made more sense to me when I recognized its analogy in the forest. What a necessary and right coupling this pulsing action of life-death-life was, there to be witnessed by any that had eyes to see and ears to hear. Faith went one step further, as I remembered doubting Thomas: "Blessed are those who have not seen and yet have believed."

I hiked for several more miles, meeting others who had chosen the other end of the trail to begin their trek. The sun was directly overhead, but the procession of waterfalls kept the air on the trail cool and misty. I emerged in late afternoon and hiked back to the truck feeling renewed, relieved, revitalized. The old growth forest that welcomed me with open branches and cascading leafy color became a highlight of the trip. Wordsworth's sonnet, "The World is Too Much With Us," found its way back into my memory: "Little we see in nature that is ours. / We have given our hearts away, a sordid boon" (*Literature*, 566–7). I knew that I had retrieved something of the natural order in these hikes and that what I felt possessed of was another spirit form. How had I allowed my own thinking to torque into believing that matter and spirit existed as separate entities? Allowing the natural order to embrace me expanded my awareness of its spiritual unseenness. It was always about vision and the level of consciousness I wanted to live within. The natural order had broken through some habituated ways of seeing to introduce a new order of spiritual awareness in me that I refused to relinquish. The regular habit of thought based on a dualistic perception of "me-them," "matter-spirit," and "nature-culture" had for the moment evaporated.

On one of my last days it rained so heavily that I stayed in and wrapped myself in an afghan in the lounge/living room area and read. The downpour was intense and as I listened to the stormy Oregon fall day, I hunkered down and burrowed deeper into a cocoon I created for myself. The afghan I enjoyed now smelled of mothballs and the love of one of the sisters' hands in the making.

Certain people are frequently placed in our path; each one of them has a reason for being in our lives when they appear. I thought, following my friend, Dianne Skafte's book, *Listening to the Oracle*, that these souls were oracles in familiar clothing. Conversation often brought out just exactly what we needed to learn from them or, contrarily, what we were to say to them that they needed or were ready to hear from us. I now believed on this pilgrimage that every person I met had given me some gift that I needed. My hope was that I had given some of them what they were seeking. Such is the working of God's grace in the lives of one another. Sisters Dorothy and Jean, as well as many others, both living and dead, had been assistants to me here. "Pay attention," says Christ. What we need is in front of us more often than not, but its visibility is often blocked by intellectual pride, selfishness, envy, anger, regret, desires, appetites—a host of impediments that blind the soul and deaden the spirit.

As I prepared to leave Shalom Prayer Center, I finished reading Shusaku Endo's novel, *The Deep River*. Not a great work by any means, but very forceful on the power of passion and of being called to a life work but often resisting it because one wants his/her own will fulfilled rather than the destiny that beckons.

In the evening I watched a fine videotape from the center's abundant library. Anthony DeMillo is a very funny Indian writer and speaker. He claims that to be detached is not the same as to be disinterested. Rather, it was to be free, to have more energy. He offered the memorable Chinese story of an archer who possesses all the skill, but cares for nothing, especially winning the archery contest. As a consequence, he hits the mark every time. Then there is the archer with skill who yearns to hit the target. He hits it less often. A third archer, equally as skilled, has a relentless desire to win the prize; he hits the target even less frequently. The fourth archer, equal in skill as the others, prays continually: "oh, let me win." He seldom hits the bull's eye. DeMillo's story highlights the different levels of detachment in the first three. Detachment seems to be necessary for keeping in check the ego's distracting force. Surrendering the ego to God's work, to destiny's dictates, is part of one's life of prayer. How to pray without ceasing, yet not demand anything for or from myself, placed me in a different attitude toward God's mercy, one which kept me interested but far less grasping for achievement.

On the evening of the last day I strolled out after dinner to visit one last time the graves of the sisters, where they continued to enjoy a long and peaceful rest after a life of service. I imagined what this cemetery looked like in the spring, when the apple blossoms fell around them and covered their tomb sites with the soft pink and red petals, preparing for another fruitful year.

I sat quietly with these women and wondered about how I could better balance a quiet life of solitude and meditation, writing and reading, with more service to the world. I had in the past taught special education classes, continuing adult education courses, been a Big Brother in several cities, served meals at homeless shelters, and tutored students in high school. I gained something from these experiences, but was it more about activity than activism, more about serving something in myself than the world? I sensed that acts of service borne of compassion could assume many forms. Monks prayed for the entire world from their cells, and their time of worship was from early morning to dusk. They too were serving the world.

I also reflected as I packed my bags and loaded the truck, that each day God offered me as gifts what I needed in profound and simple abundance. The burdens were not impossible, the pleasures not sustainable. I am not very good at separating out what God wanted me to have and to do and what I pounded into myself in often-ceaseless activity. Could serving others also take the form of doing nothing, of being silent, of not contributing to the manic and noisy life that seems to typify the world I moved within?

I was drawn to this Buddhist/Christian idea of detachment, of emptying myself of desires and wants and of allowing to die in me what was needed to fertilize new life. The decaying and newborn trees surrounding me observed this simple truth. In a culture giddy for distractions, thrills, and sensational or hyperbolic behavior as witness to a desperate desire for something deeper, I thought about how this pilgrimage had muted so many desires in me: for recognition, security, love from others, even the desire to be angry, outraged, frustrated, impatient, judgmental, self-righteous, useful, wanted, needed, desired, and called-upon. God invited me instead to mute these desires so that I could more reflectively love the proper things in a fuller measure. In such action resided more, not less, freedom. Desires, wants, cravings, and addictions were what encouraged me to abandon the world on a deep level. I sensed that they were also forces that led me to abandon myself.

These feelings of detachment made me appreciate St. Augustine's dislike for what he called his "own seething passions" (*Confessions*, 136). Converting one's dislike of the passions into a meditation on the wounds of Christ, which he claimed can "heal men's inner wounds" (167) was central to the act of pilgrimage. Christ most displayed his charity for a shortened vision of humankind in his five visible wounds, poultices for the invisible lesions we harbor within. Another paradox: the wounds of another can become our cure. Christ's wounds slice two ways: to reveal both his willingness to be wounded for our shortcomings and his desire to heal us through His own afflictions. If we are to know who we are, Augustine's insight evokes, we must grasp the deep incisions of our own woundedness.

I walked one last time among the buried sisters on the stone path that divided their graves. It had just finished raining hard; now the setting sun and the emerging blue sky calmed the clean air. The old gravestones on either side of the path leading to the large white crucifix were now dark and wet. The sisters lay silent, listening to my footsteps above them. They listened as well to the passage of time skirting across the lawn and through the orchard that protected them. They were as quiet as the walnut and apple trees around them; they sank their roots deeper into the earth with each day. Like tulip bulbs, they needed to be planted deeply to grow. I saluted all of their lives individually in my walk. Their names rang poetic in my ear:

Sister Mary Sophie Thiboudeau
Sister Mary Rose O'Brien
Sister Mary Philomena Knupp
Sister Mary Michtilde Preisendorfer
Sister Mary Flavia Brandenburg
Sister Mary Ambrosia Mangisch
Foundress Mother Mary Bernodine Wachter
Sisters Mary Beatrice, Felecitas, Alyosia, Hildegard, Columba

To all of you—*shalom!*

10

St. Francis
and a Spider's Web

Franciscan Renewal Center,
Portland, Oregon

Time does not take time off, nor does it turn without purpose
through our senses: it works wondrous effects in our minds.
—St. Augustine, *Confessions*

S<small>T. AUGUSTINE</small>'s *Confessions* offers these great insights on the
nature of time above. Time, I had discovered, carries its own
mystery, its own relations to divine presence. I wondered, as I
became more "time sensitive" at this juncture because of how rap-
idly it had accelerated in my journey, if my own relation to God
could be shifting as time sped up.

I drove north toward Portland on I-5 and watched for the signs
for Lewis and Clark College, across the street from which sat the
retreat center. The Franciscans purchased this magnificent estate,
with the immense brick Corbett mansion as its centerpiece, in 1942,
and subsequently made it into their Western Province headquarters.
To the right of the mansion was the retreat wing, with rooms on the
first two floors with bathrooms down the hall. The ground floor,
where I stayed, was remodeled on the order of a posh motel, with
bathrooms in the rooms and new furniture, including a luxurious
reclining lounge chair and a fine tape library with a reading room in
the middle. All meals were taken directly across the grand lawn in
the large dining room.

Again, situated squarely in a noisy urban area and close to college traffic sat this bustling source of a steady stream of public lectures, seminars, and retreat conferences. The works of Fr. Thomas Keating, especially his writings on Centering Prayer, were central to their mission.

I met Sister Mary Jo, the conference center director, who introduced me to Sister Carmel, the general manager. She immediately invited me into the main dining room for lunch. It was a very special occasion today: a farewell party for several sisters who were departing the center permanently, leaving only six. The diminished size would place the center in jeopardy as an institute open to retreatants seeking sanctuary. By contrast, in 1945, when the center was founded, there were twenty-five sisters, the highest number.

Sadness and jubilation conspired thickly in the room; they made a space at the table for me, a perfect stranger. Adaptable and honored, I entered into the unique moment for this order as best I could. Sunday was the feast of St. Francis; he was remembered once more as the sisters prepared to depart. One of them reminded us that Francis died in 1226 at the age of forty-four. The mood of the gathering was both celebratory and somber; grief trafficked with subdued gaiety.

Toasting the departing women, one of them told the story of St. Francis founding his order on a Portiuncula, or "little portion." Portiuncula was a tiny bit of ground at the base of Assisi. Francis rented it for a basket of fish and several loaves of bread per year. Here he founded a place for his followers to live. "A Little Portion" is the name of the retreat house where my room and the library were. I liked being given this context for my stay and felt at the same time the sadness hanging in the room over the departing residents. Their leaving seemed to mark the end of an era for the congregation at this location. They were generous in allowing me to be part of this little portion of their changing lives. I enjoyed their spirit and spent two hours in their company before returning to unpack and set up my room.

After lunch, I followed one of the trails that meandered in the general direction of Lewis and Clark College. The day was sunny and in October, usually by now in the rainy season. I sat by the creek and listened to the flow of water and enjoyed both the warmth and the deep silence that was both within me and in my surroundings. A sadness and depression, which had haunted me for several days, began to lift, and I entered a new and revitalizing rhythm of joy and gratitude. I moved throughout this pilgrimage from feelings of fierce loneliness to moments of epiphanic gracefulness, where I believed God was revealing to me His dark and light sides. I felt His moods, His shifting divine atmosphere coursing through me like the river I sat beside. I no longer fought off the loneliness but let it enter and find a habitation. I learned to trust that it was not permanent and that it too was teaching me something about God's presence and myself in His deep silence.

The tape library in my retreat house was excellent. Tired of reading, I took several tapes and a recorder back to my room, kicked back in my lounge chair in absolute plushness and enjoyed the voice of another. Ever the utilitarian, I selected the popular monk Brother David Steindl-Rast's *A Practical Guide to Meditation* and laughed at the "how-to" slant of the title. I hoped it was not the prototype of what might be *The Idiot's Guide to God Through Meditation* (and thought what a moneymaker that could be).

Brother David's voice was animated, vibrant, emotional and joyful. I enjoyed his style as he outlined the qualities he believed constituted meditative prayer: wholeheartedness, leisureliness, faithfulness, authenticity, and gratefulness. All of these qualities involved the heart rather than the head. The heart, he suggests, stands for the whole person, the deepest root where a person is of one piece, the realm where one exists with self, others, and God. A God experienced in the heart constituted the ultimate reality. All of us, he claims, are made for happiness; this condition grows directly from discovering and creating meaning in our everyday lives. Religion is the human quest for ultimate meaning, "so the term 'God' is not necessary" (*A Practical Guide* cassette tape). There are, for Brother David, many deeply religious atheists in the world also searching for meaning.

His idea of the difference between free time and leisure was helpful; on my pilgrimage I had an abundance of free time, but it was not a synonym for leisure. Leisure "is to allow time to work for its own sake wherein I allow myself to be open to what is happening right now" (*A Practical Guide* cassette tape). This leisurely attitude is a virtue because it allows one to give time and to take time. The heart in its rhythmic beating pumps and rests, pumps and rests. It gives and takes, gives and takes, and so it is the best model for leisure's rhythm: a constant give-and-take in time.

Our lives and vocabulary, Brother David revealed, is full of "take" language with very few "give" responses. For example, I take a test, a seat, a nap, a vacation, time, a shower, and a drink. Some despondent souls even "take" their own lives because they cannot not "take it" anymore. Our learning must include the word "give": to give ourselves, to give over to . . . to give in. Giving in, giving ourselves over to God, giving up old habits—"dead branches" he calls them—can help us incorporate the "give" back into the "give-and-take" of life to restore the heart's rhythm.

Brother David's simplicity in such a profound meditation stirred my own heart, giving it more time to make me aware of its rhythm. And then his punch line on for-give-ness (as opposed to always taking-offense, which was one of the most destructive forms taking can, well, *take*). For-giving, by contrast, is one of the most generous forms of giving. Christ, he suggests, took on the sins of humanity and for-gave them. Christ was the fullest model of the give-and-take of suffering and forgiveness, the great gift-giver. Grace was a given; it was freely given to us as a gift. We can take it or shun it. Somewhere I recalled here that it is better to give than to receive, to give rather than take.

Grace may then be God's way of showing us a gift without measure; and we can take it, accept it, or reject it. Our choice would determine how we entered into this give-and-take relationship with God. I thought too of Meister Eckhart's writings on compassion. Forgiveness is one of the highest expressions of compassion. In compassion we give—or for-give; in consuming, we take. How to allow compassion to replace consuming was a large challenge for me, one which I wished to transform into action.

I "took" his thoughts with me next day when I drove north of Portland to Souvie Island where I "took" a hike along the Columbia River on a beautiful cool sunny day, a gift God had "given" me without conditions. I watched enormous cargo ships glide up the river as I hiked to a lighthouse through the forest and through herds of cattle that made me skittish. These cud chewers looked at me suspiciously from above rheumy noses. I climbed a fence and walked gingerly by two bulls that suspected me of having an eye on their hefty harem. I tried to appear deferential, to give them a clear sense that these beautiful cows were just not my style.

I observed and moved within such a welcoming natural terrain with new eyes. It was a revelation to see throughout nature how the living and the dead existed side by side and how new life sprang from the decay of old matter. Some clotty soil suddenly let go along the bank of the river and slipped into the flowing stream. Motion and stillness, give and take, new life from old—the patterns continued to surface and I sensed that what had been invisible to me for so long was now revealing itself. All is revelation, all is relation, all is realization. The leaves, covered with dirt, reentered the earth, having fallen from great heights. It was fall and all was falling, returning to the earth and participating in an ancient cycle. Many of them already crispy brown, returned to replenish the soil for next year's growth.

As I walked, a leaf, acting very forward, spiraled down and landed on my cap. It wanted a last horizontal ride before finally falling on to the bank of the river. I obliged it. Water spiders jerked along the slick calm liquid surface as the Columbia River, deep and silent as God's presence in the stream of my own life, flowed without a ripple. We are each given a certain amount of time on this earth; we can spend that time taking or giving or combining the two. To give of one's time or person to another is one of the great gifts a person can bestow. Perhaps I must take the time to give it.

Leaves that had fallen into the water floated along the top, while each shadow followed and mirrored in shadowy similitude its twin floating along the shallow water close to shore. Dead logs and branches lined the muddy bottom. Leaves quietly hosted the sun, palms gently facing out. A leaf bobbed and weaved its meandering descent into the river. Sounds began to increase under the thick bushes to my left. A spider's web caught the sunlight in its gentle sway, and for just an instant, out of the corner of my eye, I noticed the filaments of perfect symmetry. This scene was too delicious to pass by, so I sat for a moment on an adjacent log to enjoy the patient and confident engineering of the web, still wet from last night's moisture.

This doubling of nature awoke in me the belief that I—each of us—was a double of God, a double of divinity; that what took place in the visible order was duplicated in me in a divine way. I waited for these instants of insight in the natural order, where God spoke quietly but clearly, if only I had the eyes and the ears to take it in by giving myself over to God's conscious presence.

Then, as I gazed at the web, it suddenly disappeared. For a moment I thought I had hallucinated it. But the sun's light had shifted just a shudder to the right to make it disappear. I knew the web was right there, almost where I could reach and touch it in its invisible presence between the two small shrubs to which it was anchored; an invisible presence now, yet I knew its existence was a matter of inches from my face. How many other webs were right in front of me, which I did not see because the attitude of the light, or because my angle of vision blinded me to them. I recalled once more the physicist's belief that we have visible to us only about four percent of the created order.

OK, but there are moments, like this one, as I shifted my position mere inches on the log, when again the spider web appeared to me as the sun once more caught it to make it magically visible to sight. So it must be that we can, depending on our disposition, see parts of the universe that may become visible when we are seated correctly or find the right angle for their appearance. It needn't move, but I must be willing to. I thought that this phenomenon could also reveal God to us through moments of grace, if grace were understood as a gift by which we are given an angle of vision of God. Grace is a light which, when slanted in the right attitude, reveals what is invisibly before us, pulsing its own reality, daring to be seen by anyone with sufficient grace to see. I felt welling up in me a gratitude inspired by grace and the gift of the imagination to be aware of what is now invisible, now visible. This, I thought, is what poets write about: those instants of vision when the light catches the invisible and allows the full measure to be seen for a moment in time.

St. Francis and a Spider's Web

Sitting alone on a log next to the deep flow of the Columbia River contemplating a peek-a-boo spider web and delighting at how little prompting I needed to enjoy the mystery of the world, no boundary existed between the physical and spiritual realms, between the natural order and supernatural presence, between the world's tangible body and its invisible gracefulness, between time and eternity. It was an instant of grace, freely given and gratefully taken; I found myself in the thick of the give-and-take of creation. All the low points, the loneliness, the feelings of depression, of sadness, of grief, of emptiness, of loss, of wanting to head home, evaporated in the face of this spider web, which had once more playfully disappeared. Its ability to remain on the margin between visibility and invisibility was its strength as the eyes of the insects it wanted to ensnare were so multi-faceted and keen that only a web that could disappear would ever snag them. This web's presence, when perceived, was akin to the effects true praying and authentic poetry had on the senses. Both of them made visible what was hidden in plain view, just in front or next to us or coming up from behind. Our failure was in lacking the right attitude by which to see it.

Both prayer and poetry make visible what is hidden in plain view, just in front of or next to us. My weakness was not having the right attitude by which to see it. I shifted my position.

Zen Web

The spider's mandala
rests serenely anchored like a large enmeshed
wheel between two scrub bushes linking forest
and river.
The sun gives it shape and an angle of clear vision.
It vanishes when the sun blinks behind
a swaying leaf.
The spider rests zen-like at the center, in perfect
zasen, waiting, praying, proud of its design it
spun from a memory it did not recall it had.
Only when the web fades, becomes clear
force, does the spider move wavily in mid-air
above the ground toward a small moth

flapping against the sticky filaments
of two scrub bushes, keeping the tension of the moth
between them, bow slightly toward one another.
Buddhists of the forest embrace the flame of death.

One evening I attended a *Lectio Divina* session hosted by Sister Jane. I had become interested in this traditional way of reading sacred texts out loud, slowly and repeatedly, as a way of praying more deeply. In this method, one meditates on (rather than analyzes) the words to allow what is evoked to surface for further and more deepened contemplation. I had no idea what to expect but decided long ago not to cower from any opportunity that presented itself on my journey. In attendance with me were three women. Sister Jane lit a candle, and then asked each of us to choose a stone from a box of stones and hold it quietly. She then proposed a question to us: what speaks through the stone to you? We each conveyed a thought or feeling that for us came through the stone. Then she gave us copies of Psalm 18 and we read it once, aloud, after which we were then asked to listen for anything that called our attention. The Psalm begins: "The heavens proclaim the glory of God / and the firmament shows forth the work of His hands. / Day unto day takes up the story / and night unto night makes known the message."

After each of us had spoken once, we were asked to read it again to deepen our reflection, and to express any further thoughts or feelings generated by it. On a third reading, we tried to amplify what we had already said, to repeat a line, if we liked, and to move into a slow, gentle, and deep breathing with our eyes closed. I found the verse "The rule of the Lord is to be trusted, / it gives wisdom to the simple" and repeated it to myself several time until I heard further into it. In the fourth reading we were asked to recognize in ourselves any deeper move to God through the Psalm's language and imagery. We were asked at each interval to voice aloud our own thought or insight; such public utterances deepened for each of us our own authentic revelations, making visible what had remained hidden. A calm and almost hypnotic atmosphere descended on us.

I loved this intimate connection between participants and between poetry and prayer; I found this exercise with the five of us insightful. I also recognized through it the layers of consciousness we are capable of moving through to deepen our reflections. This too was a form of prayer, by using an old method of praying through contemplating scripture, the psalms, or poetry, which opened the heart to new discoveries. The words, uttered to myself in the silence, began to alter my awareness of God through the words *trust* and *simple*. Much too complex did I tend to craft God; rather, what simplicity is the grace of God if it were accepted on those terms. My mind complicated what the heart knew to be a simpler truth. I meditated on these two words for several minutes in the silence and the warm community of the women and sensed that it was an act of creative imagining in which the myth that moved silently within me was invited to voice itself.

After this communal session, I was drawn to Father Keating's book *Open Mind, Open Heart,* in which he constructs a solid bridge between psychology and prayer, observing that as we recognize the traumas of our past life and the destructive tendencies in our present life, "contemplative prayer fosters the healing of these wounds. . . . If you are faithful to the daily practice of contemplative prayer, these psychic wounds will be healed without your being retraumatized" (*Open Mind,* 95).

Contemplative prayer, like the *Lectio Divina* exercise with the Psalm, was poetic in its nature in that it allowed the heart to be mindful and the mind to include the effect, the emotional response, as well. But to be open to the fullness of God, Keating suggests that on "our spiritual journey, the first thing the Spirit does is start removing the emotional junk inside of us. [God] wished to fill us completely and to transform our entire body-spirit organism into a flexible instrument of divine love" (96). His word *flexible* drew me back to the give-and-take elastic quality of Brother David's talk. Is it possible to sustain such a feeling and return to the everyday world with this feeling of being emptied of junk? Of feeling this gratitude to divinity for the simple pleasures I am now more attuned to? I knew that it could not be forced; either it became a part of me or it did not. What might decide its real efficacy was the presence of grace as a sustaining energy, to sustain the peace of mind that attended meditation.

I enjoyed a fabulous walk in the adjoining state park yesterday afternoon. Splashed yellow light fell on all the waiting leaves. I expected or longed for or desired nothing, content just to accept and love what the world offered. Was this that paradoxical sense of an empty fullness? A full emptiness? I was perfectly at peace, empty of desires. The gifts of time and circumstance became a wonderful few hours hiking in the woods, tramping along the soft spongy earth, listening to the birds scattered in the sunlight within the trees, and simply paying attention to everything I saw and heard, smelled and felt.

Later in my room I put on the headphones and listened to Sister Jose Hobday's audiotape, *The Spiritual Power of Storytelling*. She asks the simple question all of us who teach have repeated a thousand times: "What gives life in the classroom and how do we bring it to life?" She suggests we make life itself in the classroom by putting all the disparate parts of our experiences together. We might show students how to drink from their own well at the same time and not to drink solely from the well of others. We accept the loss, the drift, and the uncertainty of our lives and then pull all these pieces together into one narrative. Stories, she claims, are always happening; they have the power to affect our attitudes in every part of our day. She asks then a provocative question: "What do you linger over or lay your own life against?" To even begin an answer to it, one must deliberately take oneself out of the noise of the world and enter the space of contemplation. I took her advice to heart and thought about it for future teaching. Prayer was a personal narrative, a being present to the plot of one's own life and making it conscious. Plotting a prayer life, praying can become a way of remembering and retrieving that stitches parts of the variegated plot of my own life together into some coherent whole. In prayer I can welcome the ways my own plot thickens.

Wind and rain a day later introduced a fierce storm that dissolved the sunny, warm days of a protracted Indian summer. The change was a delight; I was happy to hunker down in my posh room, with its new curtains, thick carpet, and welcoming recliner that I coveted. I enjoyed the time to rest, to be leisurely and to move with the spirits' wishes. I listened to some more audiotapes, homing in especially on a fascinating one by the Jungian analyst John Sanford titled

St. Francis and a Spider's Web

Dreams: Your Royal Road to Healing. My tendency was to shy away from anyone promising me a royal road leading anywhere, but once I began listening to his animated voice, I yielded.

I especially liked his developing the connection between dreams and the realm of spirit. I recalled the dreams visited on Penelope by Athena in Homer's *Odyssey* or the dreams delivered by an angel to Joseph as he escapes with his family to avoid the murderous insecurity of Herod, or the dream of Pilate's wife who then warns her husband early the next morning to have nothing to do with this rebel Jesus, whom he will condemn in a few hours.

Sanford relates how both Sigmund Freud and C.G. Jung used dreams as the cornerstone of their respective psychotherapies. Dreams have historically carried the energies and images of gods and goddesses. The Biblical era called this realm of the human psyche a spiritual terrain. As a therapist, Sanford listened to thousands of his clients' dreams and discovered that no two were identical, though their themes and motifs had many cross-references. I soon realized that dreams, poetry, prayer, contemplation were all susceptible to the same impulse of the ego to interpret and limit their respective meanings in order to satisfy its own narrow impulses. Praying from an ego perspective sets oneself as the guide to whom one is praying.

Sanford relayed the novelist Isak Dinesen's belief that dreams are like smells; they decline to yield up their innermost Being to words. "In dreams," she suggests, "we forsake allegiance to an orderly, controlling maintained world" (*Dreams* cassette) Instead, we give ourselves over and even swear loyalty to a creative, imaginal force of the universe, what could be called God. Some authentic move to wholeness was at play here. These elements—dreams, poems, and prayer—shared common qualities that revolved around the imagination's place in our spiritual and emotional life.

Jonah, as Sanford related the myth on a second tape, is an important biblical figure chosen by God, but he resists, tries to hide, seeks shelter, and is eventually discovered by Leviathan rising unexpectedly out of the water. Who can hide from God? Adam and Eve tried to avoid His presence in the Garden. The Bible, Sanford related, is full of figures trying to escape their calling, their particular and unique vocation, like trying to live a life without suffering or sorrow (*Through the Belly of the Whale*). The bigger question for me was: When one suffers or falls into grief, what sustains the soul? When one is pulled into service, does one refuse or accept this task freely given by God to be taken or rejected? Perhaps the world needs to be served in just the unique way each person can offer, so refusing the call diminishes the entire world order. Would my own reluctance to surrender myself to a life of service rouse the whale? I watched my back.

Behind the large building at the center were the Stations of the Cross, set far apart on a meandering walking path in the woods. I had been drawn at the last several monasteries to the fourteen stations as mysterious stages for contemplation, rest stops on a journey of suffering and renewal. In grade school, I remembered their porcelain images along the interior walls of Holy Cross Church. Every Friday afternoon during Lent, all of us were marched to the church to recite the stations together. As an altar boy, if I was hungry, the incense steaming from the lit black wafer in its golden container would make me swoon. I hated lighting the hockey puck-sized clump because I would have to look directly over its ignition and breathe in the strange, otherworldly aroma directly. The red glow of the puck would ignite nausea in me. Swinging it back and forth in the air only increased my dizziness.

We all had our station booklets and would settle into the sing-song monotonous repetition of the same prayers as the priest and servers made the rounds from station one, Jesus is Condemned to Death, to fourteen, Jesus is Laid to Rest. Two figures always attracted my imagination when we came to their stories: at station five, a man called Simon of Cyrene is pulled out of the crowd by a Roman soldier and ordered to carry Christ's cross so that the prisoner would have enough life in him to be crucified on Golgotha. The second figure appeared like a mystery at number six. I was attracted to the young woman by the name of Veronica, which in Hebrew means "image of truth." She suddenly and voluntarily steps out from the crowd with a cloth or veil to wipe Jesus's face in a gesture of compassion. I imagined her as beautiful, dark-eyed, with smooth olive skin and a graceful figure. In spite of his deep suffering, Jesus would gaze with love and compassion at her as he offered her the only gift of which he was capable: an image of himself imprinted or embossed on her veil. Veronica and Simon were full and complex embodiments of the give-and-take of a spiritual life. Although Veronica gave of herself willingly, Simon had to be taken by force in his reluctance to ease Christ's burden. They remained the most intriguing figures for me from childhood on, and as I now walked the cinder path along the Via Dolorosa at the Franciscan center forty-five years later, I discovered that my earlier interest in these two figures was reignited.

Veronica is not mentioned by the evangelists in the gospels. Simon of Cyrene, however, is identified by Matthew, Mark, and Luke but not John. John reports that Jesus carried his own cross all the way to the top of Golgotha. Mark believes that the Romans "enlisted a passer-by, Simon of Cyrene, father of two sons, Alexander and Rufus, who was coming in from the country to celebrate Passover. He was quickly enlisted to carry Jesus's cross" (*The Jerusalem Bible*, 87). Minding his own business, perhaps, and drawn to the crowds lining the streets of Jerusalem to witness for himself what the commotion was about, Simon, I imagined, is any and every one of us, suddenly taken off guard, thrown off of our familiar path of complacency, and ushered into service, sometimes kicking in resistance, like Jonah.

Unlike Jonah, however, who initially offers one response to God's calling—flight—Simon steps forward. We don't know if he was frightened at being singled out, but one could bet he was. He was also quite possibly reluctant, resistant, and uncertain of what he was being forced to serve. Nonetheless, he shouldered the cross and thereby became one of the most intimate witnesses to Christ's anguish, his charity, and his sacrifice out of love.

Simon remains a powerful figure in my imagination. He embodied a response to a call to serve. Sooner or later, his story teaches, each of us is called out of the crowd to serve, to shoulder a cross, or to take on the burden of many crosses. But God, I believe, knows our limits and selects for each of us a cross of a particular size, weight, and textured roughness that we are capable of carrying, perhaps sharing the burden with someone who is incapable of taking up his/her cross without the aid of others. Crucifixion is both individual and communal.

Simon's image and response reminded me that so often in my life I could not carry my cross alone; I needed a Simon to come forward to assist me in the same determined way as I had followed others, shouldering their cross when needed. Perhaps we required a certain humility of giving over our cross to others at moments on our life's journey. As Jesus said in another context, "Inasmuch as you do this for the least of my brothers, you do it for me."

Simon accepts it and burdens himself with the cross of one who appears weaker than he. Perhaps, then, the image of Christ on Veronica's veil is *her* cross, one she might wear across her shoulders. Cloth, not wood, is her medium. The image is what she bears, one she reached out to cleanse in a humble act of love and courage for one oppressed and beaten. Christ offers her a gift, a miraculous one that mirrors her own unselfish heart. Her gesture is returned to her in his suffering image. If it were indeed a veil for a face covering, then the image of Christ on it would be one she saw through as she moved about in the world. Her image is a way of seeing, as Simon's is a way of being burdened. Christ's anguished bleeding sweaty face is her veronica.

Both the image on the veil and the cross shouldered are gifts freely given, freely taken. These stations depict simple but profound moments of faith that offer a passageway into the mystery of suffering and acceptance. In both image and cross resides the deep mystery of belief revealed. I saw for an instant the deeper purpose of these stories: an opportunity to step out of the certain and often predictable world of everyday life and intuit for an instant some deeper layer of this world through the presence of another reality just behind Veronica's veil and Simon's splintery cross. The spider web suddenly caught the light, and returned me to its full vision.

I thought too of this image, where some ironic twist is present in Simon's situation: here is this Roman centurion, part of the political system that will crucify Christ to protect itself. Christ's antagonist selects, seemingly at random, this pilgrim from Cyrene to serve as an assistant to this political execution. The centurion does not ask Simon; he orders him. Simon is not a fool, so he acquiesces; but I thought of the ironic way in which God moves in the world. Jesus's antagonist selects Simon so that the execution is properly carried out, a prophecy fulfilled. Rome cannot crucify a dead man; he must be at least partially alive for the punishment of political crucifixion to have its emotional impact on others.

Something about Simon I loved. He is called to help Jesus stay alive long enough to be sacrificed. He then sets the burden of the cross on his shoulder and, as an intimate witness, follows Jesus through the labyrinth of Jerusalem's streets, out the gate and up to the top of Golgotha. In the process of carrying the cross, I wonder, is Simon splintered by the wood's rough texture? Is there blood on it from previous crucifixions? Is Christ the first man? the second? the fortieth to be nailed to this wood? Does Simon linger in anguish and ambivalence for having served Rome and Christ at the same time, in order to witness the crucifixion that he has directly assisted in making possible? Is he changed on the journey as he observes people spit on Jesus and jeer at him while the suffering man bears it all without bitterness or hostility? What does he think when Jesus's own mother, along with other women who mourn for him, step forward to comfort the prisoner? What does he think of the courage of Veronica who steps forward out of the crowd, pulled by no soldier, to offer in her gesture immense compassion in a selfless act? Surely both women risk the whip from a Roman soldier as well as condemnation from those who line the streets calling for Christ's blood in hopes it will make their lives less threatening.

The story's mystery thickened as I shifted to Veronica's station, immediately next to Simon's. Who are these two souls that we should meditate on them as major figures in this drama of suffering and death prior to resurrection? They are ordinary, like me, yet they perform extraordinary acts of compassion in the face of cruelty and affliction. They are both powerful and sympathetic guides to anyone who steps onto the Via Dolorosa. Veronica's courage is different from Simon's. She cannot carry Christ's cross so she finds instead another way to serve him, to lighten his burden by offering him a small respite from his suffering. She thus comforts him as he walks. These two moments, the one taking the burden of the cross on himself, the other in a gesture of compassion comforting Jesus and being given his image in return, are simple but potent acts of courage.

The stations were themselves a complete micro-pilgrimage into deep psychological and spiritual truths as well as a sequence of poetic images to the life of Christ's example and teaching and now to his suffering and death. Both Simon and Veronica bear witness to this suffering by participating in it. Their examples reveal that I did not need to be crucified as Christ was; my life will have its own forms of crucifixion. But I did need to bear witness and to understand suffering on the extreme and brutal level that Christ lived it and to become more aware by bearing this witness. I felt too that I was approaching the heartbeat of the Christian mystery as I watched, from my cinder-covered path, this drama unfold once more between divinity and mere mortality and to witness the two coalesce. The stations suggested that this drama was to be witnessed as a form of direct participation. Simon and Veronica were figures that taught us how to witness by engagement. They did not just represent us; instead, they called us to share in the suffering of the world toward crucifixion so we might each contribute to the resurrection of ourselves and others.

As the light began to fade and the stillness on the path increased, a strange darkening descended on me, along with a jubilant feeling of illumination. I had sensed something unfold in this narrative with fourteen scenes that till now had been hidden. The fourteen instances of sorrow and compassion had illuminated some part of my own life that related to the suffering and compassion I had just witnessed.

My time in such a generous and deeply spiritual place tapered to a close as I packed my truck the night before leaving the center, the Portland area and Oregon. I would now travel east and south toward Utah as my journey created an arc. The drive would take at least two days. I hastened along in order to avoid the slippery predicament of an early snowstorm in Colorado. The weather here remained unseasonably sunny and dry. I did not want to push my luck. I bade goodbye to those who had treated me so well and headed out the next morning to pick up Highway 26 east.

I now understood from direct experience the great attraction people have for Oregon. It was a magical land, full of tiny towns with the friendliest people I met on the trip thus far. I drove through stunning ancient forests and into high desert terrain, by clear, fast-running streams. If I looked at just the right instant I would see a speckled trout propel itself out of the water into the sunlight. A clean and spacious state, it enjoyed a wide variety of terrains and weathers. That its entire West Coast abutted the Pacific Ocean was another of its joys.

On my truck stereo Celtic music increased my attraction to the open road and the leisure to enjoy it. It had been worth waiting twenty-eight years of teaching for this sabbatical; I cherished every day and realized that I had settled deeply into the groove of the pilgrimage's own devising, for it now possessed a life of its own and I was simply in the passenger seat, along for the ride. I did not ask if this pilgrimage was changing me, torquing my soul more toward God or making me a less self-absorbed person. Instead, I lived right now, for the Celtic music, for the harp and flute, for the wispy drum beat and the energy carried crisply in its ancient rhythms; I lived for the hot cup of coffee I had just bought at a diner tucked deep in tall pine trees next to a rushing mountain stream. I was satisfied with life and with my own spirit and with the rhythm of time that defined this universe I had been blessed to travel through. Some mysterious sense of the being of things pervaded each and everything I looked at, as if some veil had been lifted for a time and I could peer into the strange energy that surrounded all of creation. Something mystical hovered in the air and I tried not to breathe too deeply for fear of breaking the atmosphere open.

My first night out I discovered the town of John Day, named after a trapper with an interesting history. The town had the kind of aura that if one were drifting around the country looking to nest somewhere, this town might exert the strongest call. On October 12, my birthday, I treated myself to a rib-eye steak, baked potato, and a glass of musky Merlot. One of the patrons began a conversation by relating how John Day, a trapper in the 19th century, was found dead at the mouth of a nearby river that flowed through the town. Indians had stripped him naked; some insisted he was raped, then killed. The town bearing his name related the story that he was a villain at heart, and that his death was good riddance. After dinner, I walked the town and enjoyed the cool air at this altitude as well as the friendly open responses of its citizens.

As I walked I realized something stunning. I no longer believed in God. The word *belief* now seemed weak and inadequate. Instead, I felt his presence in every corner of my life. I had temporarily journeyed beyond belief. Within a deep sense of hope and joy, I realized this felt presence of God had been absent, pushed out in the service of busyness and career promotions. I rested comfortably and congratulated myself as I thanked God for allowing me to reach my fifty-fourth year on this earth. Tomorrow I would drive toward Utah and look for a campsite south of Ogden. The prospect of being on the road for several days excited me and kept me up much later than normal, but it was my birthday and time to exercise some liberties.

I fell asleep thanking God for looking out for my family, for protecting me on the road alone and sent a prayer of gratitude for sparing me from flat tires, mechanical problems, illness, sprained ankles or broken bones hiking, being robbed, beaten up, cheated, snickered at, lied to, or otherwise pummeled by a world that could be cruel in the extreme when it wanted to get one's attention.

On the way to Ogden, I paused at rest stops and information centers for suggestions for campsites along the way. Two women inside one of these centers were silently knitting when they weren't tending the adjacent restaurant. They hardly glanced up when I entered and I in turn hesitated to disturb them. One of them paused after a few moments and looked right past me: "Can we help you?" I glanced behind me to see if they were addressing someone who entered after me. They reminded me immediately, with their knitting, of the sisters of Fate knitting one's future in their quiet motion. One of them had deep brown furrows in her face, like those ridged ripples of skin under the jaw of a humpback whale. The other, more moon-faced, was fleshy, jolly, and did most of the spare talking. Both were kindly; deciding I was not a threat, they enthusiastically directed me to a campsite not 15 miles south, my direction. They were certain I would like it. I put my fate in their hands and decided to follow their directions after stopping for a quick lunch before continuing on to a sparsely-populated campground.

St. Francis and a Spider's Web

I entered the restaurant to get a sandwich and coffee. The young woman who waited on me had something on her tongue which glistened and clicked when she spoke. I stared at her mouth until I spotted the source of the light's reflection: a gold post pierced through the front of her tongue. I could not take my eyes off it when she spoke and decided, when she brought my coffee, to ask her why she wore it. Her story was poignant.

She related how she was twenty-two years old, married, with two young children. When she came to work each day, she passed her local high school and noticed most recently that many of the young women had body piercings, especially through the tongue and on other parts of their bodies. She then confessed in a lower voice, downrange of the regulars sipping coffee and watching us: "I needed to do something *for* myself and *to* myself to make me feel younger." I asked her if the tongue post accomplished that for her; she smiled and left to fetch my sandwich.

I wondered about her tongue, the organ of speech, and if she had thought of what the post did to her speaking but refrained from quizzing her further. I paid and pushed on to the campsite since now it was approaching late afternoon and I disliked pitching camp in the dark. I thought of this young woman as I drove and wondered if she and I shared the same desire to retrieve something from our past. Part of this pilgrimage's intention was to reclaim some feeling, some felt sense of wholeness and serenity that I had experienced before but seemed to have misplaced. I thought too that I was attempting to retrieve a time of a deeper, simpler faith and that I had been led on this pilgrimage to do so. The young mother/waitress had given her body something it could feel every time she spoke. I can still hear the post gently clicking against the back of her teeth when she uttered certain words.

I found Three Island Crossing camping park and was delighted to find that it was not crowded; in fact, only three other campsites were occupied. I pitched my tent close to the river and looked across its narrow expanse to a cliff that climbed at least one hundred feet. Close to the top, I spotted adobe huts carved directly into the mountain. My binoculars showed me there was no one inhabiting them; I liked the idea that these old Native American homesteads would be gazing down at my campsite, even as the thought passed that I might try to scale the mountain and sleep in one of them tonight. Only then did I realize how tired I was.

Firewood was plentiful; the air was still, birds gathered in the trees above my tent, and I delighted in my surrounds with the sound of the river making low swishing sounds as it passed within a few feet of my tent. I fell asleep slowly, looking through the nylon tent's roof to the adobe dwellings above me and wondered what people built them and when. I slipped back in time and deep into sleep.

Next morning I broke camp and headed south and east to Salt Lake City. I must camp or stay in a motel one more night before my reservation allowed me to enter the monastery. I stopped once again at an information center close to the causeway of the Great Salt Lake. An old woman, alone and palsied, who served as a volunteer every Tuesday and Thursday, directed me to "Primitive Camping" over the seven-and-a-half-mile causeway to Antelope Island. I thanked her before heading across the sulfur-smelling water of the Great Salt Lake, where I eventually found the campsite. Were those buffalo grazing? I tried to follow the map and sight-see simultaneously. The sun was bright, the air a pleasant seventy degrees and only a few campers inhabited this primitive area that ran right to the shoreline of the Great Salt Lake. A Porta-Potty served as the only restroom facilities. I vowed to make the best of it and pitched my tent in an open space close to some small trees and scrub bushes. I had a modest rib eye steak left, a potato that I sliced and fried for dinner, and one last corn on the cob I steamed. I saved one cookie from a small packet for desert.

I built a fine fire in my site; I noticed that the wind was picking up across the water so I let the fire burn down. Everything was tinder-dry and the landscape looked more like a desert with a thin lather of grass. These plains were once the home of thousands of bison that roamed freely as part of one of the biggest herds in North America. Many were grazing near the camp when I arrived. Two campers occupying a site close to me dismantled their tent and gear, filling their van, and left just before dark, leaving only one other camper and me. I wondered why they would leave at this late hour, as I arranged my own tent and climbed in just before nightfall. I was soon to learn they knew something I didn't: the weather forecast. The wind increased steadily and began flapping the tent in answer to my query.

By the light of a candle I tried to ignore the noise from the flapping tent and read of the nature of sabbatical. It included a phrase I liked: "the wisdom of dormancy" as Wayne Muller described it (7). Biblically, "to pray," means "to come to rest" (25), which this journey was allowing me time to do. As I began to fall asleep, I thought of the monks in the places I had stayed and their special relation to time, their rhythmic days of prayer, work, solitude, contemplation, rest and when in the days' rhythm they occurred. What does this rhythm promote or cultivate in them over many years? I wondered. Some new relation to time had infiltrated me. I felt time's powerful and invisible flow, its forceful and silent movement, like the movement of God through matter. Eternity in time was the sensation that overcame me as I fell into a hard sleep.

Around 11 p.m. three carloads of rowdy revelers sped into the camping area, across from me just on the other side of the small dirt road. I realized then that it was Saturday night. They were drinking heavily and soon had a massive bonfire roaring in the wind, its sparks carried dangerously into the surrounding brush. At times they sounded like they were right outside my tent, a thought that disturbed me greatly, as did the possibility that sparks from their huge fire would blow on to my nylon housing. Slowly and quietly, I dressed in case there was trouble. I was alone with no other campers around me. The wind, however, had been accelerating; what I thought of as a growing threat as I fell asleep I now felt was my ally. Their voices rose to compete with the wind gathering momentum from across the lake. The temperature had dropped and I sank deeper into my sleeping bag, fully awake, listening for any unwelcome guests' footsteps outside. It sounded like there might be between eight and ten people; the wind carried their voices so swiftly that at any given time I was certain they were just a few feet from my head.

By 1 a.m. the wind had risen to a howl. The walls of my tent blew in and out like small explosions of cloth. Truck doors slammed and two of the three vehicles squealed out at high speed. The others had pitched a tent and settled in. No more voices now, only the wind rattling my tent in its attempts to lift it out from under me. Its sides continued to pop and explode with the erratic wind. I knew that I would not sleep at all if I remained in it.

At 2 a.m. I capitulated, gathered my sleeping bag and stumbled out of the tent into a violent wind that pushed me over against a series of scrub bushes before I was able to climb into the driver's seat of the truck, where I dropped the seat back and wrapped the sleeping bag around me. The truck rocked in the wind like a sailboat on aggrieved waters. The best I was able to do was doze for a few minutes at a time. Eventually dawn began to show itself through the blowing sand and dirt. The lake's shallow waters were whitecapped and hostile. When I could see enough to look around, I noticed the last campers had left during the night. I was the only survivor of last night's storm.

My tent had blown down, but a large rock I put on its floor kept it from sailing to Colorado. I turned on the radio to hear a report that the winds had been blowing at forty-five miles per hour; storms were coming in bringing snow of up to eight inches above seventy-five hundred feet. I was at six thousand feet here so I would miss the first snow blast of the season. No moisture yet, but the wind's strength had covered the road with sand, making sections of it invisible. The sky was a pure blue.

I found a bathroom after breaking camp and cleaned up the best I could, then headed out toward Huntsville, due east. Grit and sand were still in my teeth, eyes, and hair. The truck's heater was a gift, and I warmed up for the first time since the previous afternoon.

My spirits lifted, I marked the event as the only occasion on the entire voyage when I felt frightened for my security. White fluffy clouds that followed the storm coated the sky in the storm's residue as I drove to the monastery's entrance, a beautiful snaking lane lined with cottonwood trees. When I pulled into the driveway and looked at the entrance, I felt safe and renewed; I had arrived at another home. Bluster had transformed into Blessings.

11

Lowing Cows
and Abandoned Heifers

Our Lady of Trinity Trappist Monastery, Huntsville, Utah

> My narrative self (the culprit who has invented) wishes to be dis-
> covered by my reflective self, the self who wants to understand and
> make sense of a half-remembered story about a nun sneezing in
> the sun. —Patricia Hampl, "Memory and Imagination"

PASSING THROUGH the barrel-shaped entrance that opened to a courtyard and housed the bookstore and registration office, I was grateful for two things: one was having stepped out of the monastic world for a few days to assess what I was doing (if not beginning to answer some of the whys for doing it). The other was gratitude at reentering the world of solitude, serenity, and silence. Or so I thought.

Michael ran the bookstore where I registered. He invited me to look throughout the store at the various honey containers pro- cessed by the monks as one source of income. An interesting and engaging fellow, Michael taught for a time at Fordham University but believed he had found his home here. He showed me to my room on the second floor of the guesthouse, which had bathrooms at the end of each hall. I noticed that many of the doors were open, a sign that few souls were retreating here.

First impressions were always important on my journey, and I liked my room immediately. It had a rounded ceiling, which sloped quickly down one wall. I rearranged the bed, chairs, and table to suit me. I was in number seventeen, called "All Saints Room." Next to me was empty number fifteen, "St. Patrick Room," and I thought for a moment of shifting to my baptismal name's site but realized I could use *all* the saints who gathered in my room, so I settled in.

The monastery was in ranch and cattle country. Founded in 1947 by the Trappists, the spread was massive, with hundreds of cows and calves grazing in infinite space under a blue Utah sky. Behind the monastery, mountains loomed up as a wall to shelter it from weather. About twenty monks now made this place their permanent home.

Later in the day I talked with Father Gerald, who lamented the big money coming into the area to develop the valley into a ski resort. He and the other monks realized that the days of solitude and open space would in a few years give way to tourists seeking to ski down the mountains, which were currently virginal and silent grazing land for the herd. He related how Nada Hermitage, which happened to be next on my itinerary in Colorado, had to shut down its Sedona, Arizona monastery and their Nova Nada Hermitage in Nova Scotia because of developers and logging companies. Solitude and silence were big draws in empty spaces; the developers revealed an excessive appetite for wanting to saturate these pockets of solitude with recreation sites. We spoke about how this compulsive behavior was so much a part of the culture generally. I was grateful to be here to enjoy the expansive solitude and silence before they were stolen from one more occasion for sacred renewal.

God's presence was much harder to sense when I was out of the monastic setting. The noise and distractions of the world competed with the silence of God, and the racket often won. He was blotted out. God comes not always in a firestorm but in whispers, in a slanted voice so still that I thought I heard something whispering to me as I sat reading in my room. Prayer was a means to open the heart to hear this whispering God, the God most often present in the soft breeze, not in the whirlwind; in the darkness of night, not in the bright sun of midday. At night, after dinner, I walked along the road that led to the main highway and enjoyed the animals grazing in their fenced enclosures on both sides of the drive.

Lowing Cows and Abandoned Heifers

Absent for a while, my father visited me again and walked with me. He told me how his alcoholism had prevented him from doing much with his sons and that drinking, or the thought of drinking, kept him self-enclosed and blotted out most leisure for hiking the woods, camping, playing ball or seeing a movie together. I remembered with sadness how I had never been to a ball game or to a movie with him. So consuming is the disease of alcohol that even when not drinking, one still lives incarcerated in the disease, which forecloses on most other activities. My response to him was that I had watched him struggle in his spiritual life to be better and that I had picked up this positive habit of his. As a result, I was on this pilgrimage and happy to have him accompany me. Guilt and shame also accompanied me as part of his heritage, but his death had somewhat diminished the power of these two crippling emotions.

As the sun began to set over the spacious and sacred landscape, I came upon a magnificent horse that wanted to talk, her head thrust over the fence, gazing at me. I approached and petted her face for a moment. Her large black oily eyes stared into mine and I saw a miniature of myself, convexed. Later I thought of the divinity in animals, how God was in all things of His creation, and perhaps in a special forceful way in animals. Their unself-conscious nature, their graceful gestures and movements embodied a peace and tranquility I admired and envied. The gaze of the horse soothed something wild in me as I remembered her look with fondness:

> I wonder if the Palomino
> standing in deep meditation
> among the wheat the color of her,
> tail taut in the shape of a
> large graceful question mark
> that begs no answer,
> knows just how beautiful she is
> in a gaze as serene as divinity
> itself.

How was writing itself an act of contemplation? Even more, how was it or can it be a form of prayer? Later in my stay I listened to a tape by the spiritual writer Anthony Padavano in the library of the monastery. He explored this question of writing and contemplation and the place of these exercises in Thomas Merton's life. His thoughts coalesced some of my feelings relating writing, poetry, and prayer to meditation.

Padavano believed Merton had two passions in his life: writing and the monastic vocation. He was an impulsive monk who wanted to accept all invitations to travel but was pulled back into solitude because of a competing desire to allow silence to ripen and sustain his spiritual life. But that same silence intensified his longing to communicate to a wide audience through words: "Thomas Merton believed there existed a relation between writing and non-violence. Wordless people are violent because they cannot express themselves any other way. Wordlessness leads to violence; silence to non-violence" (*Thomas Merton: A Life for Our Times* audiotape).

Where was prayer in this idea? I thought of prayer as a way of giving God a voice in my life to suppress violence. My father visited me again as I thought of violence and non-violence. His own enraged outbursts that often ended in physical violence every weekend during my youth surfaced after he had drunk enough to become verbosely inarticulate; his rages were futile but persistent attempts to find his own voice, unlocked now by the booze, but it was a voice of violence suppressing great shame and timidity. My own tendency to rage easily occurs without the booze; I did not need to drink to enter the chaos of rage, the door to which seemed always to be just a few feet away and always ajar. The dark side of being traumatized is a seething rage each family member entered, like a dark tunnel, which breathed in and then expressed in our own style. Rage, I realized, had a unique style, its expressive design. I was beginning to see mine up close.

I was shocked into recognition as I listened to Padavano state that the most real thing about us might be how we feel. Domestic violence had a voice too, a form of distorted or grotesque prayer, for it too was asking for divine assistance. I thought of how this pilgrimage continued to offer me the grace to deal with my own feelings of rage, which I sensed was a patterned response learned at home. Merton's own words helped me here when he claimed that prayer works not when it tries to reform others but when we see our emotions and feelings in a keener way. Praying may be an imaginal act in which what has been reduced, muted, or hidden from us in our lives—making us numb in parts of our response to the world—is again reanimated. Praying is an act of a resurrected imagination seeking God in all things.

So proud of how different I was from my father, this retreat was revealing to me the painful truth that I might be more like him than were any of my brothers or sister. What a revelation! Like Oedipus, I thought I was avoiding the confrontation with the father, being with and like the father, and in the process of escape I careened directly toward him. Prayer was my guide that brought me here; I could hardly breathe as this recognition suffocated me. My father's image continued to surround me during my entire stay, even finding its way into my dreams, where I envisaged specific scenes of violence buried now for over forty-five years. A deep darkness wrapped itself around this revelation that I made a conscious decision to carry with me, like a cross, not in self-loathing but in self-awakening. This incident revealed yet another way the cross appeared to me now; I bore the cross of my father's rage and violence as well as his impulse to the spiritual life. The tension between these contrary impulses made him suffer intensely in silence. I carried it behind him and felt both the wickedness and the blessedness of this burden and where I was in the crux of the cross, where the two beams met.

The dark and light of him was always together, but trauma forced us all in the family to dwell on the darkness. I laughed out loud to realize that I was here because of his alcoholism and his quest for freedom from it through a spiritual corridor, which may have been more like an escape hatch. I recognized as well that, like Merton, I had a similar hunger to write, almost an obsession to scribble. It may be excessive, which fits the pattern, as excess is so frequently a byproduct with adult children of alcoholics. We found another form of booze, another excess, but one that I could make peace with if it helped me to control my rage—the real weight of the cross. When I felt the encumbrance of the cross, I felt less shame, more a part of a continuum of excess, both in my emotions and in my spiritual hunger. To separate the angels from the demons would do a great disservice to the soul, so I had to learn to live with both of their powerful energies. The tension between these conflicting impulses made both of us suffer intensely in silence.

IN SERMON NUMBER 3, Meister Eckhart used as the source of his reflection the words of Matthew: "Do not be afraid of those who kill the body but cannot kill the soul; fear him rather who can destroy both body and soul in hell. Can you not buy two sparrows for a penny? There is no need to be afraid; you are worth more than hundreds of sparrows" (10:28–31). Trust rested behind this insight. Could I trust with my whole heart that the directions I believed I chose were really a cooperative between God and myself? Fear cancelled out trust. A desire that grew in me here with the Trappists was to learn to know and to trust, and in the process to damp down fear-based thought.

As I sat in deep meditation in the library after listening to the tape in my room, a man entered with a transistor radio that he held close to his ear, but the music could be heard throughout the room, violating the silence. He saw me look up when he entered and asked: "Does the radio bother you?" Stupidly, I responded that it didn't when it clearly did. Wrong generosity. He sat for a moment on the couch across from me and flipped through a small pile of magazines, with one hand while holding his radio to his ear with the other. Then, restless, he rose, perused the shelves for a moment, then headed out the door. Silence slowly and stealthily crept back into my space. Silence, I thought, can be terrifying even in the security of a monastery.

At dinner that night this very retreatant told us all that he came to this same monastery from California every year for a week. I sensed, when he launched into an argument with another retreatant over Bill Clinton's behavior with Monica Lewinsky as well as Saddam Hussein's terrorism, that the meals we enjoyed together would allow no silence or even modest conversation. Finally, another retreatant, a quiet priest, suddenly exploded in our midst: "Why do you have to bring all that crap to the table? Can we not eat in peace?" The two men arguing behaved as if the priest never spoke and continued arguing.

I quickly finished my meal, cleared my place and walked into the hall. I planned to help clean up but could not abide continuing in the toxic space created by the few. How grotesquely frightening anger looked and sounded like and how empty the conversation became when it centered on arguing, with each side deaf to the words of the other. I learned later that the man from California with the radio stuck to his ear would be departing in two days; I offered a short prayer of gratitude. How fragile was the contemplative atmosphere that most of us had come to cultivate and deepen. The tension caused by arguments over political topics of the day deflected the contemplative life and reduced social interaction to just short of a brawl. I tried to quiet myself by retreating to the solitude of my room to read.

The next day snow was forecast. It rained heavily as the temperature continued to drop; winter slid across the tops of the mountains and into the plains. The library was an inviting space when quiet, with its old floor lamps, its puffy soft couches, an old faded red carpet on the floor, and the built-in wooden bookshelves sagging slightly under the weight of well-used texts. I sipped hot tea with monks' honey sweetening it and read Merton's engaging *Contemplative Prayer*. Silence at this moment was complete and full; it carried a delicious quality of peace with it, like the honey made by the bees. Their thick liquid had now dissolved in my tea and made it more pleasurable to drink. I could not resist an analogy to the prayer life, which appeared like the honey in my tea life. It gave life itself a texture and a sweetness not possible any other way. Invisible, swirling out of sight in the tea's dark water, it nonetheless changed its character by enriching each sip.

Merton cites one Abbe Monchanin, whose words spoke directly to me in this moment of deep serenity: "For us let it be enough to know ourselves to be in the right place where God wants us, and carry on our work, even though it be no more than the work of an ant, infinitesimally small, and with unforeseeable results" (qtd. in *Contemplative Prayer*, 12). Great solace emanated from his words. I still did not have a clear purpose for this pilgrimage but had made progress by relinquishing a nagging desire to make a checklist of things to accomplish. More than two months now away from home, I yielded completely to the rhythm and the power of the pilgrimage, letting it guide me rather than my assuming control. I trusted with absolute certainty in God's plan for me and found solace in the uncertainty of it. Tolerating uncertainty brought comfort. Accepting or embracing uncertainty endorsed a deeper sense of freedom. I recalled once again Simon of Cyrene, who took up Christ's cross in a cloud of unknowing and who accepted the burden as part of his calling, however unwillingly he may have initially received it. Such a surrender into freedom was an act of the will, which began by accepting uncertainty and ambiguity. If monastic prayer "is prayer of the heart" (20), as Merton suggested, then that is the place from which I felt my trust in God had its rich genesis.

The first monks who appeared in Egypt and Syria practiced prayer in phrases or sentences, not in elaborate rituals. For example, they might say "Oh, God, come to my aid." My own brief prayers included "Dear God, protect us from harm" and "God, give me strength to do your will." These short sentences contributed to a sense of well-being. Even writing them now, I feel their calm and centering power. Through them early monastics learned to empty themselves so they could devote their entire lives "to love and service of God. This love expressed itself first in their love for God's word" (21), especially in the Psalms, God's own poem-prayers. The Psalms had the power to "reveal the secret movement of the heart" as it struggled against negative forces that sought to disrupt this emptying. The early monks believed that the heart alone expressed one's deepest inner truth.

I delighted in this connection of prayer to poetry and how the Psalms and *The Song of Songs* blended spirit and soul through a form of imagining that wedded two immense worlds. Prayer and poetry shared a kindred recognition of how important it is to move the imagination into a meditative space, there to transfer one's normal mode of perceiving and moving into a deeper seeing than ordinary perception. In addition to the Bible, nowhere is this connection sustained with poetic beauty more than in Dante's epic poem of one's soul pilgrimage from obscurity to sanctity, his *Commedia*.

For example, at the beginning of Canto 11 of *Purgatory*, Dante begins with a poetic rendering of The Lord's Prayer:

Our Father, dwelling in the Heavens, nowise
As circumscribed, but as the things above,
Thy first effects are dearest in Thine eyes,
Hallowed Thy name be and the Power thereof,
By every creature, as right meet it is
We praise the tender effluence of Thy Love. (1–6)

His entire journey, which he engaged as a pilgrim and then recollected as a poet, illustrated on every page how the heart slowly progresses toward accepting itself and God's grace at the same moment in love. It became clearer how reading or chanting scripture in the morning with the monks, as well as reading, writing, and meditating on poetry, may have a similar salutary effect on the heart: to move it to a state of emptiness where wishes and desires are temporarily quieted: prayer as nada, poetry as a path to nothingness. St. John of the Cross, whose *Dark Night of the Soul* had been calling me to be read it, writes that in contemplative prayer, "the soul, stripped of desire, moves in peace and tranquility" (82) and receives thereby "a secret, peaceful and loving infusion from God" (84). Poetry, uttered aloud and meditated upon rather than analyzed, could usher the soul into a state similar to what John of the Cross suggests. The key word was *infusion*.

The poet Rainer Maria Rilke offers a beautiful poem that unites poetry and prayer in simple language, in

The Poet Speaks of Praising

Oh, speak, poet, what do you do?
                    —I praise.
But the monstrosities and the murderous days,
how do you endure them, how do you take them?
                    —I praise.
But the anonymous, the nameless grays,
how, poet, do you still invoke them?
                    —I praise.
What right have you, in all displays,
in every mask, to be genuine?
                    —I praise.

And that stillness and the turbulent sprays
know you like star and storm?
                    —since I praise.
(*Rilke on Love and Other Difficulties*, 65)

The world's particulars, in whatever form they assumed, are objects of praise, a form and a forum for prayer, which resonate a persuasive healing quality. In the stillness of my walks where hundreds of cows and calves grazed, I yearned to be more fully in conversation with God and the natural world poetically. Some boundary had collapsed between the world's matter and me. The mystical writers of the church appeared to share one common belief: prayer was a way to connect with the mystery of divine love. But a certain harmony of heart was needed to reach this mystery as well as recognition of the world's matter as sacred. Rilke's praising poem earlier witnessed this mystery's accessibility.

In *Contemplative Prayer* Merton meditates on how interior prayer heightens the importance "of the activity of the Spirit within us" (49). Prayer became a way of imagining God's mystery, an attempt to fathom God other than through sense perception. When I entered it in openness, it nudged me to the edge of mystery and to the ineffable, to glimpse a deeper, more fully-formed view of the world. In prayer a veil was temporarily pulled aside and the heart's knowing revealed the seamlessness of creation and God's love within it. Reason was suspended momentarily, the intellect quieted, so that a response to what Merton believed was "the deepest ground of our identity in God" (46) could emerge. The Psalms drew me to them, both in the morning office in the chapel with other retreatants and the monks, as well as when I hiked the hills surrounding the monastery. Sincerity, simplicity, and even a deep silence, out of which all authentic prayerful and poetic speech originated, comprised the core of prayer, as silence resonated from our prayers uttered aloud.

What I learned in this meditation was that any residual resentment, anger, remorse, guilt over past mistakes, all worked diligently to block and cloud this clarity of vision and feeling. They were obstacles that occluded any deep communion with God and my life's purpose. Dissolution was a necessary act for me, to let dissipate into the air these negative and destructive energies that retarded renewal with God and forgiveness of myself.

The Psalms were poems that in their subtle power collapsed the gap between poetry and prayer, almost as a salve will assist a wound in healing over. Psalm 4, like so many, contained both a plea and a petition:

> Answer me when I call, O God of
> My right! You gave me room when I was
> In distress. Be gracious to me and hear my prayer.

These simple lines reminded me of how much of identity was tied to voice and ear. Being heard by God was as important, the Psalm suggests, as simply being. I recognized how important it was to me that God heard me in my deepest desires:

> God has set apart
> The faithful as God's own.
> God hears when I call.

The poem affected me in a couple of ways: it is both a meditation on faith as well as a poetic response to that fidelity. It also invited me into a reverie of God's mysterious actions, which I was not asked to understand but to accept. God's own order of being opened through the Psalm to inspire a hope fuller than I had known or felt before. Some level of gratitude and thanksgiving united me with a ripening awareness, which seeped through the poem as a prayer, much as ground water occasionally breaks to the surface to moisten a parched land.

The monks intuitively knew this connection between poetry and prayer. Merton notes that the monk abandons the world "only in order to listen more intently to the deepest and most neglected voices that proceed from its inner depth" (25). To listen intently is to withdraw from the source of the noise, even to abandon it so that one can hear what one needs in being guided. Pilgrimage was certainly moving into a new space, but it also included retreating from some places, things, or persons in order to clear a ground to see more and to gain a clearer apprehension of their meaning. Memory allowed this to happen. My own question was: will I have been gone long enough to gain this new place of seeing and understanding? Again, as I placed my trust in God, I ceased worrying about the "right time" or the "right distance" in order to give such a shift a chance.

Very difficult breathing last night. I awoke at four after finally falling asleep only a few hours before the monks awakened. The bells were just outside my window, so I was up with them each morning, willing or not. The thin oxygen at this high altitude had begun to take its toll, along with the bells. I rose in the dark stillness and flicked on the desk lamp, folded my sleeping bag and rearranged the furniture in the room again, trying to get the space right. The ceiling sloped quickly down to bump my head as I performed early morning housecleaning. When I sat in the wooden chair by the desk, the right side of my head came to within an inch of the ceiling. Jonah in his tiny ship cabin.

The shower this morning felt good, in spite of someone's hair trying to gob the drain. I liked the fact that the monks made coffee for us very early, so there was always a fresh pot brewing, even before five, and its aroma crept upstairs. The early hours remained my favorite time of day, when my thoughts were clearest, my meditations closest to God, and a sacred sense of a new day birthing renewed my thoughts and feelings. I wrote in my journal each morning and allowed whatever presented itself to be recorded, along with any thoughts or images that attended them. I had learned to trust this play of analogy in the imagination for what it might yield. This morning the following words were waiting: "we each in our own way must suffer the passion, rejection, and scourge of Christ in our own way. It will insist on being part of every one of our lives. The cross is the crux of a life fully lived." Then, "no crisis occurs without some good coming from it—it is always a sign of God's compassion for us."

I continued to read Julian of Norwich's *Revelations* and discovered in her praying over the wounds of Christ a deep insight into his afflictions being occasions for divine grace. She comprehended the connective tissue between illness, affliction, woundedness, and revelation. What I learned from her is that not only do wounds grace our lives but that grace also wounds our lives. Grace as a wounding experience startled me, yet it had the scent of something right about it. Christ's own destiny needed the five wounds he received, wounds that covered his entire body from head to feet. Julian forced me to consider more deeply the wounds the world inflicted on me, as well as the wounds I had inflicted on others; they were both opportunities for change, for becoming conscious of what a pre-wounding consciousness did not allow me to be aware of. Grace could be present both through and in affliction. Where and when we are wounded or where we wound the world might be the most cogent occasions of grace's intrusion into our lives.

This morning, however, the atmosphere was turbulent outside. From the large grazing fields arose the sound through my window of hundreds of cows lowing like a sustained choric mourning, even grieving. It was light enough now, so I gazed out my window into the distance. The rain last night had frozen and iced the domes of the black mountains. What a magnificent sight in the grey light: confectioner's sugar sprinkled generously over the mountains of sweets. But why the doleful sounds from the cattle?

At breakfast I learned that last night initiated the annual ritual separation of the calves from their mothers. When I had watched yesterday evening from the barbed wire separating the fields how the mothers and calves were all herded into a large pen, I did not know what was soon to follow. As they entered together, each calf was quickly plucked from its mother's side before she could react. Then there ensued a slow rustling that transformed quickly into a turbulent panic as the mothers were released back into the field minus their babies.

Now, Thursday, they walked out of the barns and into the fields to stand individually or in groups of two and three, all of them looking at the ground and lowing in unison. Their grief reminded me of the image of Rachel standing in the field of wheat weeping over the loss of her children. Then, as if sensing that they each needed more room to moan in singular grief, the cows separated out all over the field, no longer taking solace in one another's loss. Each called in her own unique voice across the acres and into the frozen ice resting on the mountains. It was a sad time; no one escaped the deep sound of their loss that echoed off the mountains and returned amplified to the monastery.

Twelve hours later, instead of quieting, their aching cries for their babies had doubled in intensity and filled the entire valley in the calm frosty air. Their children had mysteriously disappeared, and the mothers, now drifting alone across the wet fields, stretched out their necks in persistent and unrelenting sorrow, as if to disgorge some obstruction in their throat, a bolus of grief, and lowed deep into the gathering night air. Mothers in solid black coats of mourning, they did not suspect that the mourning ritual would find them attired in the color of grief and loss, engaged in a pageant of pitiful suffering. They would cry their dirge for three nights in all, the monks warned us. It was a lowly sound that even seeped into the chapel, there to blend with and then overtake the Gregorian chant. The sound was so deep it made my bones vibrate and pulled me into their grief. I grieved with them and remembered all the precious things in my own life I had had taken from me.

After Mass and a light breakfast, I dressed warmly and slogged out in the snow to hang on the barbed wire and grieve with them. Something about the presence of animals, their moods and gazes, enriches the spiritual atmosphere whenever they are present. But this herd of cows made us all feel the acute sense of loss that life never tired of presenting to each of us.

The calves, meanwhile, penned in several acres away across the road and against the other mountain range that framed this grief-stricken valley, echoed in their voices the cry of their mothers in the darkness. Grief felt deeply was such a solitary act; it seemed to defy sharing. But it could be heard and felt wherever loss created a wound and left dark acres of ache in the terrain we tread within us.

Darkness and silence reclaimed the monastery to absorb all the grief of another year's ritual separation of mother and children, another give-and-take pattern of life. These two experiences had been growing in me to try to describe God. God's dark world was working itself deep within me. The less I did, the better. I walked in the morning before Mass and breakfast amid the cloak of deep silence that covered the natural order. The cows were all in the barn, resigned now and silent, completely exhausted after three full days of grieving. Their babies were gone and the mothers' ritual mourning had ceased. Yeats's poem, "The Stolen Child," carried the refrain that captured these sad days:

> Away with us he's going,
> The solemn-eyed:
> He'll hear no more the lowing
> Of the calves on the warm hillside;
> Or the kettle on the hob
> Sing peace into his breast.

As the dawn began its subtle shading from darkness into a pallid light, I hiked up a large hill close to the monastery; I could hear animals rustling in the thick bush. Then all became silent, and this silence wanted to be heard. I looked down as I hiked and saw something of a different color, which made it stand out against the green shrubs. I picked up the lower hind leg of a small deer. All the skin still clung persistently to the meager flesh, soft and hard against the bone, like a very thin but elegant carpet without padding. Its black and glossy split hoof was still intact, smooth to the touch and elegant in shape.

The leg had been gnawed off, perhaps by coyotes or wolves. I doubted that the leg had been detached for long; its tan-and-white hide was still fresh, clean, and alive. I fingered the dainty split hoof, so thin and elegant. Too thin, I thought, to support the weight of such a large animal. The smell of it was of a live rather than decaying animal, gamy and musky. I placed it by a rock and sat down beside it. The silence immediately wrapped me in its thick embrace. In this instant I felt the presence of God's grace. I loved sitting here, in solitude, with the firm companion of silence protecting me and the leg of a deer for a marker.

Later that day I would read in Merton's *Thoughts in Solitude*: "There are few who are willing to belong completely to such silence, to let it soak into their bones, to breathe nothing but silence, to feed on silence, and to turn the very substance of their life into a living and vigilant silence" (87). Hard words. An implicit challenge. If God called each of us to Him in and through something that person was attracted to, then He calls me through silence.

I turned my attention back to the gnawed leg of the deer. What was so fascinating and frightening about its dismemberment, its separation from the whole? The rest of the animal had surely been eaten so that others could live. The leg was a remembrance. In its severed state it revealed both life and death in one appendage. What would it be like to wear it, to drill a hole through its bone and loop it from a chain around my neck, to carry something of the animal's spirit against my chest? The sheer shininess of the black hoof looked as if it had been buffed by hand with a soft oil rag. I felt a reluctance to leave it, but I dropped it back to the earth. The leg had a mythic quality to it, some magic, like a talisman.

Was this desire to carry and wear the animal, to be the animal, part of ancient people's mythologies to connect them in story to the animal world and the animal spirit? I could not deny my feelings of attraction and awe over the dismembered leg. Amputated, it carried a mysterious power that I felt through my hand when I held it. I thought too of the separation of the calves, the dismemberment of families, of wounds that give life, of the man who could not separate himself from the noise of his radio. Silence itself can be a dismembering experience.

I liked Merton's words: "to belong completely to silence." I can belong most to silence in the early morning darkness, where God's presence is felt with greatest porousness. I asked myself: *Where does silence lead me? What does it nourish within me? How am I nourished by silence?* Even when I say the word—*silence*—I can feel it enclose me in a condition of openness. I think of all the sounds in the world, including speech, and realized that everything was born out of the deep sea of silence. "In the beginning was the silence before the first sounds," a variation on John's Gospel where the word is revealed as the origin of the world. My friend Charles Asher had been thinking and writing about holy darkness for many years. I thought now of its corollary, holy silence, silent night, sacred silence, the place of emergence of all life and sound. How close he was to the elegant mystic, John of the Cross, whose mysticism was almost brutal in its depiction of "infused contemplation," which is the dark night as an act "of inflowing of God into the soul, which purges it from its ignorance and imperfections" (100). One does nothing; God alone works in us. St. John believes that at such an opportune moment God "secretly teaches the soul and instructs it in perfection of love without its doing anything, or understanding of what manner is this infused contemplation" (100).

To let this action occur without knowing was frightening; it bred at various times suspicion, fear, or trust. I felt this desire to submit, to yield to the grace of this secret teaching; perhaps it was the same desire and fear that the monks faced each day in their contemplative lives. In the darkness I knew its necessity. The question for me was: *Will I allow it? Do I have the courage to do nothing even while programmed to act on everything that occurs, even in thought?*

The sky was full of snow clouds this morning; they rolled in across the mountains in a deep and powerful silence. Silence and eternal darkness: these were the qualities of God that surrounded and penetrated me most deeply as I prepared, reluctantly, to leave this holy and satisfying abbey after five days.

Silence made everything happen, or it allowed happenings that were otherwise muted by noise. The subtlety of silence was the source of its power. God was nuanced in silence; silence gave God a space to speak directly and softly as a way of responding to my prayers. Silence was a prayerful way of being present to God, just below the level of a whisper; the natural order was where this silence could still exist in its deep and untethered state. Silence evoked a presence and I entered the dark mystery of solitude through its welcoming beam.

Out of silence comes a subtle "push" that was profound and shifted me into another dimension of being without my immediately knowing it. Poets and mystics put us most deeply in contact with silence. So too did a particular form of prayer. If I listened closely to every sound heard or made, especially in speech, I could attune my ears to the silence that surrounded and grounded every sound; might this be what is meant by the phrase, "praying without ceasing"?

As I sat in the library reading in solitude, the following poem pushed itself to the surface and insisted on being heard; its insistence was subtle and sustained:

Every Word Recalls Its Silence

Every word recalls its own silence,
from whence it came. Poetic words
carry a keener memory;
uttered they contain the strongest memories.
Each speech, a call to remember;
each poetic muttering a mythic memory.
If I were to utter "Beatitude," say, would
the power shift in the east for only a
moment so the meek could feel what it
is like to inherit the earth?
And if I were to say "Beatrice"
would she suddenly emerge placing a token
into the subway turnstile and enter the
darkness of the underworld,
a token gesture in a delayed pageant?
A strength in even a
gesture taken, slaking thirst?
I find the word "Beatific" truly memorable
on a grand scale for what in the heart
flutters when I utter it.
Darkness descends on every word—a divine
Darkness that carries the dust of words at
Dusk—
Solitude seems indifferent, like the desert's
right to ignore any footprint that breaks
the silence of sand and stone and
grey-green sage—ocotillo and saguaro.
Memories always play darkness
against the light. Silence, glowing
with a natural blush against the word incarnate.
Silence surrounds Him like a shroud, a shroud
of silence cloaking the skin, an Incarnate
Word with a linen as white as it is breathless.
No soul could ever again clash with
such a splintered reflection. The eye of
Beatrice is the glass of silent memory in
a splash of reflection.

Lowing Cows and Abandoned Heifers

I felt an inner urgency to write when the day was most silent, for in its deepest silence God was most patiently present to me. The membrane between sense and spirit was thinnest and most porous at these moments. My dreams were still in the room, hovering just behind my right shoulder. I read Merton citing Psalm 109:3: "From the womb before the daystar have I begotten thee."

As I enjoyed my last day at Holy Trinity monastery, a parish chapter of Alcoholics Anonymous came tumbling through the front doors for a weekend of talks, companionship, and a nonstop contest of who could fire up and smoke the most cigarettes. They were a wonderful, polite, raucous, and considerate bunch who reveled in one another's fellowship and sobriety. They did, however, set up a command post in the library for their meetings where the cigarette smoke was so heavy that I, like others, declared it off limits. I liked these men, each struggling every day to stay sober, to put themselves into God's hands and to enjoy each hour of sobriety. The monastery was their haven for three days, a time of renewal and rededication to a sober and spiritual life of mutual support.

I said my good-byes to Michael, Alan, George, Russell, Mike, Jay, Father Emmanuel, Greg, Joe, David, Dennis, and old Father Kinney, now 90, who cruised the monastery in his wheelchair, making sure nothing was out of place. In the morning I chipped the ice from the truck window and finished loading. The ice on the roads had begun to melt when I pulled out after Mass and breakfast. Jay, another retreatant, was packing up to drive to Solvang, California, close to where I lived. He would study horse training with the famed Monty Roberts whose horse ranch, named "The Flag Is Up," is where he wrote *The Man Who Listens to Horses*. I offered to show Jay around Santa Barbara when we met upon my return.

Snow was forecast for the next few days. I felt the push to head south toward Colorado, where I would stay with a friend for one night in Colorado Springs before heading to Nada Hermitage, a Carmelite order in Crestone, Colorado. I found Interstate 15, which led me south to Interstate 70. From there I crossed east to Denver and over to Colorado Springs. I spent one night in Craig, Colorado. Hunters in bright orange uniforms were as thick as deer because my day of driving was the same day that inaugurated the hunting season. The scenery in its beauty was too much to take in as the truck climbed to twelve thousand feet. I stayed in the Westward, Ho! Motel and wandered the streets of upscale and artsy Craig in the afternoon.

The next morning I drove south, passing a group of hunters who had just killed and then dragged a magnificent large buck on to the road to strap it to the bed of their pickup. I slowed down and saw the blood of the deer running out of its side. The kill must have just occurred; the buck's soft black expressionless eyes looked up from the pavement. The men looked at me silently, then down at the buck. Pride? Guilt? I could not tell. At least these men and their families would be eating the animal they killed. I waved to them and drove on. The large, oily, black eyes of the deer appeared to follow me down the road.

My friend in Colorado Springs offered the living room couch to sleep on. We were staying at the home of a colleague he was sitting for. We spent a good part of the evening at Pat Quinn's Irish Pub and enjoyed their delicious corn beef and cabbage dinner. Next morning, while my friend left to teach for the day, I packed up the few things I brought in from the truck and explored downtown Colorado Springs, hunting out a place to eat. An inviting little breakfast nook beckoned me. The only other person eating there was a distinguished looking man, mid-sixties, dressed smartly in a business suit.

We soon fell into conversation. Jim was the pastor of the Presbyterian Church across the commons area close to the restaurant where he had breakfast every morning. His desire was to retire soon and study Counseling Psychology. I gave him a catalogue from my Institute and invited him to visit the campus. As I rose to leave, he looked at me squarely: "You were sent to me by God to give me this information." Startled and pleased, I said goodbye. How can doing God's work be so easy, at times even pleasurable? His words secured me further in the thought that the people we come across in life are not accidental or random; they are more often than not placed just there to be helped or to help us. I left feeling good about what had just happened and already at this early hour counted the day a success.

Lowing Cows and Abandoned Heifers

I drove west on 24 to Buena Vista and then dropped due south to Salida, an old historic mining town, pausing there long enough to take a walking tour through it and then along the Arkansas River. The tour guide recommended an inexpensive and wonderful Chinese restaurant for lunch; I indulged myself. I had noticed recently that my truck's automatic transmission was shifting hard, so I checked the automatic transmission fluid and added a pint. I saw from underneath that it was leaking. I would have to find a shop that could replace the seal. I continued on down 285 and branched off at 17 to Moffat where I turned east again and headed directly toward the Sangre de Cristo Mountains and Nada Hermitage, elevation eight thousand feet.

In this high desert terrain I could see seventy-five miles in most directions. The mountains loomed up before me like a thick, dark curtain as I negotiated my final turn into the hermitage. My expectations and excitement on entering a new retreat center increased as I wondered what souls would present themselves at this famous Carmelite retreat center.

12

Breathless in
the Darkness of God
Nada Hermitage, Crestone, Colorado

Nada is Spanish for nothing. The experience of nothingness lies at
the heart of the whole spiritual life. It is the beginning of the mystical journey.   —William McNamara, *Christian Mysticism*

N OT A SOUL WAS VISIBLE as I parked the truck in the gravelly
parking area and walked toward several buildings the same
color as the sandy earth. Silent and spare in appearance, the
high desert Hermitage offered little welcome or direction. I began to
wander around, hoping to be seen. After a few moments a man
emerged from a low-slung building and waved to me. Brother Peter
was one of the Carmelites living here full time; he directed me to the
first floor of the main building, called Agape House, which was also
the communal kitchen, meeting room, and library where I would
eventually spend some intimate times in meals, reading, and conversation. Right now, though, everything was strange, uncertain, and
exciting. Sister Theresa greeted me when I entered the building; she
pointed out the window to a building hunkered low in the rolling
hills about two hundred yards away, which was to be my hermitage,
and suggested I get settled. She had anticipated by my look if I would
share the space with another retreatant. Laughing, she said: "No,
these are individual hermitages and there is only one other guest
staying on the grounds for another day, so that one is all yours."

I thanked her, feeling jubilant at having my own house to myself, received a schedule of Mass and services and then drove my truck along a steep road, where I backed it down to the building. It was a beautiful and inviting cottage of sorts, donated as an offering to the Hermitage by the parents of the actor, Ted Danson, from the television show, *Cheers,* and more recently, *Becker* and *CSI.* They were devout Catholics, I was told later, and they donated the money to have the hermitage built for them and for use by others. Altitude sickness and their age now kept them from making retreats, so the Hermitage regularly used it for retreatants. For the next week I was to be the beneficiary of their largesse.

Crossing the threshold of my hermitage, I was struck by the southwest beauty in its design and colors, and I knew this place would be difficult to leave. Its privacy and intimacy brought a feeling of joy as well as nostalgia already at the thought of departing. Huge cords of wood were stacked just outside the door. Inside was a spacious sitting room with cushion nooks by the windows, a table and chairs, a desk, a fireplace tucked into a corner of the room, and a galley kitchen, completely stocked by the previous retreatant with food from the communal pantry. All the floors were of a brown tile, with throw rugs scattered throughout.

A half wall divided the living room from a spacious bedroom and two single beds. A bathroom led off to the left. A large heater hunkered against one of the walls. A door off the bedroom led out to a tiny private patio that had a grand view of the high desert shrubs and trees stretching to infinity. As I unloaded the truck in the cool morning air and set up house, I felt as if all the other monasteries and retreat centers I had visited were preparing me for this beautiful desert place resting almost directly against the Sangre de Cristo mountains, named for the red color that emanated from them as the setting sun reflected itself off their ancient surface. They loomed high and silent like a gigantic wall separating the hermitage from the rest of the world. Clouds surrounded their upper surface and drifted slowly south, kissing the brooding gray stone faces of the grand mountains and forming puffy beards along their faces.

A tremendous force of solitude rose within me. I stopped all my busy actions of setting up house for a moment: complete and deep and unmitigating, almost a relentless silence, suffused the atmosphere; it was a silence I had never heard before with such assertion. I thanked God I did not come here first because the power of the silence alone would have been too overpowering. It deafened me in its completeness and finality. It carried with it the presence of eternity, some quality outside of time itself. I found myself moving more slowly and quietly in order to find a deeper accord with it.

I finished unloading the truck and brought in armfuls of wood to stack in the wooden box immediately inside the front door. Large windows on two walls connected me to the desert immediately outside. All of the hermitages had been consciously built in slight depressions in the ground, so that when I looked out I could see only the roofs of several others. Clearly, the natural order was viewed here as a corridor or pathway to God's immortal silent presence. Landscape, architecture, and spirit wedded in a harmony I had not felt so keenly anywhere else.

I learned from the Carmelite sisters and brothers that I was situated on the eastern edge of the San Juan Alpine Valley, the largest in North America and about the size of the state of Delaware. The Sangre de Cristo Mountain range had peaks topping fourteen thousand feet. To the south was Sierra Blanco, one of four of the highest peaks in Colorado and sacred to the Hopi people.

Nada Hermitage was co-founded by Father William McNamara, who with Mother Tessa Bielecki, continued to direct it. He was heavily influenced by the teachings of Thomas Merton, with whom he had many conversations in the 1950s. Both Father McNamara and Sister Bielecki came here after their southern Arizona hermitage felt the encroachment of developers destroying their solitude, a fact I had learned from the Trappist priests in Utah. I also learned that very recently the Carmelites had lost a protracted battle with other developers at their location, Nova Nada in Nova Scotia.

The Carmelites who served that site had just joined Nada Hermitage, so the men and women were still adjusting to the new living arrangements when I arrived. Their history again pointed out the endemic problem of monastic retreat centers nationwide attempting to fend off the rapacious appetites of developers who seemed to respect the rights of no one as they sought without moderation to build ski resorts, cabins, amusement parks, and housing units in pristine areas of the country, places where they continued to assassinate silence. Not silent assassins but assassins of silence. Bulldozers and backhoes were their weapons of choice.

But all of these stories faded in the excitement of the moment: this was my first hermitage and I was excited about living self-contained and in complete solitude. I visited the kitchen and gathered some fruits and vegetables to further stock my shelves. Before I left, my task was to clean the place thoroughly and re-stock what I had used so the next retreatant began with a full larder. Each monk had his/her own hermitage. I could see from my window the roofs of several that did not encroach on the living space of others. I was invited by one of the sisters to Sunday Mass, followed by a communal breakfast in Agape House. She related that this meal was the only time during the week that the monks gathered for communal talk and fellowship; it was a gathering I eagerly looked forward to. When I asked her how many other retreatants were staying here at the time, she responded: none, Nada.

My pantry was now stacked with bread, cheese, cereals, coffee, tea, vegetables, but no meat since the monks were vegetarians. I arranged my books on a wooden built-in bookshelf, built a smart and frisky fire, put on water for afternoon tea, and settled into the glow of the place. But too restless and giddy to sit for long, I ventured outside to wander the desert landscape around the building. Deer trails laced like cross-stitching through the low scrub foliage of the high desert floor. I could see no one and no houses for many miles.

The entire complex completely absorbed me into itself, and the silence moved in to cover the few ripples I had created by my arrival. Silence was much like that: when I stopped being busy, fixing something or moving about, silence immediately absorbed all sound back into itself like a gravitational force field. After a time, its only disturbance was the crackling of a log in the fire and the hiss of flame moving up the chimney. The fireplace became the central area of my stay; I kept fires burning in it morning through evening unless I was out hiking the forest trails.

Sister Nora, newly arrived from Nova Nada, visited me on one of her long morning walks to see if I had everything I needed. Originally from Ireland, she told me the story of the hermitage they were forced to abandon; what she missed was how she could walk out from her hermitage in Nova Scotia and find herself immediately in the deepest wilderness where she would see no one even if she hiked all day. She also explained that this particular week was special, honoring complete solitude, so that I might see no one for days. I realized when she told me this how consistent God is. He had given me an itinerary that for the most part had kept me in solitude throughout my pilgrimage. I was grateful for being given the royal divine treatment and once again being cornered into solitude. So be it; I relished it with each new locale.

I was drawn to Sister Nora and the entire order here because, as she told me, the community kept the mythic and poetic dimension alive in their lives. For example, they would read J. R. R. Tolkien's books aloud to one another when they gathered. Other works of fiction became their mainstay to instruct and entertain them in their communal gatherings.

As she left, she warned me that fires were a constant hazard in this arid region. She also invited me to sign up in the chapel for an hour or two of vigil on Saturday night. Individuals committed to sit before the Blessed Sacrament and pray for world peace until the next person replaced them. I told her I would add my name to the vigilant book that very day.

What a gift! The desert's stillness held a deep mystery, forcing me deeper into my interior life and eliciting a profound, serene solitude. Some retreatants, I was told later, left after one night, claiming extreme boredom for lack of anything to do. The monks believed it was actually the fear of solitude and silence that drove them to seek noisier climates with more distractions to keep the loneliness at bay. Desert silence tended to push itself into me, to open me up to myself and my relation to God as no other retreat center had. The power rested in the land's silence and in the great brooding stillness of the mountains that I often gazed at from my window nook. I loved to watch the darkness descend on them in the evening as the fire behind me crackled and competed for attention. The darkness and silence of God revealed themselves here in abundance; I wondered if my soul could withstand their power for six days. This darkness met my own internal darkness and silence in a kind of sublime marriage. I felt so small in relation to its forceful presence and sustained mystery. Silence cannot be explained or even analyzed; it is there to guide meditation and to promote contemplation of the mystery of life and of our tentative but sure connection to a benevolent Creator. Silence was like a field of energy that enwombed me in a welcome solitude.

At the same time I loved what affect it had on me. Life here was both austere and rich; the cheerful and vibrant attitude of the monks I met and occasionally engaged in conversation reflected their joy and sense of abundance. How lean and basic and yet so full. The soul is hungry for and feeds readily on silence and solitude, both anathemas to our culture's impulse for frenzy, busyness and noise, yammering cell phones and repeated distractions. Yes, I was preaching; but what I yearned for was to fall back into the abyss of silence that harbored no fear or anxiety or desire.

I found and began to read some of Father William's writing on mysticism and learned of the appropriate naming of this place: "Nada is Spanish for nothing," he writes. "The experience of nothingness lies at the heart of the whole spiritual life. It is the beginning of the mystical journey" (*Christian Mysticism*, xiv). So to begin with nothing is to begin the true journey of a mystical life.

I walked the grounds of the hermitage and felt the desert pulling at me, taking me into a shadowy desert below the sun. Dryness too had its own sacred quality, so different from moistness. John of the Cross could have had just this geography of the soul in mind when he meditated on the aridity of the spirit. Aridity was a sign, he believed, that the senses were being purged. "The cause of this aridity is that God transfers to the spirit the good things and the strength of the senses which, since the soul's natural strength and senses are incapable of using them, remain barren, dry and empty" (*Dark Night*, 65). No wonder the desert in its spare, dry condition had historically been such a powerful place of prayer, temptation, and comfort for those seeking the sacred in solitude. It was a perfect locale and image for the soul's condition as God worked in and through it, drying out the senses and emptying the self. Moisture was precious, but at times it could impede the soul's growing awareness. In the dark night of dryness I found an attractive and yearned-for condition.

This crackling brittleness surely reflected the character of Elijah, patron saint of this monastery and the Carmelite order, or the austere toughness of John the Baptist, a desert survivor and lover. Dryness and austere bounty offered its own form of love in a demanding way, in the way the desert loved its plants, coyotes, chipmunks, ground squirrels, wolves, trees, and cacti. All of these living things exhibited an affectionate form of subtlety, a subtle sacredness, but quieter, more like a small desert chipmunk eating a piece of green sprout from a plant, sitting back on his tiny haunches on top of my woodpile. His eyes were as black as 3 a.m.; slowly he would move the piece of green twig into a fast-moving but subtle jaw. Such a quiet nourishment was a sign of the subtlety the desert expressed. I felt more at home, secure in my own hermitage than in several other of the places I had stayed. I soon realized, however, that all of the monasteries I already visited had offered me an assortment of hospitable homes in which to retreat.

Life here was nuanced in its desertness. I realized that in walking, talking, doing things, or being busy, this subtlety evaporated into the dryness and with it, its sacred quality. Aridity had its own unique band of smells, which entered the nostrils with the grace and quickness of a field mouse's movement. I breathed in the air coming in the screened door and felt so much of what I had only been reading about: the power of presence, of being still, patient, open, attentive, watchful, where the soul was in rhythmic time and space with the life around it. God revealed himself in this subtlety, in a glimpse, a side-glance, something out of the corner of the eye, or in a marvelously still instant in time. I believed the opening into eternity occurred right here, right at this moment:

Solace

The desert does not demand,
it does not even beckon.
What it whispers through the porous sand
and monotonous slippage of small sages,
Angel Trumpets and Yellow Peppergrass,

crawling lizards and
Kangaroo rats scuffling in its forbidding
Silence is:
"There is no place to go. No place into it and
no way out of it"—
The morning desert light
glints so much promise
and the still red fading light
casting the shadows in evening
impress on my tired dry body the same refrain:
"Really, there is no place to go."
Perhaps its heat and savage
stillness I should read as oracles
of a truth I slip in the deep sand to deny.
"There is, really, no place to go.
Now, try to sit still and I will find
a blessing for you."
If solace is silence, then I cannot breathe
hard enough to make the right sound.
(*Casting the Shadows*, 51)

I loved my hermitage, called Juliana by the Carmelites, especially when I had one candle lit early in the morning. This meager flame had the strength to push the darkness back a few feet all around it. Some mornings I rose, extinguished the candle, and sat quietly in the eternal darkness, or opened the door and stepped out into the clean desert air and its foreboding, inviting blackness with a sky so full of chips of white light it illuminated the fields below and stunned me with its plenitude. That was the first couple of nights. If I remained still, I could hear the deer grazing just a few yards away. Mornings of solitude and silence allowed all sorts of images, feelings, and memories to loom up out of the darkness of my past, to align themselves, somehow, into patterns or ordered arrangements. It was as if the darkness allowed my memory to find homes for the scattered bits and shards of my past, to allow each of them a homecoming in the pattern of my life. Before fire, before electricity, what an uncertain and terrifying world mortals must have moved within. But I wondered if they were not closer to the numinous night of the soul than we are now.

On my second morning at Nada one of the sisters directed me to a popular meditative footpath along a creek just off the property. I set out mid-morning after sitting quietly in solitude in the chapel, where I enjoyed the beautiful stained glass windows and the rugged and crooked figure of the wooden Christ hanging from the wall over the altar. The chapel was small, intimate, and peaceful. It was almost always empty and allowed me to find a peace and serenity under the suffering, anguished face of Jesus. His twisted crucified face and body offered in its suffering and woundedness a silent peace within me, as if through His suffering gathered my serenity. What a paradox about suffering: that it could be a terrain of solace for another. Christ's anguished and distorted body healed some twisted part of my own soul as I meditated and gazed up at his tortured face.

The path invited me to venture along its thread; I enjoyed the crisp air and bright sunshine at this altitude. After walking for some time, I saw ahead of me a farm of sorts, with many horse stalls lining one of the barns and I took it for a riding stable, though I saw no horses. I had seen no one on my walk and delighted in the solitude, a gift of the morning. In another moment, however, I would be yearning for company. All was quiet as I approached.

The silence was suddenly fractured by the alert and aggressive barking of two dogs who a moment ago were sleeping on the porch but were now running straight at me from about one hundred yards away. The gate was wide open so no obstacle separated us. Panicking, I turned to the gravel road driveway and began to run as hard as my prosthetic left hip would allow me. I heard the dogs behind me barking as they continued to close the ground between us; suddenly, however, I ran out of air and fell heavily onto the gravel path. Completely winded, deprived of oxygen, I had forgotten that I was over a mile and a half above sea level. Anticipating the approaching teeth of the dogs, I covered my head with my arms and prepared to be bitten, too exhausted and about to black out to even care.

But the dogs did not attack me as I lay there. Maybe I ran out of their territory and they retreated or someone had called to them. Whatever the reason, I was grateful as I lay there breathing in quick shallow bursts. I then felt a strong desire to fall asleep right there, on the road, but knew I had to make my way back to the hermitage. After a few minutes, I rose and walked carefully back to the Nada property and Juliana, content to spend the rest of my walk within the security of their gates.

That night, after only three hours of sleep, I awoke feeling as if someone were sitting on my chest blocking my breathing. I sucked air in great gasps. Then my breath fell short, into several shallow intakes before I involuntarily lunged heavily for more air; a shiver ran out across my back and down my legs, followed by a brief moment of calm. For an instant I thought I might be having a stroke or a heart attack. In a few minutes I attempted to drop back to sleep sitting up, but when I did the same unnerving breathing pattern resumed, forcing me into complete wakefulness, gasping for air. Now, fully awake, I remembered the long hike I took to explore the area earlier the previous day and felt the fragility of my life. I knew I had exercised too rigorously in the thinner atmosphere.

Almost as an instinctive survival response, I began to pray to calm myself in the deep desert darkness which surrounded me with the thickness of water. I was in a fish tank of darkness. I prayed for all fragile life, for my sons and wife, for my family and for my colleagues, for my friends, and for the beautiful souls I had met on this pilgrimage; I prayed for all of suffering humanity who were reminded because of afflictions each day of the terrible fragility of their lives, but who got out of bed each day to begin once more fulfilling their daily tasks. How, I wondered at 2 a.m., can life be at the same time so simple, so basic, so on the edge of death and yet be so abundant?

My gasping and erratic breathing continued, accompanied now by chills. Through it I grasped that poverty of spirit did not mean a poor or depleted one; it meant to be one in everything by not being owned by anything. To love possessions and to be detached from them were not contradictory. A pure spirit was one not soiled or spoiled by ownership of possessions or the greedy habits of acquiring more of them. I felt as if I had entered a wilderness where even air itself was scarce, its forfeiture a reminder of mortality.

What I believed frightened the Pharisees and Roman government in Christ's life was the power inherent in his poverty of spirit. He was terrifying because he had *nada*. He breathed nothingness; to face nothingness was as terrifying as facing the deep silence and darkness of one's own self. This is the condition in which I found myself in the middle of the night, thoughts racing around my gasping breathing and evoking images of scarcity, mortality, and a crushing disappointment at the thought I might have to leave this place for a lower level where oxygen was more abundant but where solitude was limited.

I lit a candle and sat up in bed, abrogating completely any attempts to control my erratic breathing and the chills that accompanied it. Christ's one great aversion was complacency. A complacent or mediocre or self-satisfied and self-absorbed person existed in a grand illusion of mediocrity. Behind such narcissism might be a fear of silence, solitude, and unknowing. A reflective life of faith inevitably required that I confront the desert that resided within me. Nada Hermitage proved this to be brutally true both day and night. What had appeared as the most abundant of my stays to date had now offered in the darkness and stillness of night the greatest scarcity—lack of air and a feverish and chilling reaction that might drive me away almost a week earlier than I had planned. I lamented the possibility.

Silence placed me beyond words and allowed me to hear a profounder voice of God in His darkness. I sensed that in the desert I came closer to death as a human action or condition than if I were, for instance, seriously mangled in a car accident. Perhaps this was because in the desert I am fully conscious, not numbed in my capacities to know. The desert was a beckoning and daunting and menacing and exhilarating state of being, powerful enough to take my breath away. In its simple and austere space it was a place of full and open consciousness, along with a feeling of boundlessness, close to eternity itself, where in the silence of eternity life began, ended, and ever was.

All these thoughts seemed to ricochet around the room and in and out of me. At one point, feeling exhausted, I knelt by the side of the bed and let my body fall onto the blankets. This posture actually worked for a short time, until I dozed off. Again came the gasping for air, the short breaths, and then a pause where I ceased breathing for an instant, followed by the chills through the back and down my legs. The situation was impossible; I resigned myself to remaining awake all night. Sleep remained evasive with a fatiguing certainty.

Finally, semi-conscious, I noticed the slightest lifting of the darkness into grey morning light. Depleted, with little strength, I was both exhausted and grateful to see the light begin to reveal the dozen or so deer grazing in complete silence around my hermitage. I had never been as ready to embrace the dawn as it pushed back the suffocating darkness. I could not live this way for five more nights; thoughts of leaving began to push themselves on me. A headache that formed during the night was now full-blown. At 4:30, with a throbbing head, I built a loud, snapping fire and brought light and sound into the dark silence as I made some morning coffee and toast. I began to feel alive again.

In such an arid setting, which left me spent, I was drawn ever more to the mystics, to John of the Cross, William McNamara, Julian of Norwich, Teresa of Avila, Annie Dillard, and Joan Halifax; they all understood the profound relation of earth to spirit and possessed the grace and craft to express it forcefully. Their prose crackled like the fire across the room and consumed me in the heat of their visions and beliefs; I was consoled, even refreshed, reading their works over the next several hours as I gained strength and solace from a cup of morning coffee and slices of toast with two coats of jam. They and the fire conspired to increase the dryness to my soul and abundance to my spirit. The headache faded and I felt mysteriously rested, having slept no more than three hours.

I stepped out onto my private little patio and was stunned by the number of stars that could still be seen in the fast-fading night sky. It was creamy to the gaze and so deep, as if I could see for the first time into its farthest reaches. A heavenly view among the terrible stillness had befriended me.

I knew that last night's terror in struggling to breathe marked an initiation into something awesome, fierce, and everlasting. The dark night of the soul so poetically expressed by John of the Cross had in some small way entered me. Remembering the ordeal of hours of waking grief flooded me with a sense of dread. I dreaded tonight. Did it take coming to feel so close to death to break through into this region? The price was high, yet I felt anything but bankrupt. The land, the thin air, the place all spoke of an abundant austerity, a desert that poured forth riches but in a demanding and harsh way. Nada was offered without payment. To confront nothing was a sure act of courage and faith.

I found solace in the mystical writer Joan Halifax's *The Fruitful Darkness*: "In silence and solitude, in the emptiness of hunger and the worthiness of the wilds, men and women have taken refuge in the continuum of bare truth" (24). Her words reminded me that I was at Nada Hermitage where the nothingness of God reigns and emptiness reflects this form of the sacred. Last night, in a terrifying initiation, I had been emptied completely, stripped down to barren dry bones and shallow breath. The air itself was knocked out of me, leaving me gasping and chilled in darkness. I began to grasp, slowly, how much the desert resided within me as much as outside my hermitage window. Such recognition brought with it a deep and inexplicable gratitude; it was a profound feeling of thanksgiving. Desert as place of prayer and of thanksgiving, desert as home in its austere beauty, desert as the place of origin of silence and the silence of all origins. Desert as the dark emptiness of God's presence; not malevolence, just demanding as Hell. Desert as interior life subtly nuanced.

Something else loomed up out of the darkness the next morning. My father, who had not visited me for several days, suddenly appeared again in a memory. When his drinking became acute, he lapsed into bizarre, even terrorist behavior. Saturday night was always the worst part of the weekends; often he would stumble into the basement and remove the fuses from the fuse box, sending the entire house into complete darkness. We should have learned but we never prepared for these descents into darkness. We did not stock up on candles or flashlights. That would be to prepare for what we feared, so we denied protecting ourselves. There we would be, those of us who had nowhere to go, in complete darkness, with father stumbling through the house, often past shouting in words. His grief, now fully unleashed into the darkness, would turn into a howl, like a wounded animal. This combination of darkness, not knowing what he would do next, and his rage turned inward into grief, filled the house with terror. Until well into my adult life, I was terrified of the dark, for it was a monstrous atmosphere, full of foreboding. These dark scenes visited me at Nada Hermitage and intensified my fear of not being able to breathe.

After a few hours I walked up to Agape House to browse the library. There I met Sister Connie who asked how I slept. When I told her of my fitful night she responded: "Oh, oh, altitude sickness." Completely in the dark, I asked her what it was and she ticked off the symptoms like a physician. "Some call it Shyne-Stokes Syndrome," named after the two doctors who studied its symptoms and causes. Another term was "high-altitude pulmonary edema. The central nervous system is depleted of oxygen, so the body compensates by sucking in more air with irregular breathing, then tries to retain it by shallow breathing. How much water are you drinking?" I confessed: "not much." Her sage advice: "take aspirin, avoid hard strenuous exercise, and drink gallons of water." Grateful, I asked with some hesitation if all retreatants ought to be told this when they arrived. She agreed. Before I left after my week's stay, all hermitages for retreatants included a 2-page handout in the packet of information describing high altitude sickness and what to do to minimize its effects. For the present, I began her regimen immediately and felt better in a few hours. I also felt good about the results and began carrying and drinking water all day. Its medicinal effects were noticeable and sustained me for the rest of my stay.

On Saturday night I arrived at midnight for the Peace Vigil. Walking beneath the stars in the cool, still night air awakened a deep wonder in me; through the night air I heard the deer grazing quietly, large bodies so close to me I could almost touch them in the darkness. As I walked down the few stairs leading to the entrance, I stopped and touched the ceramic mask of Elijah, created by a local artist and gifted to the monastery, hanging on the outside wall. Elijah had a ferocious face; he was a guardian icon marking a passage from secular to sacred space. The patron of Mount Carmel and the Carmelites, Elijah did not suffer a mortal's death; instead he was taken up to heaven in a fiery chariot—a symbol, I learned, of the absolute freedom of God. His face revealed one who was consumed by God and who transported that same energy to anyone who gazed on him. I could see in his eyes that Elijah knew the meaning of nothingness.

I felt his bumpy face and gazed into his fiery eyes, full of the energy of God's unconditional and ferocious love; his austere, dry nature reflected the landscape of Nada that I so enjoyed. I crossed myself and entered the empty chapel, found a place in the pew close to the Eucharist on the altar, and prayed for cessation of violence in the world. As long as I was awake, I noticed that the altitude sickness seemed to remain crouched behind the desert bushes, harmless and docile. I enjoyed this time alone, at midnight, with the Blessed Sacrament and breathed easily in the deep solace the chapel offered as a gift. I felt as I witnessed the Eucharist that I was protecting it and at the same time was being protected by it. My thoughts drifted to Jerusalem, site of the Via Dolorosa, the crucifixion and the resurrection. Its history was scarred by violence both before and after Christ's presence there; nonetheless, he chose it as his place of persecution; the ripples of that crucifixion lingered there with even more fury today, connecting millennia of violence.

As I sat with God in the Eucharist, I wondered what this mysterious intimacy was throughout history between violence and the sacred, between devastation and divinity. Was there in the nature of violence something sacred that wished to be uttered and heard? I gazed at the Blessed Sacrament and sought some insight to help me grasp this antagonistic, mysterious companionship between them, between holiness and holocausts that seemed to find a common ground and unwavering energy in the soul of people.

My own identity these last months had been acutely defined by the landscape I inhabited, but nothing matched the intensity I found at Nada. I felt a keen kinship with both Israelis and Palestinians over their identity as part of the soil and their wish for a homeland. My thoughts turned to my own ancestral homeland, Ireland, with its own bloody traumas over land and a sense of identity that promised to stretch to eternity itself. What was missing that violence so frequently entered and replaced?

My vigil ended, but since no one arrived to replace me, I settled in for another hour. I recalled in solitude Christ's words to his apostles, who settled by the entrance to Gethsemane but soon fell asleep as Christ anguished over his destiny; he admonished them for their weakness in not being vigilant to his anguish. I was comfortable and connected with God in this chapel, lit only by a few candles and dim lighting. Feeling a desire to stay and pray longer, I looked up at the mysterious and beautiful wooden and bronze crucifix and gazed at the suffering Christ just a moment before his death, where the effects of the violence done to him and his mortal, frail, and holy nature gazed down at me.

This body, composed by the artist Dan Davidson, captured Christ's human and divine natures. His flesh sagged away from the cross as he suffocated under his own weight. I could feel him gasping for breath, feeling depleted and exhausted, drained of all human vitality. Violence and salvation peered down at me; the Eucharist's presence sustained me. The cross, I sensed, presented the ultimate desert setting, where Nothing no longer mattered. On it and through it, everything was stripped away to reveal the barren landscape of the soul. No wonder Christ cried the question to his Father, "Why have you forsaken me?" in feeling completely abandoned to the desert of his own destiny. No wonder it was so difficult to follow him; his free choice to accept the crucifixion was beyond the ability of most mortals without a strong presence of grace to sustain it. Such a voluntary choice of the will was to choose the ultimate desert of suffering. What could be more peaceful than loneliness and despair if enshrouded in faith?

In *The Way of Perfection*, Teresa of Avila, a contemporary of John of the Cross, offered another way of imagining the cross as an ultimate symbol: "Take up that cross. . . . In stumbling, in falling with your Spouse, do not withdraw from the cross or abandon it. Consider carefully the fatigue with which He walks and how much greater His trials are than those trials you suffer, however great you want to paint them and no matter how much you grieve over them" (125–26). She expressed the suffering of love for humanity's frailty, for my own imperfect and stumbling nature. The cross was a beloved to whom one was wedded, not an enemy to be avoided.

Later, in *Life*, Teresa confessed that in her faith, "there is no other reason for living than to suffer trials, and this is what I most willingly beg of God" (127). Harsh and hard for me to wish for. What I realized is that the culture of which I am a part flees from suffering and pain with the same alacrity that it flees from silence and solitude. Some value grows from suffering, some form of knowing that suffering incites and provokes cannot be acquired without it. Suffering may be the most effective road leading one to nada, to a sense of nothing, to emptiness where the ego's desires are muted. In the ten weeks I have been on this pilgrimage, I felt an emptiness that was not about lack but instead had a strange abundance surrounding it. This paradox would stay with me long after I returned home.

The next morning I joined a jubilant and boisterous Mass celebrated by Father Denny, who entered the chapel barefoot wearing green vestments. The chapel was full to overflowing with people from the surrounding community. It was a joyous celebration and the people were more responsive and energetic in their singing than I had witnessed at Mass in many years. After, in Agape House, several of the Carmelites cooked and served a communal meal where everyone pitched in to set the table, prepare the food, and clean up afterward. About fifteen people gathered around the large oak dining table. Only two of us were retreatants. We laughed, shared stories, and created a warm community for two hours. This meal was my one chance to get to know the hermits who had made this desert retreat their permanent home: Father John, Sisters Nora, Connie, Josephine, Cecelia, Ann, Susan, Connor, Kitty, Brother Ross, and others. Their high spirits were contiguous and contagious; they loved one another's company and used the meal as an occasion to talk about their lives, what they were reading and thinking. The entire experience of Mass, the Eucharist, the community's presence, and this meal, made me feel intricately a part of the community, which renewed me.

Back in my hermitage, after I had taken a short rest, I enjoyed a long hike on the Rio Grande State Park trails which I had been hiking since I arrived. It had proven a safer route than the one guarded by my canine friends earlier. At the park's trailhead was a large wooden sign warning of bears in the area and how to respond if one crossed their path in the forest: "Don't run, but back away from it. If attacked, throw anything you are carrying at it—camera, binoculars, backpack and yell as loud as you can. Carry no food on your person when you hike." My bear fantasies roared into high gear, but as long as there were other hikers on the trail, my bear images remained manageable.

Following the trail, I noticed that the Rio Grande River, with its icy cold clear water rushing downhill over dark rocks and white boulders, paralleled it. From the high desert landscape to this lush forest region full of water was such a short distance that I understood why the area was being inundated by developers. New homes lined the two-lane highway to the forest. The Carmelites told me of their constant worry that the Hermitage would become a tourist attraction and spoil the solitude they had worked so hard to cultivate and protect. They too felt their days of quiet desert peace were numbered.

As I set out on my hike along the forest path I tightened my belt. I realized that I was using notches that witnessed how much weight I had lost. The absence of sweets, meats, carbohydrates, and other high sugar and starch foods had rewarded me with the loss of fifteen pounds without ever dieting. Walking as many as five hours a day for the last few months had made a major difference in my weight and general health. I realized how much I loved being in the natural world; these hikes at nine thousand feet had as a side benefit a thinner me. On them I seemed able to enter a deeper level of meditation than when I sat reading or journal writing. These hikes filled me with a resonant joy at being alive. I thanked God for his generosity even while I dreaded the night's darkness because my sleep had improved only modestly the past few nights.

After several days of sunshine, the weather turned dark and gray; rain became more constant. Regular downpours emptied the trail of other hikers during the week. On a cold and wet Monday morning I arrived at the trailhead; the parking lot was deserted. Within twenty minutes of beginning my hiking, I entered the milky mist of a rain cloud. My umbrella kept most of me dry as I hiked up a steady incline into the white darkness of the cloud. The smell of the soft black earth, the dead leaves turning into mulch, and the river below made me dizzy with delight. I realized that, given the twisting nature of the trail and decreased visibility, I could stumble onto a bear on the path and not know it until we were almost nose-to-nose.

I pushed on, determined not to be intimidated by such fantasies. The air cooled. No birds were singing and I was completely alone. The path turned sinister and the clouds unfriendly as my bear fantasies stood on their hind legs in front of me. I berated my fear and pushed on, talking aloud to myself as the rain increased. Soon it made so much noise striking the umbrella that I realized a family of bears could come up behind me and I would never know it until they had me arm to paw.

Have I literally entered the Cloud of Unknowing, where between a steep drop of the narrowing trail to my right and the perpendicular hill on my left, I walked precariously through the rain cloud with decreasing certainty and pleasure? Here I confronted my fear of the unknown; it rose in the middle of my chest where I felt anger for being frightened, along with the fright of vulnerability. How fragile I was in this natural world, which until today had been a source of sustained solace and joy. This was nature's other face, its shadow side and its sinister obscurity, but it was also my own interior geography that emerged as well.

Fantasies of bear spotting finally won out after about an hour's climb, so I capitulated and retreated back to the truck, feeling how insecure and frightened a creature in the immensity of nature I actually was. I forced myself, as I accelerated down the soggy soft path, to slow down and breathe easy. I asked God to calm my spirit in the face of panic and help me breathe with measured breaths. "Our heart is restless until it rests in you." Augustine's line I repeated to myself until I descended out of the cloud. Deep solitude and silence carried within its folds a marked terror.

Solitude can also invite inner demons that haunted me to surface; one of them was fear of the unknown. This too was part of the pilgrimage, where terror, fear, vulnerability, facing death and the force of nature's potential all congregated in my imagination for a full service. The deep wilderness, I knew, was within; I confronted it for a time but then retreated from its power. I felt more prudent than ashamed but recognized another part of my heritage and marked it. The greatness of the beginning of Dante's *Paradiso* rests in the warning he issues for those who believe they are brave enough to attempt the journey through the third cantica:

O you that follow in light cockle-shells,
For the song's sake, my ship that sails before,
Carving her course and singing as she sails,
Turn back and seek the safety of the shore;
Tempt not the deep, lest, losing unawares
Me and yourselves, you come to port no more. (II, 1–6)

Such a journey both toward God and into the interior regions of one's own psychic reality should not be ventured lightly. If one chooses it, Dante reveals a few lines later, then don't look back; push ahead to completion, a pilgrimage which can last a lifetime. I turned back toward safety. I realized how crucial his caution is, for entering into one's fears requires not only individual courage but also the presence of grace as a guide.

When I reached the Hermitage, Connor, the Irish setter and mascot of the center, cantered to my truck to greet me and usher me back to Juliana. He was a beautiful, sweet dog who liked to hook up with retreatants arriving or leaving and walk just ahead of them as their welcome host. Keenly observant, he also seemed to know who belonged in what building. I informed him in a steady stream of what I had been doing. His look suggested he was interested. He came with me and liked to sniff out the woodpile in front of my door because he knew little critters had condos blocked out throughout the pile. Uncovering the tarp, I loaded a few good pieces into the wheelbarrow and filled the box inside the door with fresh wood for tonight's fire. Connor headed back to the Hermitage as I put on the tea kettle and lit a fire, glad to be home. I thanked God for this dry, clean, and safe place in the world as the fire caught hold after a few hearty pops. From the fear in the cloud to the feeling of comfort here was an entire cosmos that I had traversed.

I began to read a new book by the scholar and minister, Belden Lane, *The Solace of Fierce Landscapes*, and was startled at the outset by what he wrote. Organized "after a classic pattern in the history of Christian spirituality, the three stages of the spiritual life [are] generally described as purgation, illumination, and union." Each of these has a corresponding geography or landscape that accompanies it and forms its exterior expression: "These are symbolized, respectively, in the experience of the desert, the mountain, and the cloud" (6). The desert strips one down, the mountain allows a height of greater understanding, and the cloud, what mystics have called a "brilliant darkness," allows God alone to shine in the soul (6). Such a beautiful blend of nature and spiritual awakening rested in these three images.

Unknowingly and however imperfectly, I had been moving at various times through these spiritual and psychological geographies. It was as if one took a journey, traveling according to what one's intuition dictated, then to discover after the fact that one had been following a famous ancient route but without any markers. Lane's story, full of descriptions of his own spiritual search as he comforts his ailing mother suffering from cancer and Alzheimer's in a nursing home, is a poetic and mystical narrative of one man's journey seeking the refinements of God's love. More personally, his story continually bumped up against my experience of solitude, darkness, and silence as well as their accompanying terror.

I sat in the window nook and paused in my reading to gaze at the complex behavior that now roared in its stony setting. I saw in it a rich analogy to the movement of spirit. The wind's invisible changing velocity outside passing over the chimney was made visible by the rising and lowering of the flames in the fireplace. I could not see the wind but saw its analogy in the fire's behavior; the oscillating movements of the tangible flames seemed to me not unlike how God's grace moves invisibly but finds tangible expression in the material world. I also imagined my own soul's need to shift, to find the right angle or attitude, in order to sense God's presence.

That power to shift my soul, to turn it in the fire, was the action of grace. Could it be so simple that every act of nature, if followed closely in calm observance, revealed something of grace's movement, of the power of the invisible God to make Himself manifest? The created order was always speaking, always disclosing itself, if our angle of ear and eye were turned and tuned to apprehend its nuances. The now-glowing embers of the woods' last hurrah covered me with the glow of contemplation where I was opened to receive what had remained hidden, but which in solitude exposed an entire world.

St. Paul writes: "In Christ, all things hold together." I would add to his insight that of Dante early in his journey with his beloved Beatrice through the planets of the celestial spheres. When he converses with one of the souls early in *Paradiso*, he asks her if she feels cheated by her low status in the realm of the heaven she inhabits. Her response is both simple and elegant: "In His will is our peace" (*Paradiso* III: 85). The tangible feelings of being at peace grew from the invisible will of God working on my soul. Perhaps living within this double awareness of the physical and spiritual realms held the key to a serene surrender of my own will to God's. Fire and wind conjoined to bring peace, if not greater understanding. Something lingered here of an elemental sacredness contained in the natural world.

I read Freeman Dyson, who cites St. Paul. Dyson's claim is that the more he studies the universe and the human order, the more he realizes that every human being is an original expression of the universe. His assumption is that everything has a macro and micro phase; ecology, therefore, should be the basis of all studies. Earth-reference is at its core. Dyson was astonished to learn that in all the books on Economics he had read, not one had a reference to earth-ecology. Not one addressed Earth Economy. Needed, he claims, is a dream to enchant our collective minds, a valid myth, a dream or vision that would allow us to imagine the earth economics of the world, the true origin of all economic systems. One by one, I believe these economists should come to Nada Hermitage for a week in order to be instructed by the fruitful study of earth economics.

Thomas Berry, in a tape entitled "A Moment of Grace" that I listened to one evening, calls himself a geologian. As a Catholic priest and author of *The Dream of the Earth*, he echoes Tyson's urgency by suggesting that we are way overdue for a moment of grace in which the earth's needs are evoked in our imaginations. To serve the earth and work with it, we need the right temperature, as well as a more poetic celebratory attitude to guide us to the right response. I was moved by his image that "the earth is a communion of subjects, not a collection of objects"; it is our primary point of reference. If we lose the earth's vitality, humanity will lose its reference point. Only a moment of grace as a transformative event will allow us to confront "irreversibility," instead of pretending that the earth is constantly renewable. A moment of grace includes the ability to open out in a great creative phase. Our task to heal the earth can't be mandated; it must be evoked according to three dimensions: "cosmological, historical and religious" ("A Moment of Grace").

Deeply affected by these writers, I wondered how effectively religion or a spiritual life might be developed and nurtured without a corresponding respect and sustained regard for the natural world in its sacred and often secret variety. Much of current spiritual writing was truncated and ineffectual because it often denied the world's body that was so deeply wounded and on the brink of exhaustion. No wonder Nada Hermitage and hundreds of others across the country and the world cling so fiercely to their natural solitude; they know in their bones that remaining intimately related with the earth is part of spiritual growth and renewal. My walks in the desert, the forests and plateaus had convinced me that my spiritual life was incomplete if it withdrew from or excised this corresponding connection to the natural world. William Blake's "world in a grain of sand" was my pearl of great price. I knew I must return to reading the gospels, and to meditate more deeply on the images offered there. The Kingdom of God is offered by way of a mustard seed's growth. Christ's poetic parable stories are most often based on some simple life or action in the natural world.

From Agape House I called my older son, Matt, in San Antonio. He told me that he had quit his job and dropped out of college, all in the same week. This exodus, following on his mother's being let go from her job, completely disoriented me. I told him, as I fretted over his future, that I might drive to San Antonio and see him; he was fine with my coming. I walked back to Juliana and stood in the middle of the living room and asked God a very basic question: "What should I do?" My first instinct was to load the truck immediately and drive southeast, a two days' hard journey.

I called on Father Denny, who visited me in the evening, listened to my plans to abort the remainder of my stay here in order to be with my son, who seemed at the moment completely derailed. Father Denny asked if I could be more effective for Matt there than here at the hermitage. I did not know but my impulse was to be with Matt in person.

Father Denny sat back in the chair and gazed at me in silence for a moment. Then he said: "You came here expecting one kind of desert experience but you got another." Bingo. I felt that my family was disintegrating and felt myself thrown on the needles of a cactus in the desert. I wept over their losses and felt in my grief a complete nada, a nothingness, and completely bewildered about whether to head out or stay put. Father Denny's words were true but failed to console me. But he did clarify for me what condition I was in.

Alone, feeling helpless, with no rules, no guide, no plan, no props, I felt as if God had found me and wounded me through my family, which was worse for me than any wound I might sustain in my own person. When I arrived here, a voice uttered: the previous two months have been preparation for this place. It was in its first impression the most attractive of all the places I had stayed; now it had become the darkest and most painful. I felt the cross of suffering bearing down on my shoulder and was stooped over by the weight of both my son and wife.

With Father Denny's help I discovered a compromise: I would stay to the end of my time here, two more days. Then, instead of going to the next planned retreat center, I would drive to San Antonio and be with my son. I felt exhausted and planned to go to bed early; I knew the night was going to be difficult with breathing and the creation of this new plan. But in the terrible dryness and pain I felt for my son, God granted me my first night of full rest. I slept at peace for nine hours without waking. When I awoke I knew that my breathing difficulties had passed; I had acclimated and been initiated. When I awoke I prayed in gratitude as I put on the morning coffee to the sound of continuing rain, the first signal of snow not far behind it. Outside it was as black as the world was capable. Soon I had a friendly fire roaring in the fireplace.

Someone knocked at the door; I saw Sister Nora's face through the window. She loved her morning walks in darkness and saw my early light on. I related my conversation with Father Denny, which she listened to with great sympathy. She affirmed my decision to visit my son; then she was off, refusing my offer of morning coffee. I was grateful for her visit out of the darkness as I watched her disappear into the storm. The fire I built crackled into animated conversation. A deep joy pervaded me. I looked out the black window and saw myself standing there, in complete solitude and in a fullness of life beyond measure. Sounds as loud as the pop of a gun being fired cracked out of the dry firewood; comets of embers blasted against the metal screen, trying to burn the throw rugs on the brick-tiled floor.

My breakfast was spare—cereal, some fruit, and two pieces of toast. I recalled at this moment the miracle of the loaves and fishes. What wisdom was in that story: in little, having little or what appears to be insufficient was in fact the presence of abundance. Abundance was not having plenty but having what "looks like" not enough but in fact was bountiful, even having something left over. I saw how on this pilgrimage having little was more than enough, if the appetites were quieted, so that I could see clearly what I had. Perhaps there was contained in the soul something that could be called an ascetic imagination, where a certain poverty was actually the reflection of a fuller fruitfulness and abundance if only our angle of vision could rotate a bit on its axis to bring it into view.

God is paradox. Not "God is *a* paradox," but God *is* paradox itself, with occasional irony blended in. I sat in my favorite padded window nook and gazed across at the chatty fire. I believed that my love of poetry was so pronounced in part because the poets fed on paradox, on God himself.

Silence Springing Toward the Word

Behind every word we utter
hides a silence, like the coyote
behind the scrub bush watching the deer
grazing serenely close by.
Fear is a felt quiver that the
Word we utter last could be the last
Word spoken anywhere.
The silence will crouch slowly behind
the innocent bush and spring toward a
deer who looks up suddenly, ears fanned,
with green sprigs of leaves dangling from
her lower lip at the last word uttered

leaping at it through the night air.
It will know the terror of oblivion,
and all sounds will be swallowed by
the animal silence of the springing coyote.
Silence is the last act of the final word
Uttered.
Who will be given the privileged place
in the closing mouth of the universe
when it has said all that is in it?
(*Casting the Shadows*, 91)

As the light began to push back the stubborn darkness, it revealed a dozen deer within three yards of my window. They were there the entire time but the dawn light now made them visible. They looked up at me but were in no hurry to run, so accustomed were they to visitors staring out at them.

A small chipmunk that lived in the woodpile made his morning appearance, sitting on his hind haunches atop the woodpile and staring at me, paws in prayer. Quick, fitful energy without limits, he ran with his tail high, like a spoiler on the back of a racecar to guide him and keep his posterior from becoming airborne. He sped down the log pile, across the sand separating my window from it, and perched on the opposite side of the window, looking in at me through eyes no bigger than the period that ends this sentence.

He was curious about me and I him. Beautiful, elegant, with light brown sides the color of coffee lightly creamed, his back sports racing stripes of black and white, slick, vertical and low on his soft body. In his glee over having made contact, he suddenly shot to the woodpile in his natural friskiness. Home and safety. I related to his feelings viscerally. He moved at the speed of silence, impossible to be contained. When he returned in a moment he carried in his mouth a blade of green grass. Staring at me from his perch on the window ledge, he guided the straw into his mouth with one paw—a real show-off—as his jaws moved like a video tape put on fast-forward. Here God greeted me in the morning and had breakfast with me through one of his creatures. I felt honored by the visit.

What is it that animals want to reveal to us of our own spiritual and animal nature? Mary Lou Randour's *Animal Grace* reflects what

Breathless in the Darkness of God

I felt in the presence of these creatures: "Animals have a wisdom that is, as yet, largely undiscovered by some. . . . In many ways their sensory world is vastly different from ours. In that difference, animals have access to levels of reality that might remain hidden to us without their help" (xxi).

My own imaginings, as I watched him, fed on the silence, like the quiet that surrounded the dawn riding on low dirty-white clouds, bringing a barely perceptible light. Silence stilled the heart and evoked images looking for a home. Silence throbbed in my ears, coursing the blood to the level of feeling. Silence indeed had a voice, one not heard often because other sounds kept her buried deep in the heart's soul, pulsing softly, expectantly, waiting to be born.

Nada

The morning light comes down
from the Sangre de Christo peaks with
somber certitude.
Silent and slow-moving, a cloud
the color of dirty snow, luminous,
crouches before the purple mountain
face in the stillness of morning's
new light.
Slowly, like an apparition,
the cloud splits in grief
when it crosses a bump in the
mountain's face, a cloud
not of unknowing—it knows.
And like the arms and hands of
lovers so reluctant to let
go, it slips apart in
a dissolving Shakespearean grace,
the motion of a deep sonnet
without sound.
Now it is separate from itself,
two clouds dying a death
to each, its own life.
Cloud bank, cloud interest, cloud
splitting, mirroring itself

against the mountain's close visage.
I watch this silent violent separation
from my hermitage window.
What have I seen?
Two clouds peek at one another
in their longing languid shapes, the
shape of longing, from where they
rest easily against the hard rock of
the mountain.
They long to become snow.
I breathe the thin air of the high desert
and wonder if the clouds at such height
are now breathless for one another?
(*Casting the Shadows*, 35)

Rain fell steadily as I packed the truck once more. I planned to drive to San Antonio to see my older son. I walked the grounds of this wonderful and terrifying place, a hermitage that I was destined to enter, where I was to be stripped of the last remaining defenses keeping me from the darkness of God's eternal presence. The deer grazing so intimately close to my window did not bolt and run; instead, they watched me curiously, and then returned their heads to the grass and sage. I thanked them for teaching me something of the silence of slow motion. I walked the path that led to the corral of Lucy, the hermitage's sometimes ornery mule. I spoke to her, but she appeared indifferent to my words, stubbornly resistant to my social greetings to the end. Connor, the hermitage's dog ambled up the path, sensing I was yet another visitor preparing to depart. I did a laundry last night in the basement of Agape house and felt right, yet disappointed, about the decision to bypass Ghost Ranch in Abiquiu and head directly to San Antonio by way of Dallas, where I would stay with a friend for a night. Another pilgrimage would allow me to retrace my steps to Ghost Ranch.

I drove out of the hermitage property and paused for a moment to glance back at the hunkering buildings lying low in the desert mounds. Happiness melted into a reluctance to leave, the same push-pull emotions that punctuated the end of every stay. I took with me the tough austere friendship of the brothers and sisters of this Carmelite home. I took with me the disappointment at not having met either Father William or Mother Tessa; both of them were away teaching at Colorado College. But I took with me as well Father William's penetrating raw book on mysticism, especially his profound grasp of nothingness, nada. "The sense of nothingness is heightened and intensified and becomes most salubrious and fruitful when absolute reality or ultimate being is recognized as God. In comparison with him, in the light of his stunning reality, we are literally nothing" (*Christian Mysticism*, 70). There is no place for egocentricity if one accepted his claim to God's stunning reality. Yet it was mysteriously liberating and instilled in me a feeling of joy to accept my own nada in the face of God's silence. I did not feel humiliated by God; rather, God's presence humbled my own sense of self-importance.

My dark breathless nights struggling with altitude sickness were occasions not only to sense deeply the absolute presence of God as darkness; they also helped me unload the tedious dead weights of my own preoccupations enough to feel the nothing that is at the heart of this hermitage and the heart of human life itself.

I reentered the world and drove through the rough-edged heated landscape of the desert southwest and across west Texas into Dallas. The next morning I traveled the three hundred miles through the late summer heat of late November to San Antonio where I enjoyed the precious time with my two sons and worked with Matt on his future plans. I knew as I headed west again after three days of a short visit, and found a little restaurant in Del Rio in which to eat breakfast, that I could not have continued on this pilgrimage with my son's condition as it was. My choice was right.

I now retrieved the concluding leg of my pilgrimage by driving Route 90 to Van Horn, Texas, then picking up I-10 west through El Paso, Las Cruces, New Mexico and on to I-25 north into south Albuquerque and the Dominican Retreat House where I would be on the lookout for Sister Rose to help get me settled.

13

A Hermit in the Fridge

Dominican Retreat House,
Albuquerque, New Mexico

Look, in short, at practically anything—the coot's feet, the mantis's face, a banana, the human ear—and see that not only did the creator create everything, but that he is apt to create *anything.* He'll stop at nothing.—*Pilgrim at Tinker Creek*

I FOUND MYSELF DEEP within a rural part of southern Albuquerque, a neighborhood in transition from farm and cattle country to residential complexes. The driveway into the adobe buildings that made up the retreat center was narrow. Old and well-worn, the buildings and grounds were spotless. I drove back to a structure standing alone next to a large green space lined with a sidewalk. I entered the side door of an old Spanish-style ranch house the sisters of the Dominican order purchased years ago and converted into a home and retreat center.

The Dominicans opened up the first retreat house for women in the United States in 1882. Structured weekend retreats brought many individuals and parish groups for conversation and prayer. The conference room, in the same building where my room opened from the outside walkway, was a converted hangar where the previous owner kept his private airplane. I found myself once again, and without any surprise, the only retreatant on the property. The weekend, however, promised to bring in a large parish group, but for the moment I enjoyed complete and exclusive use of the property, the book and tape library, and the dining hall. Sister Rachel directed me to fix my own breakfast in the morning if none of the sisters were there to cook. I liked this familial atmosphere and their immediate trust in me to take care of myself as I roamed freely from my room to the main building.

How could I not love these women, fussing over me like a son who had been away from home for years? I had all their attention and decided to enjoy all their pampering. Sister Rose, from Mexico City, took it upon herself as a vocation to fatten me up with over-sized daily meals, convinced I looked too thin. I told her that my appearance had been dearly bought and paid for in long hikes and a careful diet and was proud of the results, but she wouldn't hear of it; her cooking was so exquisite that I indulged myself and saw that it pleased her. I visited a tiny chapel with a low ceiling and was invited to morning Mass there, where only the sisters, a few neighborhood parishioners, and I attended.

A storm had followed me, accompanied by a blasting, windy cold front. I walked the grounds and noticed on the adjacent property about eight Black Angus bulls alternately grazing and gazing at me with about the same degree of indifference as did the deer at Nada Hermitage. My walking was restricted to an oval asphalt path along which were posted the Stations of the Cross. I felt too enclosed, almost trapped in this neighborhood, but had to adjust my sights from the expansive terrain of the high alpine desert plateau of Colorado to the desert floor of New Mexico, and to absorb the give-and-take of pilgrimage stays. The sisters immediately made me feel at home, but I missed a place to walk and hike that would give me some solitude in natural landscapes.

Sister Amata informed me after a few mornings that the sisters had dubbed me "The Hermit." I was happy to let them have their fun and told her I felt very eremitical in my journey up to now. They began the habit of fixing my meals and putting them in the refrigerator so I could eat when it suited me. All of the food designated for me was marked in ink on masking tape labels in large letters, "The Hermit." So be it. I decided that this was indeed my calling and tried to slip more into this role by generally promoting a lean and hungry look in their presence.

I enjoyed my new status and felt that my retreat bedroom

deserved a name as well, in the tradition of Andalusia or Penhally or even William Faulkner's Roanoke. I called it, without too much thought, "The Hermit's Lair" and considered painting a small sign to hang above the door. I planned to hibernate with my books until the end of my stay, at which point the food would disappear from the fridge, "The Hermit" labels would be discarded, and my presence would drift into a vague hermit memory.

A bitter wind blew steadily for a day and a half while I remained hunkered down reading and enjoying my small but elegant room that contained an impressive and busy wall heater. Alongside the new bed was a small desk and reading lamp as well as a new Stratolounger rocker and lounge chair. The room was very small so I used the conference center one door down, with large tables and access to the modest book and tape library. But my soul had grown accustomed to the expansive forest and desert landscapes; I could control neither my restlessness nor the feeling of claustrophobia. One morning I attempted walking along the road in front of the Priory, but so many dogs roaming loose began to sense my presence and took far too much interest in me. I headed back after only a few hundred yards, certain of the fact that my running-from-dogs days were behind me. St. Romuald's admonition to stay in one's cell where all would be given, however, was too much for my restless spirit. I sought an escape clause.

I took my laundry into Albuquerque over toward the University of New Mexico. A woman there told me of the magnificent Cibola National Forest in the Sandia Mountains north and east of the city and believed I would enjoy hiking there. My heart soared at the prospect of retreating once more into the wilderness.

Following breakfast the next morning, I drove from the Dominican Center up to seven thousand feet and parked at the entrance to several trails. When I turned around I could see for a hundred miles across the desert floor, which appeared like a vast, shallow bowl below me. On this trip I had grown to feel God most fully in the darkness and in the arid desert landscape. I realized that I now loved the desert as I had loved few landscapes in my life. If it was true that each of our souls is drawn to a particular natural element over others, then I believed it equally credible that each of us is drawn to a particular kind of terrain. The desert had become for me not just a geographical region but also a disposition of God, a face of God on the world, and one I found most accessible and natural in its austere and quiet loveliness. Here solitude intensified through desert barrenness. I craved the austerity and aridity of the desert because it approached the spiritual quality of nothingness that fed deep in me my own sense of nada.

A pervasive joy overwhelmed me as I parked the truck and walked to the beginning of the Piedras Negras trail, where three rangers greeted me. I noticed on a wooden sign by the entrance, as one passes ritually through a gate to the trail's origin, words from Henry Thoreau's *Walden:* "In wilderness is the preservation of civilization." Perhaps Thoreau saw that it also preserved the spirit's connection to divinity. His words were like a rich trail mix I carried with me.

One of the rangers cupped in his hand several seeds from the pinones fir trees surrounding the hillside. He offered some to me; I liked their meaty, woody, and nutty taste. He showed me a tree where they were falling this time of year. Another ranger offered directions and approximate time to hike the trail heading up to twin peaks, about an hour and a half away. He was glad to see I wore good hiking boots and carried a hat and coat with me, since I would be climbing into snow in less than a thousand feet. I thanked them and felt more secure heading into new territory with their directions. I brought with me two oranges, an apple, and a bottle of water.

I loved the desert and feared it; it conjured something of my own solitary nature. Nowhere had solitude been so pronounced for me as in this setting. When I entered, it asked only one simple question of me: "What are you willing to give up?" It also opened me to that interior wilderness that can terrify and enlighten, since God was given an opportunity to speak through barrenness. Solitude was less about being alone than about being in relation to a presence that offered nothing; nothing comes from silence. Silence, in its fullness, bred and promised nothing; on the contrary, it encouraged emptiness. It was the central core of stillness and it frequently returned my presence with a gift. I sensed God more often as the presence of an abundant emptiness, a fullness that amounts to nothing. Here was the paradox of God's presence.

Wilderness gave something back to me. It was an image of God in the way it simultaneously engaged relinquishment and retrieval—a loss and a gain. What one gave up in quantity one gained back in freedom, part of the give-and-take rhythm of Brother David's insight earlier. The silence of the desert landscape tended to swallow all of the petty concerns that kept one enslaved to trivia, to petty resentments and ego-driven desires. But what surfaced out of the stillness, as I hiked up the mountain path, was a deep and clear intuition of what mattered and what should be discarded. God spoke directly to me in this landscape, a place that reordered my life and recentered my soul so that not my will but His was most prominent in the stillness. "In His will is my peace."

I kept this one short sentence close and repeated it often as a way of discernment in my solitary treks in nature. The desert taught me that there existed an imagination of silence, even a silent imagination—some ordering principal awakened in the silence of the desert. The scarcity, silence, and indifference of the desert stirred in me a principal of order whose origin is, I believe, God-originating and God-given. In it was the deep practice of discernment: knowing what was of authentic value and what needed to be relinquished. But such discernment was only possible if one were free of what the Italian writer and one-time national president of Italian youth in Italy in the 1940s, Carlo Carretto, called "spiritual egotism," which uses "piety and prayer for its own gain" (*Letters from the Desert*, 30). Any feelings of righteousness and purity had to be scanned with a spiritual egotism meter.

Now at eight thousand feet, I saw ahead the first white thin carpet of snow on the trail, where I found and sat on a dry rock and noticed dozens of animal tracks that had crisscrossed the snow, leaving their black paw or hoof prints in a busy and dizzying highway pattern. I tried to notice what was around me as I breathed heavily in the thinning air. I reveled in the joy emanating from the stillness; contemplation seemed so natural at this altitude because the space of nature's silence opened the places in my own soul that fed on stillness that rested safely in stillness and nourished itself in solitude. Stillness connected my own fleshy nature with the body of the world in its particulars that I felt right here with the prickly pear cactus and Pinones trees.

Subtle purple burns of color appeared along the top ridge of the prickly pear cactus, the hard pods of the Pinones conifer that dropped its seeds for the animals and through them, the promise of more trees. I tasted four or five seeds in the hard shell as my teeth sank into the soft meat inside. The prickly pears all contained needles extending straight out, protecting them from predators.

At the base of the cactus was soft porous and spongy earth, ready to absorb every drop of rainwater or snowmelt in preparation for the hot sun of summer. The silent soil and the gentle sound of the wind passing through the conifers and cacti evoked feelings that I was inhabiting a subtle space of contemplation. The philosopher Max Picard wrote a beautiful and challenging book, *The World of Silence*, a sustained meditation on the power of silence. He observes that "the silence of nature is permanent; it is the air in which nature breathes" (137). Solidarity in silence, a more natural state of being for us than perhaps even speech, is more permanent, more originary. When I spoke, I sensed that my words were dying even as they were formed by and passed my lips, tongue, and teeth. Each utterance was a speaking into the teeth of death; but silence linked me permanently with everything else. It harbored a different power from speech.

Perhaps this was why, in St. Benedict's *Rule for Monasteries*, instructions on silence follow obedience, and those on obedience precede instructions on humility. I listened to the minimal voice of the wind passing through the Mesquite trees. What I heard in solitude's small utterance was min-a-mal-ist, a little voice, more like a whisper. If I listened openly and with attentiveness, I heard the little voice—not the boisterous boom of hollow speech but the stiller, fuller voice that grows from meditation. The desert emerged in that small voice; scarcity allowed its fullness to speak to me as I rested on a rock high up in the mountains, beyond the snowfall.

The silence that held the desert in place—with its tan, tawny stillness, its delicate bushes and sharp spears of cactus plants—was different and more profound. It wanted to be called an ancient silence, even a wilderness silence, or a wild silence that refused all efforts to be tamed. Part of its power would reveal itself only at night, when darkness cloaked the silence like a death shroud. Silence and darkness together—such an attractive and terrifying pair of accomplices for spiritual awakening.

In the silence beyond words gathered an atmosphere, an intuition of grace at work to shift my vision so I was able to see the spider web which needed only a few degrees' rotation for its filaments to be struck by the sun to become visible. Perhaps only a couple of degrees or less separated me from the entire invisible world. Solitude wished to be felt and sensed beyond words. In his teachings Christ put me in touch with the metaphors and symbols of speech through stories, parables, beatitudes; but his words all pointed to the deep silent darkness, which is the Father.

It brought me to that place described in Belden Lane's book mentioned earlier. Originating in the 4th century through the writings of the Syrian monk, Pseudo-Dionysius, the apophatic tradition expresses a state which transcends speech: "Reaching beyond language, beyond the capacity of the mind to entertain the divine mystery, [is] the chief impulse of the apophatic tradition, both in theological method and in the practice of a life of prayer" (64).

This economic feeling of silence and stillness pervaded me at nine thousand feet in the mountains, in solitude, as the wind delivered an increasing chill and the sun stared directly across from me in its accelerating descent to the desert floor. I had been hiking slowly and steadily for more than two hours, grateful that Nada Hermitage's elevation had helped me endure the thinner air at this level.

I ate my fruit, drank half a bottle of water, and began my descent. In this silence of profound sacred space, I realized that solitude and stillness were the apertures that allowed me to move through and into the eloquence of deep silence. In it lingered a clarity that was uncluttered, spare, and manifest—a wildness and tameness at once. I imagined it as a wild nothingness, a tame emptiness. Merton, who loved the natural order and the life of prayer with such enthusiasm, wrote, in *Bread in the Wilderness*, of his own love of the rhythms of the natural order: "Light and darkness, sun and moon, stars and planets, trees, beasts, whales . . . all these things in the world around us and the whole natural economy in which they have their place have impressed themselves upon the spirit of man in such a way that they naturally tend to mean to him much more than they mean in themselves. That is why . . . they enter so mysteriously into the substance of our poetry, of our visions and of our dreams" (59).

His words guided me to the realm of invisibles that through an act of grace captured his insight.

Melville's pilgrim, Ishmael, as he reflects on his pilgrimage aboard the Pequod, reminds us: "We live in an ocean of subtle intelligences" (*Moby-Dick*, 243). This intelligent source at the origin of all intelligences is, for me, God, both masculine and feminine, the silent white whale deep within the world's vast oceans. Nothing approached the subtlety of Ishmael's observation more than silence itself, the supreme subtlety sliding through the world's body.

I continued my descent as the afternoon sun lowered its shades and dropped out of the hazy sky. Fatigue from the hike as well as breathing the thin atmosphere left me weak and anxious about reaching my truck and heading back to the comfort of my room. I moved slowly, however, not wanting to slide over a precipice from the snowy path I was negotiating. The stillness was thick, resonant, and comforting.

It was shattered suddenly by a riot of crashing in the brush to my left. The foliage was too thick to see into, so I froze on the trail and waited for whatever was hurtling toward me through the branches and thick growth to make itself visible.

In an instant, across my path, not ten feet ahead of me, glided a magnificent brown-and-white buck with a large and impressive rack of antlers. One deep black eye, wide and polished in its slickness, spied me at a perpendicular angle as he broke noisily into the thicket to my right. I can still hear the hollow sound of his antlers battling the lower branches of the trees as he moved swiftly beneath them. They clacked like hollow wooden swords against the bare branches as he sped with great dignity into the woods, head held majestically high, followed almost immediately by a doe and then a young fawn slipping and sliding behind her.

Two large dogs in hot pursuit skidded directly in front of me, where I remained as still as the surrounding trees. They paid me no attention since their sights were glued to the three animals ahead of them. They scampered in a howl of sound, breaking the silence in their delight with the hunt. The entire incident opened and closed in less than sixty seconds.

I remained frozen, grateful that my silence and slow movement had put me just there, in that place, at that instant to witness such majesty in nature. Blessed by the solitude, it allowed me this revelation and showed me one can never prepare for what solitude might offer as a gift. Such an image as this erupted unbidden, most often unearned, from out of the stillness. For an instant, something sacred, natural and pulsing with life and the will to survive in its wildness, made an appearance in a kind of spontaneous theophany. Then, speechless, voiceless, but wrapped firmly in the deep, wild silence out of which it had just emerged, it was just as quickly swallowed by the wilderness that opened for its appearance and now closed around its memory.

I recognized all around me this pattern of yielding in nature. When water flows toward rocks and yields to them; when the dead and decaying trees and plants yield to the new life that feed off their disintegration to preserve and continue the forest's existence; when the branches of trees, plants, and flowers sway to the wind's pressure in bending away from it; or when the light of the day bows to the darkness in the oldest rhythm of day and night. This was one of countless patterns that the natural world taught me as I struggled to be still enough to receive them.

I felt both blessed and panicky as the animals' sounds faded. Not desiring, not seeking, but being simply present to what was directly in front of me, if I could tame my aggressive spirit not to grasp, to reach out, to possess it. Then something was offered gratuitously, without condition, as a gift, through the silence and solitude. I learned from this momentary encounter how solitude and silence were places, even attitudes in which other elements that I needed but perhaps could not recognize, stepped forward. Something of divinity itself was present in the magnificent body and dark, black, glistening eye of the buck—a deep darkness that solitude and silence can transport us to.

Back at the monastery I noticed that I was still the only hermit inhabitant. My companions in my room stared at me from above the headboard of my bed: one was the Blessed Virgin's sweet face, the other was of John the Baptist in his wilderness fury and sacredness, and close by were two small angels talking among themselves. I would miss their silent presence when I left.

Later, reading Meister Eckhart, I laughed on discovering this insight: "The closest thing to God is stillness" (157). This stillness is the disposition necessary for moments of grace. I was also reading the Swiss psychologist, C. G. Jung's, works on my pilgrimage because I liked his struggle to understand the movements of the human psyche and spirit in persons to engage the imagination that he suggested is both psychological and theological. He offers in one of his volumes a condition that I related to immediately: "only when the props and crutches are broken, and no cover from the rear offers even the slightest hope of security, does it become possible for us to experience an archetype that up till then had lain hidden. This is the archetype of meaning" (*CW*, 9.1:32). To experience God's Holiness and Benevolence, something in me must give way, yield, step aside, and abdicate its prominence. Grace was the power of abdication wherein I gave my own will over to the will of God.

In the morning I attended Mass, after which Sister Amata prepared a lavish breakfast. I asked her what was ailing the old priest who said Mass this morning. He had pushed from one side of the altar to the other a wheeled canister containing oxygen with a clear plastic hose snaking into his nose. Every movement was an effort, but he pushed on, even delivering a brief, breathless, and insightful homily. Sister related to me how he had retired a few years ago. He wanted to die and so lay in bed, refusing to eat and waiting for the end of his life, a passive suicide, she sensed.

But one morning one of the sisters, exasperated at his self-pitying condition, told him to get up, that he had some life still in him and some work yet to complete. Although he was deeply depressed, alone, and isolated, he nonetheless followed her command, like Lazarus obeying Christ's, and rose out of his bed. Offering Mass three times a week kept him busy. He also felt useful again as he visited the sick and despondent in hospitals and bought them the sacraments. He could speak to them from first-hand experience of their own depression and desire to die. He was an example of how one can turn what afflicts him into a gift for others.

I would miss these motherly Dominicans. They too were planning to leave the old ranch house and property for another location north of Albuquerque. It was, they informed me, newer, with more conveniences and with greater possibilities for accommodating groups. I would miss finding my meals in the fridge wrapped with cellophane and marked "The Hermit" in one of the sister's clean handwritten notes. I would miss the low ceilings of all of the buildings and the warmth of the kitchen and dining room. I would miss making the coffee at 5:00 a.m. and then cooking eggs in the old kitchen. Sometimes, early, I would sneak into one of the spacious rooms off the dining room, one with a television, and watch the national news while eating my cereal. The hospitality here had been one of God's most abundant blessings on this pilgrimage.

I planned to leave in the morning, now that the early winter storms had passed and the air was again cool and clear. I had one more retreat center on the itinerary as I headed west. My truck would take me to Picture Rock Retreat Center just north of Tucson. There I would end over three months of travel and pilgrimage awakenings, and I looked forward to its ending, though I felt already a growing gnaw of nostalgia emerge. I was determined, however, to enjoy one more stay because I never knew what or who it might have waiting, ready to teach me something I needed to know. Perhaps I had something to offer them as well.

14

Christ and
the Hohokam People

Picture Rocks Retreat Center,
Tucson, Arizona

Religions commit suicide when they find their inspiration in
dogma.   —Alfred N. Whitehead

O UT OF SOUTH ALBUQUERQUE, I found Interstate 25 and
headed south to scenic and beautiful Route 60, on which I
traveled due west through Pie Town, Reed Hill, through the
Apache-Sitgreaves National Forest, Springerville, then up and
around Show Low and into Mesa and Phoenix. From Phoenix I
dropped the one hundred miles south on I-10 to exit 248, turned
west again to Wade Road, and found the entrance to the seventy-
five acre retreat center located right at the entrance to the expansive
Saguaro National Monument Preserve.

Founded in the early 1960s by the Redemptorist priests, it now
contained motel-like rooms for over eighty retreatants and guests.
The rooms were in a series of buildings running in a row, with seven
to eight rooms per building. It was still quite warm when I entered
the main office and registered, received my key, and found the
room, which was very comfortable and had the feeling of recent
remodeling. It contained a small bathroom, a double bed, chair and
table, and a stuffed rocking chair beside a floor lamp. An individual
air conditioner filled the bottom portion of the window, next to a
sign pleading with guests to turn off the unit when leaving the

room. The space was private and secluded, yet I could hear the traffic hissing by close to the entrance of the center.

Aided by several books in their library, I began learning the plant life of the desert; as I walked on the property down to the dry river bed, I identified by sight the ocotillo cactus with its wand-like stems, the soaptree yucca, the ponderosa pine, the teddy bear cholla, and the lupine. Here I felt the age of the mighty and somehow human figures of the saguaro cacti that stood like giant sentinels in the desert topography. Some had lost their skin through either disease or age, so they stood like wire mesh figures with intricate tough interiors, mere skeletons now of their once fleshier fullness.

I walked in the desert in the early afternoon. Other retreatants were staying here but I saw them only at meals; seldom were they out walking on the property. I felt more strongly in this geography that I have two fundamental impulses in me: the desire to help, to assist people in whatever circumstances and however I am able; the other an impulse to abandon individuals in my life, part of an impulse to dismantle things. I had felt these two urges my entire life and realized that the only way to deal with the destructive force was through forgiveness, through letting go, and through generous gestures serving other people. Toward the end of his journey through the planets of Paradiso, Dante the pilgrim meets on Venus the young Cunizza, a sister of a tyrant in Italy. Though she has loved much and often, both in and out of marriage, she is placed in this realm of the Blessed because of forgiveness:

> ...and I glitter here because
> I was o'ermastered by this planet's flame;
> Yet gaily I forgive myself the cause
> Of this my lot, for here (though minds of clay
> May think this strange) 'tis gain to me, not loss.
> (IX:32–36; qtd. in Luke, 143)

Dante drew my attention to one's ability to forgive oneself with a light heart, to step out of the ego's demanding desires and engage the levity of feeling over the gravity of despair when approaching one's faults and shortcomings. Cunizza's salvation relied on her ability to treat her faults with a charity born of paradise. The desert walks brought these two forces within me into mutual relief. The desert as landscape exposed the internal terrains in me as I sensed how necessary it was to cultivate a feeling of compassion for others and myself as a saving quality of forgiveness for all my weaknesses.

When I visited the ample library of the retreat center, I discovered a book by the spiritual writer David Cooper, *Silence, Simplicity and Solitude: A Guide for Spiritual Retreat*. He offered an image to help me understand forgiveness. Pretend you are in a dark room with no light source but the matches you hold. Light one in the darkness. That light is forgiveness. Soon it goes out. Light another one and hold it until it goes out. Such is the life-long repetitive process of forgiveness. He also asks that we visualize those we have hurt, and then ask their forgiveness. We visualize those who have hurt us, and we say to them: "I forgive you." Then we say to those whom we have hurt and those who have wounded us: "Just as I want to be happy, so you be happy. Just as I want to be peaceful, so you be peaceful" (47).

This simple set of exercises had a calming affect; the destructive thoughts, feelings of resentment, hurt pride, and wounding looks or gestures I seem to store up began to shrink in size, like malignant tumors. Cooper's exercises were portable, so I practiced them on my desert walks, especially up the dry arroyos in the morning. Forgiving others was itself a form of prayer and should be done, as Cunizza realized, in a spirit of gaiety, even celebration. I asked God to allow me to forgive others and then to let the afflictions I felt from them dissipate. What a deep liberation occurred at this moment! Freedom was so profound in its simplicity, like God Himself. Self-enslavement in my own ego's slights and wishes was constructed of a subtle web that snagged me almost without my being aware. I thought while in the desert of my daily life and the ways I was ensnared because I ceased loving and forgiving others. The desert revealed the crucial ability to constantly adapt to changes, subtle and grand, stark and simple. Whenever I could imitate the growth, the space and the independence of the desert plants, I moved closer to God's will. Be stubborn, yet yield.

I walked each morning into the Sonoran desert while the light was still a restful blue-grey and before the sun rose to flood the tips of the saguaro cacti rising vertically twenty to thirty feet above the desert soil. They seemed to stretch their long, sometimes stubby arms, in welcome celebration, greeting the new day and saying farewell in the evening to its gentle passing.

I sat in front of the enormous pile of chocolate brown rocks stacked in a magnificent mound some forty feet high; on the lea side from the monastery, they were covered with petroglyphs left from the Hohokam tribe that inhabited the region more than fifteen hundred years ago. Through binoculars I studied their intriguing shapes: animals that looked like large cats smiling, their stiff tails straight out of their behinds like propulsion jets; star figures, men adorned with cosmic headdresses; adults holding the hands of children.

In the rock pile the stillness in the glyph figures transformed the region into a memorial bridge, a time corridor where AD 500 and AD 1998 met in the repose of the animal and mortal figures looking down at me staring up from the wash below, which was windswept and scat-pocked from mountain lions, coyotes, gila monsters, and raccoons. These were the brothers and sisters of the long lineage of time that gathered its vapors into the rock-hard images the wind tried but failed to erase, or my own mortal coil efface. I adopted the habit of coming out alone in the early morning to sit by the figures in the rocks and imagined those who carved them and what these mythic and cultural images wished to say to me across time. Were these their gods and goddesses, accompanied by their sacred animals that helped them on their journey through such a harsh and at times stingy landscape?

I also discovered the most elaborate and inviting sculptures of the Stations of the Cross just in front of the petroglyphs, up a slight rise accessed by a metal staircase. Large crosses twelve feet high, they spread out over the desert in a circle of perhaps a quarter mile. At their base was affixed a bronze plaque identifying each scene. Many had benches in front of them where one might sit and meditate. The stations were so close to the petroglyphs that I could revolve slowly and worship in two worlds at once to the same divine source.

Early each morning I rose and hiked out to greet the Hohokam figures. Then I journeyed into the desert with the stations as my resting spots. I walked each day, enacting a small pilgrimage through the

Christ and the Hohokam People

Via Dolorosa, a journey of suffering, but marked by individuals along the way who stepped forward to help Christ in his woundedness. They represented moments of service and generosity. The stations took on the depth of a deeply layered poem, including an underworld descent, a rise to the top of the mountain and a final decline into death. All of this suffering prepared one for a rebirth and renewal of soul. My imagination tenaciously grasped this journey because it seemed to transform before my eyes and heart as *the* human journey. Something deep in me discovered its pattern in these fourteen poetic interludes offered for meditation and renewal.

What became central was a feeling of suffering through the stations with Christ, to feel his sacrificial impulse toward humanity. The stations revealed how he entered the deepest and most isolated desert and returned to show us that death was not the end of life. Death was not even an experience we move through once; our lives were filled with deaths, some of which called my attention to them more than others. Some occurred with such subtlety that I only became aware of them through a sudden and often surprising remembrance. The images imparted to me as I walked the gravel path a deep wisdom of how a life needed to be accepted and lived.

The cross appeared to me as both a way of life and the weight of life at one moment. I asked myself: *What wanted to be seen in each station of Christ's pilgrimage toward his own death? What wished to be revealed?* The questions helped to deepen my participation in these moments of his destiny. Each depicted a deeply psychological and emotional experience through his embodiment in time and invited me to enter it as fully as my imagination allowed.

In this desert atmosphere, the stations had found me. I sat in the welcoming chapel made of cedar with full windows that opened to the landscape. In its simple but attractive architectural space I meditated on the words on the wall in front of the altar: "The desert will lead you to your heart where I will speak." The placement of the stations in the quiet stillness of the desert landscape allowed them to speak with much greater depth.

I reflected on the well-known mantra of the popular mythologist, Joseph Campbell: "Follow your bliss." Yes, provided I am also prepared to accept the consequences of such a journey that might also insist: "Tend to your blisters." To deny this suffering of the stations was to live sentimentally. I realized that my own sufferings, from whatever size cross they arose, must be seen in light of these stations if I were to grasp what divine love was capable of. What if I were to take my own emotional and psychological afflictions and give them to Christ to carry? What if I were to begin taking all of what I feared and submitted them to the story of Christ's suffering? Perhaps the narrative itself would absorb the wounds of my tattered history by giving my own plot a needed salve.

The stations invited me to meditate on my own life thus far, how I had been helped by people who gratuitously stepped forward to relieve some suffering I had fallen into, scourged by others, crucified by still others. I had known many Veronicas and several Simons of Cyrene who had aided me. The stations in their particular events revealed my life story through a larger narrative that was strangely healing and soothing through its pain and suffering. The Via Dolorosa depicted in these powerful desert stations shifted my own attitude toward my suffering.

The Via Dolorosa was a full and profound desert experience, a wilderness entry, where God's voice rang clearest. Nowhere did nothingness speak as sharply as in the journey of the stations in the desert, a poetic rendering of one soul stripped to nothing, even of life itself. Therein resided the most constant power of relinquishment. Whatever acts one performs in the world, Meister Eckhart writes in Sermon 32, one must, in order to avoid the snares of an ego-driven, merchant mentality, remain free and unfettered by everything so that only nothingness remains. Only then, he claims, "are your deeds spiritual and divine" (452). Resurrection, if understood through Eckhart, was a birth into nothingness, into a disposition in which all that one performed in life was guided by compassion that emerged from a sense of nothingness. The paradox here was that abundance, a sense of more-than-enough, was to be discovered in nothing. The desert descended into me in its profound stillness, its austere nothingness.

Christ and the Hohokam People

Stillness in Motion

Things move gracefully in stillness
Even in the tomb is movement
a sacred friend of stillness.
In death stillness has an inner
motion—
A slight turn, the flame up of
Breakdown—
A stillness comes over me in the
desert's subtle body.
In the Sonoran desert poison milkweed
grows into stillness.
No one sees its white bloom
breach from out the green waxy plant.
If I can be still as death,
then a bit of commotion emerges from under
a bottle, or beside an abandoned
truck tire,
its rubber still smelling of Albuquerque and
San Antonio, Houston and New Orleans.
Death's stillness settles over words
squiggling to life on a blank white page,
the words' wounds that dry to scars
immobile and in motion on the back of
a desert landscape,
futile attempts to scratch past death.
But the silent scrub oak and Beavertail cactus
send words home into the dark silence where
even Death's roilings are muted in time.
(*Casting the Shadows*, 45)

John of the Cross's reflections on Job encouraged me to meditate on the wounds of Christ, and through them my own battered nature. He cites Job's own cries over the pain of his wounded nature by God: "He hath broken me and set me up for His mark to wound me; He hath compassed me round about with His lances; He hath wounded all my loins. . . . He hath broken me with wound upon wound" (*Dark Night of the Soul*, 108–9). The deepest mystery is the mystery of affliction and woundedness and the possibility of seeing them as gifts from God. Forgiveness arises not from where we are attuned to God but from where our deepest wounds reside, even the wound of doubt.

Each morning, as I made the pilgrimage in the desert of the stations, I gained some new understanding of the place of wounds in my life and how easy it is to wound others through thoughts, words, and deeds. I asked for the grace of understanding the five wounds of Christ and the many wounds of my own shattered and struggling condition. The stations revealed not just what Christ suffered to liberate me from my own nature, but something of my own nature that felt the deep agony of my own afflicted life. In this recognition arose a sense of hope, a surprising response for me and perhaps closer to the miracle of being able to hope in suffering.

Reflecting on wounds seemed to invite my father's presence into the landscape. I remembered one day coming home from classes at Cleveland State University and finding my father sitting in the living room at 11 a.m. He had been fired from his job after twenty-seven years with the same company. His drinking had forced him to be absent from work too many days; they let him go. No warning, no lead up, just up and out. I felt myself falling into the basement in fear. He sat quietly, stunned, hurt, expressionless, and distraught. I did not see him drink again after that date, though he continued to live out the personality of an alcoholic, but on a lower register. Eventually, with my mother's help, he found a job at the city's Municipal Court and, good with numbers and accounting principles, worked several more years before retiring. But he remained crushed and intimidated by life, though he suffered his cross far less violently. Wherever he walked, a brooding darkness dogged him; he carried that atmosphere into every room.

When I visited home after he had retired, I learned that he would not go outside because he believed he smelled, that a foul odor emanated from him. "I can't go out," he told me, "because people will notice the stink I give off." Troubled by his reason for staying cooped up in the house all the time, I approached him once from behind and sniffed him out. No odor, no smell. "Dad," I told him point blank one morning as he sat watching television, "There is no smell coming from you. You do not stink." "Yes I do, and it is embarrassing. I cannot go out even after I change my pants and wear clean clothes. It will not wash off." He remained convinced and no reasoning would deter him from his position of feeling soiled and smelly.

What had replaced his drinking was his stinking body. Had he now begun living out the life of a stinker, even a shit, for his past behaviors and addictions? Both odious and odorous had he become through his imaginal stench. No amount of talking to him altered his perception one jot. He refused any suggestions of counseling; his condition did not improve for a very long time.

It was obvious that he could not, would not forgive himself, no matter how hard he prayed. I believe he eventually died unforgiving and unforgiven, but I hope I am wrong. I felt his presence now as I sat in front of the stations and imagined the size and weight of the cross he carried to his death. His burden may have finally exhausted all his energy. My hope, however, is that he did forgive himself as I had forgiven him; otherwise, our wounds continue to fester and the soul remain toxic, unsettled, and full of destructive impulses to wound others and self in a repetition of pain and violence.

As I ended my few days' stay at Picture Rock Retreat Center, I felt blessed in being given these desert Stations of the Cross. A piece of this pilgrimage had been offered that was essential for the completion of my journey. My father's visits had also helped me to reconcile a part of myself that was wounded by him through my childhood with his own painful and suffering nature. We had come to some agreement on this journey and told one another we never stopped loving one another. I feel that same release today. To forgive is to heal some deep affliction gnawing at the heart of our being.

This entire pilgrimage had been in the service, unbeknownst to me until the end, of forgiving my father and being forgiven by him. A third forgiveness enters here: his forgiving himself and letting me know that such an important act had occurred within him. To accept one's deeply wounded nature is to solicit forgiveness.

I packed my truck with a new anticipation and urgency as I prepared to spend my last night in retreat centers. After dinner I visited the petroglyphs for a last conversation and already felt a sense of loss. I had fallen in love with the Hohokam people through the images they traced on the rocks as memories of their presence here.

Their crafted images were so austere and beautiful and expressive of their mythology and spirituality. I then walked amidst the silent and protective cacti that guarded the stations day and night and gave thanks for what had been revealed to me in my micro pilgrimage through their stark, painful, and generous poetry. I trudged along the large rocks in the arroyo and felt the sand and debris that had washed out of the mountains. This natural highway through the property, with here and there an abandoned Whirlpool clothes washer or a rusted shell of a 1946 Ford pickup, offered a place of calm and serenity; it often pulled me farther from the noise of the highway into deeper solitude. I loved this stony wound in the earth, a special path holding the memory and the promise of gushing water running through the center's property to nourish the spare foliage lining it. Such a scene was an accurate snapshot of my entire pilgrimage.

In these last moments that ended fifteen weeks' traveling and dwelling in exterior terrains and interior landscapes, I saluted God for His bounty, His revelations, and His gentle wisdom in calling me to the road and the byways of these magnificent retreat centers and the people who inhabited them.

Peregrination. Pengrination. Both the journey and the memory of it recorded in words embodied a changed perspective toward some fundamental qualities of my own person and a recognition that the struggle to believe, to sustain a faith amid doubt, is a central part of an entire lifetime's pilgrimage. Questions of whether God does or does not exist faded into irrelevance. I was beyond belief into the land of knowing. Rather, how does the will of God show itself in what I experience as joy, suffering, intuitions, callings, desires, hesitancies, nothingness—these are the areas I wish to explore further as I learn more explicitly how to forgive myself my own weaknesses and failures and how I carry this forgiveness to others. Every soul is a wounded wriggling gift, struggling, like me, with crosses that sometimes become too burdensome, too weighty and splintered to bear. I hope the struggle continues for a lifetime.

My father died the year before I embarked on my pilgrimage. He had fallen on the cement walkway leading to the backdoor of his home and had broken his hip. He lay in bed for two days, fearful of having to go to the hospital. Finally, he succumbed to the pain and my brother Bill called 911. After his surgery we talked by phone often as he recovered in the hospital. Having broken his left hip—the same one that my own surgery replaced with a prosthesis—he was now my artificial hip brother and we joked about it. He looked forward to the calls, which I made daily. These were to be our last conversations.

One morning he died suddenly in his hospital room; his body could not withstand the trauma of surgery. My brother Bill was with him when he passed. Losing a parent changed everything. My father and I ended as friends, even expressing affection for one another, something that rarely happened in my life growing up. I was pleased that he appeared out of somewhere having decided to take advantage of having me to himself; he traveled with me for the entire pilgrimage. "I have some things that I need to say to you," he once remarked early on the journey. "I am sorry that it has taken me this time after passing over, to return and express them." His presence might be the most important part of this entire voyage. I recorded here only a small fraction of our conversations. Some things are best left unwritten. But there is no question, I sensed, that he had finally forgiven himself, me, others and that the spirit in which he traveled with me was of a loving and open companion.

In the end we shared the same body wound, an appropriate finale to a life of trauma and affliction. When all was said and done, we were in fact joined at the broken but mutually forgiving hip; we both enjoyed new ones. Wounded and united; how the body insisted on carrying the metaphors for our lives, both individual and communal!

Just having him along for the ride made the journey a beneficent and healing act of remembrance. Remembering is itself often an unknown journey, full of surprises, as this pilgrimage taught me. After our first encounter, I kept the passenger seat empty and piled all the supplies I wanted to remain accessible into the back seat. I knew that dad wanted his own seat. Now, through the images of my father, I turned to my sons and tried to imagine their image of me. I knew that I had most likely repeated some of the same destructive behaviors I had inherited from my father—how does anyone escape them? The great task ahead of me was further and regular self-for-giveness in a deep spirit of compassion.

I wrote through the dark corridor of destruction, through parts of my childhood I have not wanted to face. This record of a journey I could not have foreseen would return me to painful parts of my past that have been, I believe, redeemed, set right, reshaped, fixed in place, through an act of forgiveness that emerged only through grace. Like being fitted with a spiritual prosthesis, my life now has less pain, more stability in the wound. Now I can let all of my child-hood wounds evaporate. Writing is a human attempt to retrieve time; remembering willfully turns the clock back, yet invites today's time to wrap around it. All of this is in the service of making death less final, less a period than an ellipsis. Writing allowed me to nego-tiate my way through time in a way that speech, in its temporal and ephemeral nature, did not. The feeling of liberation reflects a moment of grace unconditionally given. Forgiveness is at the heart of it all—*I swear.*

I end this sojourn, both on the road and on paper, with a short poem from the journals of Teresa of Avila, who expresses a simple truth to help anyone who is puzzled by the meaning of it all and who seeks solace in retreat in a handful of words. When full of doubt, seek out poetry as a way to pray:

> Let nothing disturb you,
> Nothing dismay you.
> All things are passing,
> God never changes.
> Patient endurance
> Attains all things. . . .
> God alone suffices.
> (*Mystical Writings*, 15)

The spare beauty of Teresa's prayer contains an entire cosmos of understanding the force of God's active presence and benevolent reassurance if we can remain patient penitents.

And to you, Roger, my father: over and out.

FINIS (2000/2015)

Appendix I
Other Monastic Stays

St. Andrew's Priory
Valyermo, California
661-944-2178
www.standrewsabbey.com

Located north of Los Angeles off Route 14 outside of Palmdale, the Priory sits on the edge of the Mojave Desert in the foothills of the San Gabriel Mountains. It consists of an old ranch that was converted into a retreat center, with very comfortable air-conditioned rooms, tasty but simple meals, and a greathearted spirit within the Trappist Cistercian community. Its rustic setting, desert landscape, and feel of a ranch blend with the amenities of a comfortable motel.

The bookstore is ample and one of the best of any retreat center I have visited. It concentrates on the classics of the Church and contains as well a separate filled with elegant icons. The monastery also harbors a huge ceramics shop where monks make small ceramic images of saints that are shipped worldwide.

Meals are taken together in a large dining room. The pace is very relaxed, friendly, and conducive to solitude. Of particular interest are the brightly-painted steel Stations of the Cross placed along a hillside just out back from the private rooms. One hikes the desert and meditates on the fourteen stations.

Serra Retreat Center
Malibu, California
310-456-6631
www.serraretreat.com

Named after the Franciscan priest, Junipero Serra, the apostle of California and founder of the California missions, it is located

289

twelve miles north of the Santa Monica Pier along Highway 1. Operated by the Franciscan Order, it sits just up a hill from a beautiful wooded residential neighborhood. It keeps a busy schedule in its large compound that contains, in addition to private rooms, two large conference rooms and five small meeting rooms. Many parishes use it for large retreats. The rooms are private, often containing a shared bath with the adjoining room. Private individuals, married couples, recovery groups, and special group needs are all accommodated.

A modest bookstore and gift shop is open for small needs. The promontory of land that juts out of the mountain setting offers a magnificent view of the Pacific Ocean as well as of luxurious neighboring estates. While this is a large complex, one can still find pockets of solitude on the property or one can enjoy a vigorous hike to the ocean.

La Casa de Maria
Santa Barbara, California
805-969-5031
www.lacasademaria.com

In a quiet part of Montecito, a city adjacent to Santa Barbara and just off Highway 101 at the San Ysidro exit sits the twenty-six acre retreat center. The buildings convey a rustic hacienda quality amidst large live oaks and a small river that runs through the property. Programs are plentiful and the site is busy most of the year. The staff and workers here are friendly and helpful in making one's stay a pleasure. It is also a wonderful place to come and simply spend the day walking the grounds, visiting the chapel, meditating, praying, journaling, and enjoying the quiet and serene natural setting.

Our Lady of Peace Retreat Center
Beaverton, Oregon
503-649-7127
www.olp.retreat.org

The center sits in a residential neighborhood in a suburb south of Portland. It is operated by the Franciscan Missionary Sisters of Our Lady of Sorrows on a twenty-five property. Rooms are large and spacious. Comfortable beds, chairs, and a desk are in each room, all of which are housed in the same building as the chapel, bookstore, gift shop, and dining hall. The center has the feel of a suburban parish, but it is quiet and well organized.

With services daily in the chapel as well as an inviting series of Stations of the Cross for beginning retreatants, it offers a familiar surrounding that might be beneficial for one just beginning retreats before moving on to more isolated centers.

Ghost Ranch
Abiquiu, New Mexico
505-685-4333
www.ghostranch.com

One of the most famous and frequently visited retreat centers in the United States, Ghost Ranch is northwest of Santa Fe on US 84. It is also one of the largest sites in the country, occupying over twenty-one thousand acres in the high desert. The Presbyterian Church operates the conference center, which enjoys a steady stream of people coming in to study a wide variety of subjects. Georgia O'Keefe made it one of her favorite places from the 1930s until her death; she loved to paint the cliffs, the large mesas, and the desert's wild and spectacular growth.

The dining hall, which can serve hundreds of people per meal, is efficient and spacious. Food is excellent, served cafeteria-style. Walking the high desert early in the morning or toward evening reveals an almost mystical play of light on the faces of the mesas and the land. Its austere and simple beauty makes it one of the most sought-after retreat centers for people from around the country.

Monastery of Christ in the Desert
Abiquiu, New Mexico
575-613-4233
www.christdesert.org

Out of Santa Fe, take Route 84/285 northwest. Pass the sign and entrance for Ghost Ranch, and two miles further up the highway watch for a small sign marking Highway 151. Turn left and drive with care along a thirteen-mile gravel and red clay road that often runs parallel to the Chamas River. The road dead-ends in the parking area to the Benedictine monastery. Situated in the Chamas Canyon at an elevation of sixty-five hundred feet, amid breathtaking mesas, the retreat center offers a range of rooms, from rustic with bath and shower down the walkway, to more comfortable rooms with private baths.

The elegant chapel has massive windows that expose the giant walls of the mesas. The spirit of the place is serene, full of solitude and prayer. The gift shop/bookstore is one place where retreatants may congregate and converse. Thomas Merton stayed here in 1968 and felt a strong affinity for its desert austerity.

Holy Trinity Monastery
Saint David, Arizona
520-720-4642
www.holytrinitymonastery.org

Located about forty-five miles east of Tucson, the Monastery sits off US 80 about nine miles from Interstate 10 and eight miles from Tombstone, Arizona. It is fourteen miles north of the famous town of Tombstone. The Benedictine Order operates the Spanish-style center, where oblates occupy a small village of trailers throughout the property. Campers with RVs are also welcome; they can park in a large, grassy field in back of the main buildings and hook up to power and water lines. A thrift store is on the site, and the community helps the neighboring people by selling used merchandise as well as jams and jellies made by the inhabitants of the center. A fine little bookstore/gift shop greets the visitor in a small building where one registers.

Retreatants use two bathrooms at the end of the hall. A large sitting room in the middle of the building gives one an alternative to staying in one's room to read or write. A beautiful adobe chapel in Spanish style with an elegant fountain in front is a joy to visit, whether in silence or for Mass or prayers. It contains an inviting mix of priests, sisters, oblates, and married couples.

On the property is a well-kept secret: an exquisitely ornate and detailed museum of some nine rooms, each depicting a particular theme (old altars, crèches, early nineteenth-century memorabilia). I reserved a time to visit it and was given a two-hour tour by the gracious hostess and curator.

Meals, taken communally, are simple and delicious. The Stations of the Cross wander through the thick foliage. Deep in the property is one of the finest and most extensive bird sanctuaries in the region; for part of the way the path parallels the San Pedro River. Bring good binoculars and mosquito repellant. The small cemetery next to the chapel is worth a visit for its unusual and striking gravestones and markers. Finally, an opulent library of over fifty thousand volumes makes it a unique opportunity for religious studies.

St. Anthony's Greek Orthodox Monastery

Florence, Arizona

520-868-3188

www.stanthonysmonastery.org

East of Phoenix past Mesa and Gilbert, watch for Highway 60, which travels south to Florence. Beyond Florence there is a small sign identifying the left-hand turn-off. Drive back into the flat desert landscape; the road leads to the entrance of this garden paradise located in the middle of the Mojave Desert. A new monastery, it offers lush greenery and beautiful adobe architecture. No shorts allowed. Rooms are comfortable, the food good.

During services, those who are not Greek Orthodox are required to sit outside, where one can observe the services through glass windows. I found the arrangement isolating, severing me from the spiritual life of the community. My stay was short and pleasant but a very different experience.

Appendix II

Monastery Websites and Further Readings

Websites Offering Directories
for Retreat Centers and Monasteries

1. Retreats Online Directory: retreats, gateways, workshops: http://www.retreatsonline.com/
2. Abbey of the Monastic Way: http://monasticway.tripod.com/
3. OSB Association of Benedictine Retreat Centers Directory: http://www.osb.org/retreats/
4. UK Retreat Association website: http://www.retreats.org.uk/
5. Google Directory: Society>Religion and Spirituality>Yoga >Retreats: http://directory.google.com/Top/Society/ReligionandSpirituality/Yoga Retreats and Workshops/
6. Google Directory: Health>Alternative>Meditation>Retreats http://directory.google.com/Top/Health/Alternative/Meditation/Retreats/
7. Google Directory: Society>Religion and Spirituality>Budhism>Centers and Groups by Region: http://directory.google.com.Top /Society /ReligionandSpirituality/Buddhism/Centers and Groups by Region/
8. Tricycle.com: Dharma Center Directory Search: http://www.tricycle.com/resources/find-dharma-centers

Appendix II

Further Readings

For those wishing to read additional books on God, spirituality, psychology, and the imagination, the titles below may prove useful and enjoyable. Space limitations prohibited their discussion in the book.

Anonymous. *Meditations on the Tarot: A Journey into Christian Hermeticism.* Translated by Robert Powell. New York: Jeremy P. Tarcher/Putnam, 2002.

Armstrong, Karen. *The Bible: The Biography.* London: Atlantic Books, 1988.

Apostolos-Cappadona, Diane, Ed. *Art, Creativity and the Sacred: An Anthology in Religion and Art.* New York: Continuum, 1996.

Appelbaum, David, Ed. "Prayer and Meditation." *Parabola: Myth, Tradition and the Search for Meaning* 24, no. 2 (May, 1999).

Asher, Charles. *Soundings: Seventy-Five Reflections on Love and Romance, Personal Development and the Search for Meaning.* Green Bay, WI: Desert Springs Publications, 1988.

———. and Dennis Patrick Slattery. *Simon's Crossing: A Novel.* New York: iUniverse, 2010.

Bangley, Bernard, Ed. *Nearer to the Heart of God: Daily Readings with the Christian Mystics.* Brewster, MA: Paraclete Press, 2005.

Barasch, Marc Ian. *The Healing Path: A Soul Approach to Healing.* New York: Putnam, 1994.

Barks, Coleman, Trans. *The Essential Rumi.* Edison, NJ: Castle Books, 1977.

Barnhart, Bruno. *Second Simplicity: The Inner Shape of Christianity.* Mahwah, NJ: Paulist Press, 1999.

Bulgakov, Sergei. *The Holy Grail and the Eucharist.* Translated by Boris Jakim. Hudson, NY: Lindisfarne Books, 1997.

Casey, Michael. *Sacred Reading: The Ancient Art of Lectio Divina.* Liguori, MO: Liguori Publications, 1995.

Chodron, Pema. *No Time to Lose: A Timely Guide to the Way of the Bodhisattva.* Boston: Shambhala, 2007.

———. *Taking the Leap: Freeing Ourselves from Old Habit and Fears.* Boston: Shambhala, 2010.

Coleman, Simon and John Elsner. *Pilgrimage: Past and Present in the World Religions.* Cambridge: Harvard UP, 1995.

Corbett, Lionel. *The Religious Function of the Psyche.* New York: Routledge, 1997.

De Waal, Esther. *The Celtic Way of Prayer: The Recovery of the Religious Imagination.* New York: Doubleday, 1997.

Dossey, Larry, MD. *Healing Words: The Power of Prayer and the Practice of Medicine.* San Francisco: HarperCollins, 1993.

Dryer, Elizabeth A., Ed. *The Cross in Christian Tradition: From Paul to Bonaventure.* New York: Paulist Press, 2000.

Eberle, Gary. *Sacred Time and the Search for Meaning.* Boston: Shambhala, 2003.

Edinger, Edward F. *Transformation of the God-Image: An Elucidation of Jung's* Answer to Job. Toronto: Inner City Books, 1992.

———. *The Bible and the Psyche: Individuation Symbolism in the Old Testament.* Toronto: Inner City Books, 1988.

———. *The Christian Archetype: A Jungian Commentary on the Life of Christ.* Toronto: Inner City Books, 1987.

Ferguson, Kitty. *The Fire in the Equations: Science, Religion and the Search for God.* Grand Rapids, MI: William B. Eerdmans Publishing, 1994.

France, Peter. *Hermits: The Insights of Solitude.* New York: St. Martin's Press, 1996.

Goldstein, Joseph. *Insight Meditation: The Practice of Freedom.* Boston: Shambhala, 1994.

Goldstein, Niles Elliot. *God at the Edges: Searching for the Divine in Uncomfortable and Unexpected Places.* New York: Bell Tower, 2000.

Greeley, Andrew M. *Religion as Poetry.* New Brunswick, NJ: Transaction Publishers, 1995.

———. *The Catholic Imagination.* Berkeley: University of California Press, 2000.

Halifax, Joan. *The Fruitful Darkness: Reconnecting With the Body of the Earth.* San Francisco: HarperSanFrancisco, 1993.

Inchausti, Robert, Ed. *Seeds.* By Thomas Merton. Boston: Shambhala, 2002.

Jiminez, Juan Ramon. "Oceans." *The Soul is Here For Its Own Joy: Sacred Poems from Many Cultures.* Ed. by Robert Bly. Hopewell, NJ: Ecco Press, 1995.

Johnson, Maxwell E., Ed. *Benedictine Daily Prayer: A Short Breviary.* Collegeville, MN: Liturgical Press, 2005.

Jung, Carl. *Psychology and Religion: West and East.* Trans. R.F.C. Hull. Bollingen Series XX. Vol. 11 of *The Collected Works of C.G. Jung.* Princeton: Princeton University Press, 1977.

Kelsey, Morton T. *The Other Side of Silence: A Guide to Christian Meditation.* New York: Paulist Press, 1976.

Kurtz, Ernest and Katherine Ketcham. *The Spirituality of Imperfection: Storytelling and the Search for Meaning.* New York: Bantam, 2002.

Levoy, Gregg. *Callings: Finding and Following an Authentic Life.* New York: Three Rivers Press, 1997.

Lipton, Bruce H. *The Biology of Belief: Unleashing the Power of Consciousness, Matter and Miracles.* Santa Rosa, CA: Mountain of Love/Elite Books, 2005.

Louth, Andrew. *The Wilderness of God.* Nashville: Abingdon Press, 1991.

Mahaffey, Patrick, Ed. *Evolving God Images: Essays on Religion, Individuation, and Postmodern Spirituality.* Bloomington: iUniverse, 2014.

Markides, Kyriacos C. *The Mountain of Silence: A Search for Orthodox Spirituality.* New York: Doubleday, 2002.

Mauser, Ulrich. *Christ in the Wilderness: The Wilderness Theme in the Second Gospel and its Basis in the Biblical Tradition.* Eugene, OR: Wipf and Stock Publishers, 2009.

Merton, Thomas. *Opening the Bible.* Collegeville, MN: The Liturgical Press, 1986.

Miles, Jack. *God: A Biography.* New York: Vintage, 1995.

Milosz, Czeslaw, Ed. *A Book of Luminous Things: An International Anthology of Poetry.* San Diego: Harcourt, Brace, 1996.

Mitchell, Donald W. and James Wiseman, OSB, Eds. *The Gethsemane Encounter: A Dialogue on the Spiritual Life by Buddhist and Christian Monastics.* New York: Continuum, 1997.

Mitchell, Donald W. *Spirituality and Emptiness: The Dynamics of Spiritual Life in Buddhism and Christianity.* New York: Paulist Press, 1991.

Mogenson, Greg. *God is a Trauma: Vicarious Religion and Soul-Making.* Dallas: Spring, 1989.

Moore, Thomas. *A Religion of One's Own: A Guide to Creating a Personal Spirituality in a Secular World.* New York: Gotham Books, 2014.

Needleman, Jacob. *Time and the Soul.* New York: Doubleday, 1998.

Norris, Kathleen. *Dakota: A Spiritual Geography.* Boston: Houghton Mifflin, 1993.

———. *Cloister Walk.* New York: Penguin Putnam, 1996.

O'Donohue, John. *Eternal Echoes: Exploring Our Yearning to Belong.* New York: HarperCollins, 1999.

O'Kane, Françoise. *Sacred Chaos: Reflections on God's Shadow and the Dark Self.* Toronto: Inner City Books, 1994.

Osman, Ahmed. *Christianity: An Ancient Egyptian Religion.* Rochester, VT: Bear and Company, 2005.

Otto, Rudolf. *The Idea of the Holy.* Translated by John Harvey. New York: Oxford University Press, 1958.

Pagels, Elaine. *The Origin of Satan.* New York: Random House, 1995.

Pelikan, Jaroslav. *Jesus Through the Centuries: His Place in the History of Culture.* New York: Harper and Row, 1999.

Phan, Peter C. and Jung Young Lee, Eds. *Journeys at the Margin: Toward an Autobiographical Theology in American-Asian Perspective.* Collegeville, MN: Liturgical Press, 1999.

Ricoeur, Paul. *Figuring the Sacred: Religion, Narrative, and Imagination.* Translated by David Pellauer, Edited by Mark I. Wallace. Minneapolis: Fortress Press, 1995.

Rogers, Barbara J. *In the Center: The Story of a Retreat.* Notre Dame: Ave Maria Press, 1983.

Sardello, Robert. *Freeing the Soul from Fear.* New York: Riverhead, 1999.

———. and Therese Schroeder-Sheker. *Silence: The Mystery of Wholeness.* Berkeley: Goldenstone Press, Heaven and Earth Publishing, and North Atlantic Books, 2008.

Thera, Nyanaponika. *The Heart of Buddhist Meditation.* Foreword by Sylvia Boorstein. San Francisco: Weiser Books, 2014.

Sellner, Edward C. *Finding the Monk Within: Great Monastic Values for Today.* Mahwah, NJ: HiddenSpring, 2008.

Sells, Michael A. *Mystical Languages of Unsaying.* Chicago: University of Chicago Press, 1987.

Slattery, Dennis Patrick. *Day-to-Day Dante: Exploring Personal Myth Through* The Divine Comedy. Bloomington: iUniverse, 2011.

———. *Riting Myth, Mythic Writing: Plotting Your Personal Story.* Skiatook, OK: Fisher King Press, 2014.

Smith, Huston. *Why Religion Matters: The Fate of the Human Spirit in an Age of Disbelief.* San Francisco: HarperSanFrancisco, 2001.

Solovyov, Vladimir. *The Meaning of Love.* Translated by Thomas Beyer, Jr. Hudson, NY: Lindisfarne Books, 1985.

Storr, Anthony. *Solitude: A Return to the Self.* New York: Ballantine Books, 2005.

Suzuki, D. T. *An Introduction to Zen Buddhism.* Foreword by Carl Jung. New York: Grove/Atlantic, 1994.

Taylor, Mark C. *After God.* Chicago: University of Chicago Press, 2009.

Turner, Alice K. *The History of Hell.* New York: Harcourt Brace, 1995.

Van Kaam, Adrian. *The Mystery of Transforming Love.* Denville, NJ: Dimension Books, 1982.

———. *Envy and Originality.* Rev. and ed. Susan Muto. Pittsburgh: Epiphany Books, 2012.

Welwood, John, Ed. *Awakening the Heart: East/West Approaches to Psychotherapy and the Healing Relationship.* Boston: Shambhala, 1983.

White, Victor. *God and the Unconscious.* Foreword by C. G. Jung. Dallas: Spring Publications, 1982.

References

Adult Children of Alcoholics: Alcoholic/Dysfunctional Families. Torrance, CA: World Service Organization, 2006.

Aivazian, Sirarpi Feredjian. "Eastern Christian Pilgrimage." *Encyclopedia of Religion*. Edited by Mircea Eliade. New York: MacMillan, 1987.

Alighieri, Dante. *Inferno*. Translated by Mark Musa. New York: Penguin, 1984.

———. *Purgatorio*. Translated by Dorothy Sayers. New York: Penguin, 1955.

———. *Paradiso. The Divine Comedy*. Translated by Allen Madelbaum. New York: Alfred A. Knopf, 1995.

———. *La Vita Nuova*. Translated by Barbara Reynolds. New York: Penguin Books, 1971.

Allison, Alexander, Herbert Barrows, Caesar Blake, et al. *The Norton Anthology of Poetry*. Third Edition. New York: Norton, 1983.

Benedict. *The Rule of Saint Benedict*. Edited by Timothy Fry, OSB. New York: Vintage Spiritual Classics, 1998.

Berry, Thomas. *A Moment of Grace*. Sonoma: Global Perspectives, 1995.

Blake, William. *The Complete Poetry and Prose of William Blake*. Edited by David Erdman. Commentary by Harold Bloom. New York: Doubleday, 1988.

Bly, Robert, James Hillman, and Michael Meade, eds. *The Rag and Bone Shop of the Heart. Poems for Men*. New York: HarperCollins, 1992.

———. ed. *The Soul is Here for Its Own Joy: Sacred Poems From Many Cultures*. Hopewell, NJ: Ecco Press, 1995.

Carretto, Carlos. *Letters from the Desert*. Translated by Rose Mary Hancock. Foreword by Ivan Illich. Maryknoll, NY: Orbis Books, 1998.

Cooper, David A. *Silence, Simplicity and Solitude: A Guide for Spiritual Retreat*. New York: Harmony Books, 1999.

References

Dickinson, Emily. *The Complete Poems of Emily Dickinson*. Edited by Thomas H. Johnson. New York: Little Brown, 1960.

Dillard, Annie. *Pilgrim at Tinker Creek*. New York: HarperCollins, 1999.

Dyer, Wayne. *The Power of Intention*. New York: Hayhouse, 2010.

Eckhart, Meister. *The Essential Sermons, Commentaries, Treatises and Defense*. Mahwah, NJ: Paulist Press, 1981.

Fox, Matthew, ed. *Breakthrough: Meister Eckhart's Creation Spirituality in New Translation*. New York: Doubleday, 1991.

Greeley, Andrew. *The Catholic Imagination*. Berkeley: University of California Press, 2000.

Gelineau, Joseph. *The Psalms*. New York: Paulist Press, 1983.

Guggenbuhl-Craig, Adolf. *From the Wrong Side: A Paradoxical Approach to Psychology*. Translated by Gary V. Hartman. Woodstock, CT: Spring, 1995.

Halifax, Joan. *The Fruitful Darkness: Reconnecting with the Body of the Earth*. San Francisco: HarperSanFrancisco, 1993.

Hampl, Patricia. "Memory and Imagination." *I Could Tell You Stories: Sojourns in the Land of Memory*. New York: W.W. Norton, 1999.

Hanh, Thich Nhat. *Peace is Every Step: The Path of Mindfulness in Everyday Life*. Edited by Arnold Kotler. New York: Bantam, 1992.

———. *The Miracle of Mindfulness: A Manual on Meditation*. Boston: Beacon, 1999.

———. *Living Buddha, Living Christ*. New York: Putnam, 1995.

———. *The Sutra on the Full Awareness of Breathing*. Translated by Annabel Laity. Berkeley: Parallax Press, 1988.

Hart, Patrick, ed. *The Literary Essays of Thomas Merton*. New York: New Directions, 1985.

Heraclitus. *Fragments*. Translated by T.M. Robinson. Toronto: University of Toronto Press, 1991.

Hildegard of Bingen. *Secrets of God*. Translated by Sabina Flanagan. Boston: Shambhala, 1996.

Hobday, Sister Joseph. *The Spiritual Power of Storytelling*. Kansas City, MO: National Catholic Reporter Publishing Co., 1987.

John of the Cross. *Dark Night of the Soul*. Translated by E. Allison Peers. Radford, VA: Wilder Publications, 2008.

Jones, Alexander, ed. *The Jerusalem Bible*. Garden City: Doubleday, 1966.

Jung, C.G. *The Archetypes and the Collective Unconscious*. Translated by R. F. C. Hull and edited by Herbert Read. Vol. 9, Pt. 1, *The Collected Works of C. G. Jung.* Princeton: Princeton University Press.

———. *The Red Book. Liber Novus. A Reader's Edition.* Edited by Sonu Shamdasani and translated by Mark Kyburz, John Peck and Sonu Shamdasani. Philomen Series. New York: Norton, 2009.

Keating, Thomas. *Open Mind, Open Heart: The Contemplative Dimension of the Gospel.* New York: Continuum, 1992.

Kelly, Marcia and Jack. *Sanctuaries: A Guide to Lodgings in Monasteries, Abbeys, and Retreats of the United States.* 2 vols. New York: Bell Tower, 1996.

———. *Sanctuaries, The Complete United States: A Guide to Lodgings in Monasteries, Abbeys, and Retreats.* New York: iUniverse, 2009.

Lane, Belden. *The Solace of Fierce Landscapes: Exploring Desert and Mountain Spirituality.* New York: Oxford University Press, 2007.

Luke, Helen M. *Dark Wood to White Rose: Journey and Transformation in Dante's* Divine Comedy. New York: Parabola, 1993.

McNamara, William. *Christian Mysticism: The Art of the Inner Way.* New York: Continuum, 1991.

Melville, Herman. *Moby-Dick, or The Whale.* Edited by Harrison Heyford and Harry Parker. New York: Norton, 1999.

Merton, Thomas. *Turning Towards the World. The Journals of Thomas Merton.* Vol. IV: 1960–1963. Edited by Victor Kramer. San Francisco: HarperSanFrancisco, 1996.

———. *Bread in the Wilderness.* New York: New Directions, 1997.

———. *Conjectures of a Guilty Bystander.* New York: Image Books, 1968.

———. *Life and Holiness.* Garden City: Image Books, 2013.

———. *Contemplative Prayer.* New York: Herder and Herder, 1969.

———. *Thoughts in Solitude.* New York: Noonday Press, 1999.

———. *Echoing Silence: Thomas Merton on the Vocation of Writing.* Edited by Robert Inchausti. Boston: New Seeds, 2007.

Moorehouse, Geoffrey. *Sun Dancing: A Vision of Medieval Ireland.* San Diego: Harper Brace, 1997.

Morrison, Toni. "Memory, Creation, and Writing." *The Anatomy of Memory: An Anthology.* Edited by James McConkey. New York: Oxford University Press, 1996.

Muller, Wayne. *Sabbath: Restoring the Sacred Rhythm of Rest.* New York: Bantam, 1999.

Nada Hermitage Self-Guided Tour. Crestone, CO, 1995.

References

Neruda, Pablo and Vallejo: *Selected Poems*. Edited by Robert Bly. Boston: Beacon, 1993.

Norwich, Julian of. *Showings*. Translated by Edmund Colledge and James Walsh. Mahwah, NJ: Paulist Press, 1978.

Nouwen, Henri J.M. *The Genesee Diary: Report from a Trappist Monastery*. New York: Doubleday, 1981.

Novak, Philip. *The World's Wisdom: Sacred Texts of the World's Religions*. Edison, NJ: Castle Books, 1994.

Padavano, Anthony. "Writing and Contemplation." *Thomas Merton: A Life For Our Times*. Kansas City, MO: National Catholic Reporter Publishing Company, 1982.

Pethica, James, ed. *Yeats's Poetry, Drama, and Prose*. New York: Norton, 2000.

Picard, Max. *The World of Silence*. Translated by Stanley Godman. Washington, DC: Gateway Books, 2002.

Pratt, Lonni Collins and Father Daniel Homan. *Benedict's Way: An Ancient Monk's Insights for a Balanced Life*. Chicago: Loyola Press, 2000.

Randour, Mary Lou. *Animal Grace: Entering a Spiritual Relationship with our Fellow Creatures*. Novato, CA: New World Library, 2000.

Rilke, Rainer Maria. *Rilke on Love and Other Difficulties*. Translated by John J.L. Mood. New York: Norton, 1994.

Sanford, John. *Through the Belly of the Whale: The Journey of Individuation*. Kansas City, MO: National Catholic Reporter Publishing Co., 1986.

———. *Dreams: Your Royal Road to Healing*. Kansas City, MO: National Catholic Reporter Publishing Co., 1986.

Saramago, Jose. *The Gospel According to Jesus Christ*. Translated by Giovanni Pontiero. San Diego: Harcourt Brace, 1994.

Slattery, Dennis Patrick. *Casting the Shadows: Selected Poems*. Kearney, NE: Morris Publishing, 2001.

Slattery, Dennis Patrick and Lionel Corbett, eds. *Depth Psychology: Meditations in the Field*. Einsiedeln, Switzerland: Daimon-Verlag, 2000.

———. *The Wounded Body: Remembering the Markings of Flesh*. Ithaca: State University of New York Press, 2000.

Steindl-Rast, David. *A Practical Guide to Meditation*. Staten Island: NCR Cassettes.

Thera, Nyanaponika. *The Heart of Buddhist Meditation: A Handbook* of *Mental Training Based on the Buddha's Way of Mindfulness*. Translated from the Pali and Sanskrit. York Beach, ME: Samuel Weiser, Inc., 1996.

Thoreau, Henry David. *Walden and other Writings*. New York: Barnes and Noble, 1993.

Twenty-Four Hours a Day. Hazelden Foundation. Minneapolis: Winston Press, 1975.

The Way of a Pilgrim. Translated by R.M. French. New York: Quality Paperbacks, 1998.

Wordsworth, William. "The world is too much with us." *Literature: Structure, Sound and Sense*. Sixth Edition. Edited by Laurence Perrine and Thomas R. Arp. Fort Worth: Harcourt Brace Jovanovich, 1993.

"Zendo Form and Practice Procedures," 1/97. Sonoma Mountain Zen Center. Santa Rosa, CA.

About the Author

DENNIS PATRICK SLATTERY, PhD has been teaching for forty-five years, the last twenty-three in the Mythological Studies Program at Pacifica Graduate Institute in Carpinteria, California. He is the author, co-author, editor, or co-editor of twenty-four volumes, including six volumes of poetry: *Casting the Shadows: Selected Poems*; *Just Below the Water Line: Selected Poems; Twisted Sky: Selected Poem*; *The Beauty Between Words* with Chris Paris; *Feathered Ladder: Selected Poems* with Brian Landis; and *Road, Frame Window: A Poetics of Seeing. Selected Poetry of Timothy J. Donohue, Donald Carlson and Dennis Patrick Slattery*. He has co-authored one novel, *Simon's Crossing*, with Charles Asher. Other titles include *The Idiot: Dostoevsky's Fantastic Prince. A Phenomenological Approach; The Wounded Body: Remembering the Markings of Flesh*. With Lionel Corbett he has co-edited and contributed to *Psychology at the Threshold* and *Depth Psychology: Meditations in the Field*; with Glen Slater he has co-edited and contributed to *Varieties of Mythic Experience: Essays on Religion, Psyche and Culture; A Limbo of Shards: Essays on Memory, Myth and Metaphor*. His more recent books include *Day-to-Day Dante: Exploring Personal Myth Through the* Divine Comedy; *Riting Myth, Mythic Writing: Plotting Your Personal Story*; with Jennifer Selig, he has coedited *The Soul Does Not Specialize: Revaluing the Humanities and the Polyvalent Imagination* and *Reimagining Education: Essays on Reviving the Soul of Learning; Creases in Culture: Essays Toward a Poetics of Depth; Bridge Work: Essays on Mythology, Literature and Psychology;* and *Our Daily Breach: Exploring Your Personal Myth through Herman Melville's* Moby-Dick. He has also authored over 200 essays and reviews in books, magazines, newspapers, and on-line journals.

He offers writing retreats in the United States and Europe on exploring one's personal myth through the works of Joseph Campbell and other mythologists. www.dennispslattery.com; dslattery@pacifica.edu.

CPSIA information can be obtained
at www.ICGtesting.com
Printed in the USA
LVOW08*2321290817
546902LV00007B/57/P